JESUS's STENOGRAPHERS

The Story of the Red Letters

Ben van Noort

WESTBOW
PRESS®
A DIVISION OF THOMAS NELSON
& ZONDERVAN

WestBow Press books may be ordered through booksellers or by contacting:

WestBow Press
A Division of Thomas Nelson & Zondervan
1663 Liberty Drive
Bloomington, IN 47403
www.westbowpress.com
1 (866) 928-1240

ISBN: 978-1-9736-2766-1 (sc)
ISBN: 978-1-9736-2767-8 (hc)
ISBN: 978-1-9736-2765-4 (e)

Library of Congress Control Number: 2018905584

Print information available on the last page.

WestBow Press rev. date: 06/29/2018

I have been reading poems, romances, vision literature,
legends, and myths all my life.
I know what they are like.
I know none of them are like this.

C. S. Lewis (about the Gospels)
Modern Theology and Biblical Criticism, 1959

Table of Contents

Part II
Sources

Part III
Documentation and Exegesis

Part IV

Documentation and Canon

Appendix

Abbreviations
Analytical Reading:
a. r. 1, rule 1
a. r. 2, rule 2
a. r. 3, rule 3
a. r. 4, rule 4
a. r. 5, rule 5
a. p. anchor point

[] In Greek original, but not in modern translation
{} In modern translation, but not in Greek original
TDNT Theological Dictionary of the New Testament
LCL Loeb Classical Library
LSJ A Greek-English Lexicon, Liddell, Scott and Jones

Preface

After the first edition of this book, I thought that I had completed the task. Thoughts, however, don't stop but follow their own way of reasoning and find new evidence, especially in matters such as the speedy writers of Jesus, who jotted down his words on wax tablets to preserve his teachings.

For the first edition, Dean Baerwald helped me in the preparation of English texts for the American language area. After the passing away of my friend Dean, two other native speakers offered their time and skill to read and comment on my texts, for which I am extremely grateful. Julia Mansfield and James MacGregor, thank you for your interest, encouragement, and competence.

From the First Edition

> I also want to express my gratitude to the members of the high school governing board where I taught. They allowed me to speak freely about writing in Jesus's ministry and to incorporate instruction of the documentation theory into the curriculum for the higher grades. Because of that I was able to develop this approach to the Gospels into a theoretical concept.

> I am likewise indebted to the many students who have followed my classes in the course of the years. Their interest in the issues, their questions and their natural acceptance of the documentation theory were a real joy to experience as a teacher.

> The fellows of the SEON (Society of Evangelical Old and New Testament in the Netherlands and Belgium) deserve special thanks. Their penetrating questions and remarks were valuable in giving thorough consideration to the subject and in developing the documentation theory in all its details.

Concerning the second edition, the book has been divided into four main parts in accordance with the issues of the documentation theory: foundations, sources, exegesis, and canon. Significant changes were needed in chapter 1. The prologue of Luke contains more grammatical content than I could ever imagine, and that made me look also at the other key passages, especially the prologue of John's first letter and Plutarch's testimony about the origins of stenography.

Further, in chapter 6 a new date for the Gospel of Mark has been established, along with the role of secretaries in the first transmission of Jesus's words. Another addition to this chapter is a section with a summary of failing Gospel theories. And at the end of chapter 10, some consequences in text restoration are described in accordance with the documentation theory.

In preparing the second edition, again I had in mind not only those who in some way made Christian work their profession but also the wider circle of Christians who feel the need for sound knowledge regarding the Gospels. These books form the *only tangible* inheritance of Jesus Christ and deserve to be understood for what they say about themselves. With the wish that many may be strengthened in their faith through trust in the reliability of the biblical words of Jesus Christ and in the reliability of the New Testament as a whole, I rededicate this book to its readers.

Ben van Noort

Introduction

The Gospels have always provided the revelation of Jesus Christ for our Christian forebears, and they held the apostles responsible for the books and the information they contained. These books were considered to be inspired and infallible writings, notwithstanding questions about the content that might be raised inside or outside the church.

A field of theological study that has been developed in the last two centuries is modern gospel research. A wealth of scholarly observations, explanations, theories, and of course books—many, many books—have emerged in this field of study. Three theories provide the main guidelines of it: the Aramaic source theory, the documentary theory, and the oral tradition theory. The Aramaic source theory says that Jesus would have spoken Aramaic and that the Greek Gospels are actually translations. The documentary theory says that the Gospel writers used each other's books as sources and changed the information for their own purposes. The oral tradition theory says that the oral preaching of the first Christians—with all sorts of deviations—also was a source for the Gospel writers.

In the end, hypotheses—viewpoints and observations—that were proposed since the eighteenth century became scholarly results—truth. And the strange effect was that in searching the Gospels, theology lost the original words of Jesus. His sayings were changed through the oral tradition, the supposed translation into Greek, and by the Gospel writers themselves. The many different forms in which Jesus's sayings appear in the Gospels are seen as the strongest evidence for this opinion.

Theological results have been presented in such a way that this was deemed no loss, as the only thing that mattered was belief in Jesus. However, this is merely a sophism, as inadequate expositions cannot be claimed as a reliable content necessary for a serious belief. The theory of the Aramaic source of the Greek Gospels no doubt has been the heaviest blow, with the implication that the original words of Jesus were lost in the dawn of history. These theological views go around not only in the churches but also outside; they are common knowledge today, despite apologetic efforts of courageous

Christians. Even among evangelicals—to which the present author adheres—these views are not uncommon. Many don't know what to think about it, and so they remain silent—very silent. The time has come for the Christians to dot their i's and cross their t's.

In 1975 I started as a high school teacher for Christian religion to adolescents, and I was forced to reconsider the old and central problem in theology: "What about the words of Jesus?" My senior pupils leaned back, saying, "Sir, it was all written long after the events, wasn't it? So how do we know it is true?" Another remarked, "Yes, sir, it's fiction, just as we have learned with Dutch language and literature." There I stood, empty-handed after five years of academic theological studies. Of course I knew the dilemma, but it was so clearly presented by my pupils that I could only feel respect for them. This experience brought me again to the books to seek the answers. I felt that my students were entitled to clear answers, especially concerning the authenticity of Jesus's words. I started with the first verses of the Gospel of Luke (1:1–4), which contain the basic ideas about the oldest Christian transmission.

At that time I got a catalog that offered older theological books. I didn't have much money, so I satisfied myself with the purchase of old but qualitatively good theological works. One of them was the book *Syntax of the Moods and Tenses in New Testament Greek* by E. DeWitt Burton (1955). This book made me understand Greek verb forms for the first time in my life. As my attention was focused on the prologue of the Gospel of Luke, I applied my new grammatical knowledge on the verb forms to it, but the text only became more incomprehensible to me. I don't know how often I have turned the words of this Bible passage over in my mind. To make it easier, I learned the Greek text by heart so that I could meditate on it at every moment of the day. Slowly, an entirely new reality started to unfold. This text spoke of writers who promptly followed Jesus. With the new insight into the meanings of the Greek verb forms, the bits of the puzzle began to fall into the right places, little by little.

During this process, I cast a look on a second passage with a similar message, Hebrews 2:3–4, and finally a third instance, 1 John 1:1–4. These three passages together form the scriptural basis for the *documentation theory* described in this book, which says that writers followed Jesus to preserve his teachings in writing.

For the work with my high school students, my discoveries gradually made an impact. Instead of sounding weak and hesitant, conviction entered the classroom. The words of Jesus really do exist. And listening to his words is listening to him. For human beings, these words form the point of contact with the higher (invisible) world, as well as with the ordinary (visible) world: Love God (invisible part) and your neighbor as yourself (visible part). This was not more information concerning Christian theory or spiritual thinking that begs for approval. No, this evidence-based approach brought the urgent contact between practical and spiritual reality. My pupils did not lean back anymore; this was real. Gradually, much research had to be done. This necessitated taking a deep breath to understand all the grammatical aspects in the key passages and for the mass of new explanations that were required for the Gospels as books.

The sayings of Jesus cover a lot of Christian issues. It is Jesus's words that evaluate the Hebrew Bible (Old Testament) as the Word of God. It is Jesus's words that define the *meaning* of his works, his Passion, his resurrection, his Second Coming. The Gospels do not give the opinions of the Gospel writers about these matters, as is often stated with the implication that they could have been wrong. Jesus's biblical words are necessary for salvation (John 5:24), for a convincing Christian life (Matthew 7:24). And particularly, Jesus's words form the most touching inspiration for the individual believer through the Holy Spirit. Jesus's words are more than Christian principles to be followed, and they cannot be missed.

Many have written about the Gospels. Many have defended the historical truth of these books but, sadly enough, without the essential evidence that Jesus's words do still exist. For that reason the documentation theory is presented here, which makes clear that the biblical words of Jesus can be accepted in faith and without intellectual reservations, thanks to the persistent efforts of his speedy writers.

Part I

Foundations

1. Dare to Read Your Bible

In the history of Christianity, there always has been the need to go back to the sources of the faith: Jesus and his words. In the earliest centuries of the church, the question already arose concerning how reliable the books about Jesus—the Gospels—really are. Today, all sorts of theories exist about the origins of these books. But how decisive are they? Since all theories give different answers, many people are not convinced of the trustworthiness of the Gospels.

In a modern transparent society, it is necessary that Christians develop a clear vision of their origin. It is no longer appropriate to come up with obscure theories concerning the center of the Christian faith: Jesus and his words. We not only want to believe in him and his sayings, but we also want an adequate theology to fully justify that faith. That means a journey to find the right answers, an expedition through texts that sometimes don't want to yield their secrets spontaneously and sometimes do through refractory traditions of opinion; it's always an exciting journey.

1.1 Spectators of Jesus, the First Generation

In the first sentence of his Gospel, Luke gives the information on how he wrote his Gospel:

> [1] Inasmuch as many have undertaken to compile a narrative of the things which have been accomplished among us, [2] just as they were delivered to us by those who from the beginning were eyewitnesses and ministers of the word, [3] it seemed good to me also, having followed all things closely for some time past, to write an orderly account for you, most excellent Theophilus, [4] that you may know the truth concerning the things of which you have been informed. (Luke 1:1–4)

The usual explanation of the prologue is dominated by the term *eyewitnesses and ministers of the word*. Since ancient times, one has supposed this referred to the apostles. Before Jesus's departure, they became the eyewitnesses as his disciples. After his departure,

1

they became apostles or "ministers of the word," preachers of the Gospel. It is generally assumed that the Gospel writers received their information from the preaching (oral tradition) of the apostles to write their books, but is this indeed what Luke wants to tell us?

At first, a paraphrase (in italics) is given to clarify what Luke is really saying here, together with an added explanation. Thereafter, the fine-tuning of some grammatical aspects will be discussed.

> ¹ *As* many *of us* have undertaken to compile a narrative of the *Jesus events each time when they* had been accomplished among us, ² *just as delivered to us* the eyewitnesses *since* the beginning *while they at the same time were also servants of the spoken word of Jesus,* ³ it seemed good to me also, *just like the many,* having *studied* all things closely for some time past, to write an orderly account for you, most excellent Theophilus, ⁴ that you may know the truth concerning *the spoken words that informed you* about these things.

Now the read is specifically different. Luke refers in verse 1 to the ministry of Jesus, with all the great things he did and the new teachings he brought. During this great time many hearers began to write about what they experienced with him. Each time after a Jesus event, they wrote about what they had seen and heard. In doing so, they received longer-time narratives. This custom of writing was encouraged by disciples of Jesus who, from the beginning of Jesus's ministry, made short reports for the hearers to copy (verse 2). And the best is still to come. These skilled disciples worked as note-takers of Jesus's spoken word during the events. They recorded his teachings by note-taking for the people, and after an event, they provided short stories with Jesus's sayings for copying. In verse 3, Luke says that he—later on—also made use of the records provided by these writers of Jesus, to write his Gospel. He followed the example of the many when he wrote his Gospel, with one difference: His Gospel was more complete than the narratives of the many.

It should be clear that this picture is quite different when compared with the earlier mentioned traditional view on these verses. Luke didn't use of the preaching of the apostles, but he used the accurate reports of note-takers on the preaching of Jesus. These interpretations are as different as night and day. What is the grammatical evidence for this view? We first need to look at the greater picture.

Luke not only wrote a Gospel but also the Acts of the Apostles. When a classical author wrote an ongoing history in two books, he normally used one title for the entire work, calling the two parts Book 1 and Book 2. Comparing this with the Gospel of Luke and the book of Acts, we immediately see the difference. It is clear that the Gospel and Acts have different titles; namely, the Gospel according to Luke and the Acts of the Apostles. There is no indication in the well-documented history of the New Testament scriptures that these books ever had different names, so they are two different works. Consequently, the prologue of Luke is to be taken as referring to the Gospel and not additionally to Acts. This insight makes it possible to determine some specific meanings of words and expressions of the prologue (1:1–4) of Luke's Gospel.

Let's return to the translation of the Revised Standard Version (RSV) of the Bible for grammatical aspects. Luke says that many made "narratives about the things which have been accomplished among us." Their work was in writing, as Luke followed their example (v. 3): "it seemed good to me also ... to write." Further, Luke speaks about the content of his Gospel as "the things which have been accomplished among us"; literally, the deeds or events (Jesus accomplished among us).[1] Consequently, the word *us* refers to the bystanders of the events (deeds), the spectators of Jesus, those who were there (and maybe even more widely, the generation that heard about these things at the time that they occurred). In short, *us* refers to the first generation who had seen Jesus.

Before we continue, let's put verse 2 in the active form, as in the original: "just as delivered to us the eyewitnesses from the beginning [also being] ministers of the word" (the words in brackets are missing in the Revised Standard Version but not in the Greek

---

[1] J. H. Thayer, *A Greek–English Lexicon of the New Testament* (Grand Rapids: Baker, 1977, repr. 1991) *pragma*: that which has been done, a deed, an accomplished fact; G. Kittel, G. Friedrich (editors), G. W. Bromiley (translator), *Theological Dictionary of the New Testament* [TDNT] (Grand Rapids: Eerdmans, 1968, repr. 1988), VI: 639. "Luke 1:1 calls the 'events' that have taken place among us"

and are important for a proper understanding). It is said that the eyewitnesses delivered to *us*. This *us* is the same group as in "the things which have been accomplished among *us*." It is against all grammatical rules to change a reference word within a sentence, and so the second *us* means the spectators of Jesus, the bystanders, the first generation.[2] To them, the eyewitnesses delivered information by which many could make narratives in writing, as we have seen. This may seem strange—eyewitnesses who delivered information to other eyewitnesses. But no, the eyewitnesses who handed down information had a second qualification; they were also servants (ministers) of the word, *logos*, the spoken word.[3]

The question now is, what was this service to the spoken word? There is mention of two simultaneous actions: the eyewitnesses *delivered ... also being* servants of the spoken word.[4] Delivering or handing down by the eyewitnesses occurred during a service to the spoken word. This makes oral delivery (oral tradition) impossible; it would obstruct the spoken word. Delivering during the spoken word was by writing in the nature of things. In short, verse 2 excludes oral tradition and includes note-taking during the spoken word of the events of Jesus's appearance in public.

Another striking aspect of Luke's prologue is the form of the Greek perfect in "events (deeds) which have been accomplished"

---

[2] The hearers of Peter (from Acts 2 and so on) are to be taken as the second generation; the third generation the hearers of Paul (from Acts 13 and so on).

[3] The Greek *logos* is in its first meaning, *spoken word* (viva vox): speech, saying, discourse, etc. The second meaning in relation to *mind*: reason, ratio, cause, etc. The first meaning, spoken word, is used in Luke 1:2, 4. Comp. Thayer, *A Greek–English Lexicon of the New Testament*, s. v. Also, TDNT IV: 80. Further, it is not appropriate to use the term "preaching" for *logos*, as, also in verse 4, preaching is not meant for *logoi* but basically the spoken words (that have informed you).

[4] *Genomenoi* is aorist participle plural of antecedent action: *having become* servants. That is: delivered ... also having become; also being servants of the spoken word. Compare: Acts 7:32 And Moses becoming trembling didn't dare to look. That is: being trembling he did not dare to look. Acts 10:4 and having become fearful he said. That is: being fearful he said. A construction of simultaneousness with the participle *genomenos* was a popular stylistic device.

(v. 1). The Greek perfect, in general, refers to a so-called resulting state.[5] The perfect participle plural refers to a plural of resulting states. Collective terms using the perfect participle plural are good examples: Acts 20:32—those who are sanctified are saints; Acts 21:20—those who have believed are believers. Each saint and each believer has his own state of being holy, of being a believer.[6]

When a perfect participle is used, the rule is as follows: "The time of the resulting state is usually that of the principal verb."[7] And so, "many have undertaken to compile a narrative of the events (deeds) *each time when* they had been accomplished among us." The use of this perfect plural shows that documents were made after events in Jesus's ministry. It was a general custom.

Concluding, we may propose a better translation of Luke 1:1–2 (elaborated in the Revised Standard Version):

> [1] Inasmuch as many have undertaken to compile a narrative of the *events (deeds) each time they had been accomplished* among us, [2] just as delivered to us the eyewitnesses from the beginning *also being servants of the spoken word,* [3] it seemed good to me also, having followed all things closely for some time past, to write an orderly account for you, most excellent Theophilus,

---

[5] B. M. Fanning, *Verbal Aspect in New Testament Greek* (Oxford: Clarendon Press, 1977, repr. 1990), 291. About the resulting state: "This is the normal use and it is the most direct application of the threefold meaning of the perfect." We follow the "normal use" of the perfect tense as a starting point in our discussions.

[6] In most grammars, the Greek perfect participle plural seems to be forgotten, but the rule is that all members of the group (all components) have their own resulting state (distributive aspect). Whether it is about people or about things; each member or part of the group has the resulting state of being sent (Acts 11:11), sanctified (Acts 20:32), believing (Acts 21:20), each heaven (Acts 7:56) or door (Acts 16:27) is open. Matthew 23:37 and Luke 13:34 show a *serial plural* of states "stoning those *who are sent* to you," not one collective stoning but a serial plural: everyone was stoned in his own state of being sent. In Luke 1:1, a serial plural also is used.

[7] E. DeWitt Burton, *Syntax of the Moods and Tenses in New Testament Greek* (Edinburg: T. & T. Clark, 1898 3th ed., repr. 1955), 71.

⁴ that you may know the truth concerning the things of which you have been informed.

1.2 Public Records

Not all people wrote after the events, but many did. Many made narratives about the works of Jesus. From the outset, his followers saw him as the Messiah (John 1:42, 46, 50), whom Moses had prophesied would speak the truth of God in everything (Acts 3:22–23).[8] With an insatiable appetite for news and a hunger to hear about the great things God was doing among them, many were used to copying reports.

The eyewitnesses provided a written transmission for those who were present at the events. We may speak therefore of public records made by the eyewitnesses. Many people made use of the public records, as many had undertaken to compile a narrative (v. 1). Sometimes there were a few copyists; sometimes there were a lot of them. Altogether, Luke speaks of "many" (v. 1).

The eyewitnesses were active as speedy writers during the events, in order to be able to deliver the spoken word. And after an event, they had the task of composing a public record containing what they had seen and heard. Later on, Luke also made use of the public records in writing his Gospel. He says in the third and fourth verse of his prologue that he followed the example of the many: "it seemed good to me also … to write an orderly account for you, most excellent Theophilus." Luke dedicated his book to Theophilus, and in doing so, he followed accepted practice. Usually, the person of dedication was a rich person who had financed the composition of the book. Theophilus and Luke had the same desire: a history of Jesus. Of course, Luke chose from the records that were appropriate for his purpose: "that you may know the truth of which you have been informed" (v. 4). It is clear that Theophilus already had heard a lot about Jesus via the public reports that went around, but now, in Luke's Gospel, he was offered many reports in succession so that he was able to recognize the *asphaleia*, the coherence, of all that he had heard into one great history.

---

[8] Even Moses could not meet the description of Deuteronomy 18:18b–19a; see Numbers 20:10–11.

The prologue of Luke tells us how documents were made during Jesus's ministry and how they were used as sources later on (documentation theory). Here follows a question and answer summary:

Q. What things are meant in verse 1 of Luke's prologue?
A. The events or deeds concerning the life of Jesus, from birth to resurrection.
Q. Who are meant by *us* in "the things which have been accomplished among us"?
A. The spectators, the bystanders. In general, the first generation.
Q. To whom did the eyewitnesses deliver public reports?
A. To *us*, the first generation.
Q. When did they deliver the reports?
A. After an event, when it was accomplished, and the transmission was in writing.
Q. What was the content of the public reports?
A. Whatever the eyewitnesses had seen or heard, as they were also servants during and of the spoken word.
Q. Why does Luke refer to this?
A. He also used the public reports to the first generation when writing his Gospel later (documentation theory).
Q. What was Luke's goal?
A. To make it possible for Theophilus, after Jesus's departure, to know the evidence about Jesus, as all sorts of narratives, as well as hearsay stories, went around. Luke's use of the first reports made his Gospel stand for ages.

Conclusions

Three changes have taken place with regard to the traditional interpretation (and translation) of the prologue of Luke:

1. The word *us*. It refers to the bystanders of the events in verse 1 as well as in verse 2, with the result that an oral tradition is excluded.
2. The translation *things* for the deeds of Jesus is too weak; it is about events or deeds. The word *logos* is not "preaching" of the apostles but "spoken word", and this is confirmed in

verse 4, where the plural is used and where it refers to spoken words that informed Theophilus in some way about Jesus. (No doubt he had also heard public reports about Jesus.)

3. The participle perfect plural "deeds that have been accomplished" refers to a series of events and also to a series of stative aspects—moments after each deed or event in which writing activities took place.

A thorough investigation of Luke's prologue offers a new picture of the work of Jesus and his disciples. How is it possible that we have not heard about this earlier?

1.3 Clerical Confusion

The traditional explanation of Luke 1:1 is based on a set of questionable assumptions that stood for ages. One assumed, mistakenly, that the Greek perfect plural refers to a series of completed actions with one existing state thereafter: the period of the church. The second strange assumption is that one started to write late in this period of the church about the life of Jesus. The third painful assumption is that the preaching of the apostles and not the preaching of Jesus became the source for the Gospels. These inadequate clerical presuppositions have received general acceptance in Christianity until this very day.

The view has always been stressed that Luke worked as a serious historian who accurately collected his information from the apostles. There may have been some documents from Jesus's ministry, but primarily they made use of the oral tradition.[9] It is not possible in this approach to discriminate between documentation and oral tradition in the Gospels.[10]

How can it be that this traditional opinion stood for ages? The ancient Bible translators dealt with a serious problem. From the

---

[9] I. H. Marshall, *The Gospel of Luke. A Commentary on the Greek Text.* The International Greek Testament Commentary (Exeter: Paternoster Press; Grand Rapids: W. B. Eerdmans, 1978, repr. 1989), 40–42.

[10] L. Morris, *Luke, An Introduction and Commentary.* Tyndale New Testament Commentaries (Leicester: Inter-Varsity Press; Grand Rapids: W. B. Eerdmans, 1974, revised 1988), 32–33, 73.

third century onward, the classical Greek perfect began to disappear; only a few fixed forms survived. From that time on, there was not much chance that the first sentence of the Gospel of Luke would be understood properly.

Origen (about AD 250) supposed the resulting state of the perfect (v. 1) to be a conviction in the hearts of the believers.[11] William Tyndale (and later Calvin) followed Origen with "things which are surely known among us," and so did the King James Version: "things which are most surely believed among us." But this translation is too far from the simple word meaning "accomplished deeds," and therefore Jerome (about AD 400) in providing the Vulgate (revised edition, replacing older Latin versions), rejected the solution of Origen.[12] Two incorrect translations of Luke 1:1 went around for more than a thousand years, during the Middle Ages up to our modern time. During the Reformation, the Greek New Testament was rediscovered; nevertheless, explanation and translation of the texts remained fixed on the concepts of the Vulgate. Luther followed Jerome's translation, and Calvin, that of Origen. Only in the nineteenth century did new insights into the character of the Greek verb come up—especially in the use of the Greek perfect.[13] And so a new interpretation of Luke 1:1 has become possible.

The first sentence of Luke's Gospel immediately starts with a rather unusual perfect form (*peplèroforèménoon*: while they were in accomplished states) without a context. Certainly the earliest Christians (before AD 70) did not have problems with the first sentence of Luke's Gospel. They were familiar with the living context of the time of Jesus. They knew how pupils learned to read and write in the Jewish land, and they knew about the writing activities of the apostles. Apostolic letters were written down from their speech by secretaries.[14]

---

[11] Origen, *Homilies* 1.

[12] Vulgate: "quae in nobis completae sunt rerum" (Luke 1:1).

[13] J. H. Moulton, *A Grammar of New Testament Greek*. Vol. I, Prolegomena (Edinburgh: T. & T. Clark, 3rd ed. 1908, repr. 1988), 140; about the Greek perfect: "the most important, exegetically, of all the Greek Tenses."

[14] Romans 16:2 (Tertius); Paul remarks in some letters that he signed in his own handwriting: 1 Corinthians 15:21; Galatians 6:11; Colossians 4:18; 2 Thessalonians 3:17; 1 Peter 5:12 (Silvanus).

Later on, everything changed. After the destruction of the Jewish land by the Romans during the wars against the Jews (first in the years 66–70 and later in 132–135), nothing remained the same; Judea even became a province of Syria. The living context in which Jesus and the apostles had worked was gone. The church fathers, in later centuries, could not even imagine the high standards of knowledge and culture of that period through the prosperity of the Jews at that time. In later centuries, Jews were often abused in the Roman Empire, whereas they were held in great respect in the time before the wars. The absence of the living context in which Jesus had worked and the disappearance of the Greek perfect from the third century onward were no doubt the causes of the first sentence of the Gospel of Luke being misunderstood by the church fathers. They were no longer able to recognize the few instances in the New Testament documents that deal with the writing of the spoken word during the Jesus events.

The conclusion must be this: The clerical interpretation of Luke 1:1–4 hides a set of assumptions that are in conflict with the heart of the matter—our knowledge of Jesus. On the other hand, an honest grammatical interpretation leads to a more satisfying concept of Gospel interpretation.

1.4 The Letter to the Hebrews about Jesus's Writers

The opening verses of the letter to the Hebrews start with three important issues—themes that return again and again in the letter:

1. In the past, God had spoken to the fathers of the people of Israel through the prophets.
2. In these days, God speaks "to us" through the Son, who reflects the glory of God.
3. After the purification of sins, he took his place on the throne at the right hand of his Father in heaven.

In accordance with these three issues, the author of Hebrews often refers to the Old Testament scriptures to sustain his argument (theme 1). Further, he encourages his addressees to listen carefully to what the Son has spoken to not drift away (theme 2), and at last he gives insight in Jesus's priestly work as the great heavenly high priest (theme 3). For our discussion, the second theme, which starts in Hebrews 2, is of importance:

> [1] Therefore we must pay the closer attention to what we have heard, lest we drift away from it. [2] For if the message declared by angels was valid and every transgression or disobedience received a just retribution, [3] how shall we escape if we neglect such a great salvation? It was declared at first by the Lord, and it was attested to us by those who heard him, [4] while God also bore witness by signs and wonders and various miracles and by gifts of the Holy Spirit distributed according to his own will. (Hebrews 2:1–4)

Verse 1 refers to what was spoken through the Son (what we have heard). *We* is used here in the wider context that Jesus had spoken in Israel to the Jewish people in the time of the author and his readers (Hebrews 1:1b). Immediately thereafter, in verse 2, the author goes back to the past of which he and his readers had knowledge by the Hebrew Bible (OT). There was a valid statute spoken by angels to punish transgression and disobedience in a legal way—the Ten Commandments are meant as having been spoken to Israel from Mount Horeb, once in the desert.[15]

In verse 3, the author begins his main theme of the passage: the revelation of Jesus and his words. The traditional translation is again that Jesus first spoke the Gospel (a great salvation declared by the Lord), and later on it was attested (proclaimed) to us by those who had heard him. As in the prologue of Luke, however, the traditional translation is missing the clue of the original sentence. Let's take a closer look.

The phrase "*and* it was attested to us" split the entire statement into two sentences, which is wrong, as the word *and* (Greek: kai) is missing in the original. In Greek, we have to do with one lengthy phrase instead of two coordinative sentences. By splitting the phrase into two distinct sentences with *and*, the original occurrence (preaching

---

[15] The Ten Commandments were given to Moses by angels (Acts 7:38, 53; Galatians 3:19).

11

of Jesus) is split into two occurrences (preaching of Jesus, preaching of the apostles), and that is a serious intervention. Unintentionally, the translation introduces an oral tradition: the preaching of Jesus's hearers about what they heard from the Lord.

Another point is that the keyword *confirm* always has been interpreted as "to attest, proclaim, preach," instead of the original meaning. The Greek expression *bebaio-oo eis hèmas,* or "confirmed unto us," does not express a direction, as the simple meaning is "to make firm, establish, confirm, make sure."[16] Therefore, the preposition (Greek: *eis,* unto) is to be taken as "in behalf of, in favor of." When we take these aspects into consideration in the translation of the King James Version, we get the following:

"How shall we escape if we neglect so great salvation; which beginning to be spoken by the Lord, *was confirmed (established) in behalf of us by those who were hearing*; God also bearing witness, both with signs and wonders, and with diverse miracles, and gifts of the Holy Ghost."

With recent analysis of the Greek verb, it is clear that the verb forms "beginning to be spoken" and "who were hearing" imply an aspect of coincident action, together with the verb form "was confirmed (established)."[17] To speak, to hear, and to confirm (establish) are to be taken instantly, nearly at the same time, as one occurrence, generally speaking. In this translation, we meet again the writers of Jesus who were taking notes during his teaching. They were the hearers who established Jesus's preaching in written form "unto us, in

---

[16] The verb *bebaio-oo* very often has a legal meaning, concerning a matter which is legally established for the future. A *bebaioo-sis* is a legal confirmation. This legal context is also in Hebrews 2:3, visible in the use of God also bearing witness ... (TDNT I: 603). In modern Greek *bebaioo-sis* is assurance, confirmation, or even certificate.

[17] About "beginning to be spoken" and "those who were hearing": Older exegetes would call these forms as aorist participles of antecedent action; for example, De Witt Burton, *Moods and Tenses,* 63–64. N. Turner, *A Grammar of New Testament Greek.* Vol. III, Syntax (Edinburgh: T. & T. Clark, 1963, repr. 1978), 79–81 would speak of aorist participles of coincident action. Fanning, *Verbal Aspect,* 97–98 speaks of "an occurrence in summary, viewed as a whole from the outside." So the signs and wonders cover three aspects as belonging to one occurrence: speaking by the Lord, hearing, and confirming.

behalf of us." They were working while signs, wonders, and miracles accompanied Jesus's words as God's approval on his words.

Several meanings of the verb *bebaio–oo* are to be excluded: (1) *attest, proclaim, preach*; any form of oral tradition by the hearers is impossible during the spoken word of the Lord. It would only disturb his word; (2) *confirm* is not appropriate, as only God could confirm the words of Jesus, and that is said in "God also bearing witness etc."; and (3) *establishing* of Jesus's spoken word by men is to be taken as analogous to "the message declared by angels was valid" (v. 2), as the word *bebaios* (stable, fast, firm, sure, valid) is of the same root as *bebaio–oo*. The Ten Commandments became firm/valid, as they were given to Moses in writing on the stone tablets. What was said by angels was written on stone tablets; the words of Jesus became valid as they were written *on wax* tablets by note-takers.[18]

Later on, in Hebrews 9:15–17 we read that a written document, a will in writing (testament), becomes valid (*bebaios*) as soon as the one who made it passes away, and *the will cannot be changed anymore*. It is clear that the author of Hebrews points to Jesus with this comparison. After his death, his teachings in writing are to be followed, just as a will or testament. It cannot be changed anymore: "For where a will is involved, the death of the one who made it must be established. For a will takes effect only at death, since it is not in force as long as the one who made it is alive" (9:17). This testament or new covenant is made under the blood of Jesus, which makes it stronger than any other covenant. The words of it will be written in the hearts of his people when Jesus, resurrected, speaks again through his biblical words to them (Hebrews 8:10, 12:24–25). The author of Hebrews is speaking about the words of Jesus in written form and that apparently are known by all.

1.5.1 Apostolic Manifesto I

The apostle John also gave information about the writing activities of Jesus's disciples. He did so in the prologue of his first letter. To get a clear insight into the working method of the Gospel writers, it is necessary to deal with this testimony. First we will examine the prologue:

---

[18] Valid (*bebaios* v. 2) refers to the writing of the Law (in stone) by which it was put into force.

[1] That which was from the beginning, which we have heard, which we have seen with our eyes, which we have looked upon and touched with our hands, concerning the word of life—[2] the life was made manifest, and we saw it, and testify to it, and proclaim to you the eternal life which was with the Father and was made manifest to us—[3] that which we have seen and heard we proclaim also to you, so that you may have fellowship with us; and our fellowship is with the Father and with his Son Jesus Christ. [4] And we are writing this that our joy may be complete. (1 John 1:1–4)

In verses 1–2, the apostle John describes how his generation experienced the Lord Jesus Christ. The apostle John speaks for all those people who had heard, seen, and followed him. John and the other apostles become recognizable in the prologue as he describes their activities, and therefore the prologue may be called the apostolic manifesto.[19] After Jesus's ascension, John looks back on the period with Jesus as the beginning of the Gospel that came into the world.[20] A new *archè* (beginning) came with the revelation of Jesus Christ, as "That which was from the beginning" stands in unity (apposition) with "which we have heard, which we have seen with our eyes." This word *beginning* also occurs in Luke 1:2 and in Hebrews 2:3, in the context of the beginning of the Gospel, and we also see it in Mark 1:1, where it says, "The *beginning* of the Gospel of Jesus Christ."

Several times John makes use of perfect forms, which give very emphatic meanings. A perfect form always has a resulting state

---

[19] The twelve apostles became the authoritative eyewitnesses, the speaking voice of many eyewitnesses (Luke 24:48; Acts 2:14, 32, 39, 41). Comp. 1 John 1:2—"and (we) testify to it and proclaim." It is unique that John uses "we" (first person plural) in the prologue (apostolic manifesto), as he continues to use "I" (first person singular). "My little children, I am writing." (See further 1 John 2:1, 7, 8, 12, 13, 14, 21, 26; 5:13.) From 1 John 1:6, sometimes John uses "we" to identify himself closely with his hearers. So: Turner, *A Grammar of New Testament Greek*. 28.

[20] In John's letter, the only occasion where John refers to *archè* as the time of creation is 3:8, speaking about "the devil who has sinned from the beginning." Obviously, this interpretation is captured in the context.

(i.e., the state after what has happened and often continuing at the time of the main verb). John uses a double perfect twice: in verse 1 (which we have heard, which we have seen) and in verse 3 (that which we have seen and heard). In doing that, John divides the prologue into two parts; each part beginning with special force. The two parts are either side of one coin: the apostolic proclamation. The first part (vv. 1–2) is about the oral aspect of the apostolic proclamation—the preaching of eternal life—and the second part (vv. 3–4) is about the handing down of the written tradition of the story of Jesus.

In the first part, John describes how they experienced Jesus, the word of life. They had seen him, touched him, and heard him and "(we) testify to it, and *proclaim to you* the Eternal Life." The result was a lasting experience that brought dedication to the Gospel. The use of the present forms (testify, proclaim) mean that in the past, the actions of testifying and proclaiming started and continued, up to the writing of the letter.[21] As John tells how the apostles experienced Jesus, he creates authority for Jesus and for their proclamation of the Gospel, already from the beginning.[22]

Further, *proclaim* is the translation of the Greek word *apaggelloo* (bring word, send message, proclaim, preach). This verb implies more than only "to make known" (*anaggelloo*, 1 John 1:5). The prefix *ap(o)* means "from the source"; *apaggelloo* is "to make known from the source."[23] An example is King Herod, who said to the wise men, "Go and search diligently for the child and when you have found him bring me word" (Matthew 2:8). Herod charged the wise men to inform him after they found the child. This is the reporting of what one has experienced, to carry a message directly from the source.

Another aspect of the verb *apaggelloo* is that there were several possibilities of reporting: orally, by writing, or by a combination

---

[21] Compare what the oldest son said to his father: "Lo, these many years I serve (present) you" (Luke 16:29). Or "Lo, these three years I have come seeking (present: I seek) fruit on this fig tree" (Luke 13:7). Present forms referring to ongoing actions, since one point in the past.

[22] In John 1:40–52, the first disciples of the twelve meet Jesus: Andrew, (probably) John, Peter, Philip, and Nathanael.

[23] Like the word *apostolos* (delegate, messenger) is from *stelloo*, send, and with *apo-*, from the source.

of both. In the case of a written report directly from the source, a document (e.g., a letter) contains the message. Such a document either was written by the sender or it was dictated by him while a clerk or secretary wrote. Then someone took the letter to the addressee. This aspect of writing is not necessarily applicable in verse 2: "(we) proclaim to you the Eternal Life." In verses 3–4, however, John elaborates on it.

1.5.2 Apostolic Manifesto II

In the second part of the prologue, John uses two perfect forms to give force (have seen and heard):

> ³ that which we have seen and heard we proclaim also
> to you, so that you may have fellowship with us; and
> our fellowship is with the Father and with his Son
> Jesus Christ. ⁴ And we are writing this that our joy may
> be complete. (1 John 1:3–4)

The main verb "proclaim from the source" (*apaggelloo*) has a present form again, but it has a new object: "which we have seen and heard," instead of eternal life in verse 2. Here in verse 3, there is a different aspect of the proclamation from the source: what they saw and heard about the deeds and words of Jesus. That's quite remarkable, particularly as John motivates this "so that you may have fellowship with us; … and with the Father … and with the Son." John is speaking here about a second gift: community with the apostles, with all who believe, and with God through the possession of the very words of Jesus Christ. Of course, this is inseparable from verses 1–2. In both cases it is about the new life in Christ.

Concerning verse 3, the question is: How could the apostles proclaim from the source what they had seen and heard? It's not a difficult answer; only if they had written down Jesus's miracles and teachings in the short time of seeing and hearing him. This is what John suggests in verse 3 and confirms in verse 4: "And we are writing this (these things) that our joy may be complete."

According to the grammatical rule, the term *this* (or *these things*; Greek: *tauta*) refers to what precedes "which we have seen and heard," and in written form, it brings complete joy.[24] The present form "We are writing this" is to be taken in the widest sense. At the source of Jesus's ministry, they were writing what they saw and heard; until now, during the apostolic era, they were responsible for the stories about Jesus's deeds and words, and this implied an ongoing writing activity. This state of affairs was the other side of the coin of the apostolic proclamation and could not be missed, as it formulated the foundation of the early apostolic church (v. 3) and was the reason for the complete joy of the individual believers (v. 4).

Is there greater joy than the Gospel? To come into "fellowship with the Father and with His Son Jesus Christ"? Of course not. The New Testament, as a whole, reveals that this everlasting joy is in the Gospel. According to verse 4, documents belong to the full joy of the faith! The senders, who already had this joy, as well as the receivers took part in this joy (Luke 10:20).[25] So verses 3–4 form the evidence that documents always were part of the Gospel—documents about the great works of Jesus, together with his spoken words. They always have been transmitted to the people from the outset. Not only *apaggelloo* but also the *chara* (joy) of the Gospel form the evidence in the apostolic manifesto that Jesus was followed by speedy writers to preserve his works and words in writing.[26] (There are some different

---

[24] John did the same in 1 John 2:26; 5:13. "These things have I written unto you" (KJV). He referred to what he wrote in the foregoing of the letter. Sometimes the plural *tauta* (v. 4) may refer to the following if a clear enumeration is given (comp. Mark 16:17), and it is obvious that this is not the case after 1:4. Reference of a plural "these things" (KJV) to a collective singular "that which we have seen and heard" is not unusual. In John 8:2, "them" refers to "the people."

[25] J. R. W. Stott, *The Letters of John, an Introduction and Commentary*. Tyndale New Testament Commentaries (Leicester: Inter-Varsity Press; Grand Rapids: W. B. Eerdmans, 1988, sec. ed.), 71. "The fellowship and the joy are both to be a common possession between the apostle and his readers. This 'seems to suit best the generous solicitude of the author, whose own joy would be incomplete unless his readers shared it.'" With reference to B. M. Metzger, *A Textual Commentary on the Greek New Testament*, (London, New York: United Bible Societies, 1975, ed. 3), 708. Also: "And NEB captures the sense well by translating 'we write this in order that the joy of us all may be complete.'"

[26] Jesus gave two mandates for this apostolic manifesto in Luke 24:46–47 (corresponding with the first part of the manifesto, 1 John 1:1–2) and in

variant readings in verse 4, but they are immaterial with regard to this discussion.)

We now may ask, how is it possible that we seem to have neglected for ages the *full* message of the prologue of John's first letter, particularly the writing part of the apostolic proclamation? Indeed, a short response cannot be kept back.

1.6 A Serious Misunderstanding

The traditional explanation of 1 John 1:1–4 (full text, 1.5.1) usually concentrates on the following seemingly logical steps.[27] The first step (verse 1): the greatness of Jesus's appearance and how his disciples experienced it. The second step (verse 2): from the beginning, the disciples became witnesses and became messengers of the Gospel later on. The third step (verse 3): the hearers of their message came to believe and found a relationship with the Father and with the Son. And finally, the fourth step (verse 4), as most commentators suggest: later, the apostles also spread their message in written form before they died.

The explanation seems logical, as the sequence of John's statements has been followed. Nevertheless, this exegesis is not valid. It is too easy to conclude from John's prologue that the apostles started to write their messages at a later stage. If we are to accept the traditional view that written documents came many years later—after the oral preaching—then such interpreters are asking us to accept that the first preaching of the Gospel through the apostles did not give complete joy but rather an incomplete joy. According to this view, the full joy only came later, when the hearers received written documents (v. 4). Of course, John could never mean this. Fellowship with the Father and with his Son, Jesus Christ, gives that complete joy immediately. So the traditional view cannot be true, and it is

---

Mathew 28:19–20 (corresponding with the second part of the manifesto, 1 John 1:3–4).

[27] For instance, an older exegete as A. Clarke, *Clarke's Commentary, Part III, Matthew–Revelation* (Nashville, Abingdon Press, 1824), 903. But also more recently, L. Morris (Letters of John) in D. A. Carson a. o., *New Bible Commentary. 21th Century Edition* (Leicester, Downers Grove Il: IVP, 1994), 1399.

clear that the interpretation presented here not only better fits the grammatical features but also the intentions of the apostle John.

The term *full (complete) joy* is an important expression in the Gospel and in the letters of John. In John 16:24, full joy is connected with answers to prayer; in 2 John 12, complete joy is related to spiritual brotherhood. In John 3:29, it refers to the joy concerning Jesus being compared with a bridegroom. In all of these cases, it's about experiences of spiritual joy as part of the Gospel. Jesus, however, also spoke of the full (complete) joy with regard to the message of the Gospel itself: "These things I have spoken to you, that my joy may be in you, and that your joy may be full." And "these things I speak in the world, that they may have my joy fulfilled in themselves" (John 15:11; 17:13). There can be no doubt that this remaining joy also is meant in verse 4 of the apostolic manifesto.

The prologue of the Gospel of Luke, the second chapter of the letter to the Hebrews, and the prologue of the first letter of John, all give the same remarkable message: Jesus was followed by writers, and they recorded what he did and said. This insight must have a magnificent influence on our view of the Gospels—origins, arrangement, dates, interpretation ... everything. It appears that records were made by the eyewitnesses according to fixed rules. In applying these rules, a better insight into Jesus's life and work is possible.

First, we have to deal with the question of what language Jesus used to communicate to the people. Did he speak in Aramaic or in Greek? Were the first records consequently written in Aramaic or in Greek? We have Jesus's words in the Greek language, so the question is, therefore, do we have them in the original language in which Jesus spoke or do we have them as translated from Aramaic?

2. Jesus Spoke Aramaic: An Impossible Theory

It is a common view that Jesus spoke Aramaic when he taught the crowds. This idea was widely propagated during the twentieth century, within and without New Testament theology, whereas in former ages a wide diversity of opinions existed among scholars on this issue. In 1954, H. Birkeland wrote, "As a matter of fact, no competent scholar any longer holds the view that Jesus spoke Hebrew, the language of the Old Testament. They all agree that this language was Aramaic."[28] He was right; many eminent theologians took this position. F. F. Bruce declared in 1962, "It [Aramaic] was thus the language commonly spoken in Palestine in New Testament times, the customary language of our Lord and His apostles and the early Palestinian church."[29] The orthodox and learned D. Guthrie wrote in 1970, "It may be assumed *a priori* that since our Lord taught in Aramaic some Aramaic background would be found behind the teaching of Jesus."[30] In 1992, E. Linnemann stated, "The linguistic fixing of the words, deeds and suffering of Jesus occurred primarily in the same language, colloquial Aramaic, that Jesus himself used."[31] And A. Millard wrote in 2000, "On this evidence we may assume that Jesus spoke Aramaic as a matter of course."[32]

There are two arguments for the view that Jesus spoke Aramaic. The first is that Aramaic was the common Semitic language in the Jewish land (Judea and Galilee) at that time, so Jesus also spoke Aramaic. The second argument is that the Semitic sayings of Jesus are Aramaic, and so they are the clearest proof for the position that Jesus used Aramaic as his vehicle of speech. Unfortunately these arguments are always brought forward without any proper grammatical or

---

[28] H. Birkeland, "The Language of Jesus." *Avhandlinger utgitt av Det Norske Videnskaps–Akademi i Oslo,* II klasse (Oslo: Jacob Dybwad, 1954) No. 1, 6-40.

[29] F. F. Bruce, *The Books and the Parchments* (London, Glasgow: Pickering & Inglis, 3th ed. 1963, repr. 1978) 56.

[30] D. Guthrie, *New Testament Introduction* (London: Inter-Varsity Press, 3th ed. 1970, repr. 1985) 47.

[31] E. Linnemann, *Is There a Synoptic Problem?* (Grand Rapids: Baker Book House, 1992) 162.

[32] A. Millard, *Reading and Writing in the Time of Jesus* (New York: University Press, 2000) 144.

historical proof.[33] They are repeated in New Testament theology rather unthinkingly, and nobody seems interested in the question of how valid these arguments really are.

The assertion that Jesus spoke Aramaic seems scientifically correct because so many scholars have associated their names with it. On the other hand, this state of affairs may display the deplorable condition in which theology and even Christianity finds itself at this moment. We do possess the Gospels in Greek, the language in which they have been delivered to the world. That would mean that Jesus's words are handed down to us in translation and not in the original Aramaic. Let's be honest; we cannot escape the conclusion that we do not have the authentic words of Jesus if he taught in Aramaic.[34] In that case, Christianity would be the only world religion without the authentic words of its founder. And if this is so, it seems appropriate to say that Christianity finds itself in a deplorable situation. But is it true that Jesus spoke to the people in Aramaic?

2.1 The Languages in Israel at the Beginning of the Era

In the discussion of the languages spoken in the time of Jesus, the first substantial evidence is seen in the epigraph on the cross, which, according to the Gospel of John, was written in three languages: Hebrew, Latin, and Greek. There exists little uncertainty about Latin or Greek. Latin was spoken in the Roman army.[35] Greek was the normal vehicle of speech (Koinè) in the eastern part of the Roman Empire, which included Judea and Galilee. Many regions of this part of the empire were bilingual; apart from Greek, native languages of the peoples within these regions also existed.[36] The Jewish land was

---

[33] In the second part of the twentieth century in scientific literature, scholars stopped giving references for proof of the Aramaic position.

[34] Sometimes it has been stated that the Gospels in the Peshitta (Syriac-Aramaic translation of the Bible) may preserve authentic Aramaic sayings of Jesus in contrast to the canonical Gospels. But this position fails any evidence, as the Syriac Gospels are translations of the Greek Gospels and do not stand for themselves.

[35] Flavius Josephus, *Bellum* 3:5.4.

[36] Many examples of native languages are given in Acts 2:9–11. In Acts 14:11, the hearers of Paul and Barnabas reacted in their native language,

no exception: the people spoke Greek and Hebrew, according to the epigraph at the cross.

Now we must ask what is meant by *Hebrew*, the first language of the epigraph on the cross. What sort of Hebrew do we think of? Was it the original language of the Jews, the language of the Old Testament? Or was it Aramaic, the language of Syria and Babylon at that time. It is generally assumed that in Judea and especially in Galilee—the homeland of Jesus—the people spoke an Aramaic dialect, closely related to Syrian Aramaic, because Galilee adjoined Syria.

Let's have a look at the theory that Aramaic was the vehicle of speech in the Jewish land in the first century, in addition to Greek. This thesis generally is brought forward as fact, and it seems that no one dares to cast doubt on it. Anyone who has the courage to ask how we know this likely will get the reply that Aramaic, at that time, was the Semitic *lingua franca* of the Middle East and of Judea, or that Aramaic was spread over a wide language area that included Judea and Galilee. Of course, that is not an answer to the question of how we know that. The problem is that it is very difficult to give sound proof for this thesis. In the Jewish land, inscriptions (especially epitaphs on ossuaries and tombstones) have been found from that period in Aramaic vernacular but also in real Hebrew vernacular. It's often not possible to distinguish between the two languages of the inscriptions because epitaphs usually are extremely short or of only fragmentary preservation.[37] The second problem is that there are few Hebrew and Aramaic documents from the first century found in the Jewish land, although the Dead Sea Scrolls were found in Qumran, and they contain Aramaic as well as Hebrew material. Most of the material is Hebrew, and since the discovery of the Dead Sea Scrolls, it is no longer tenable to state that the Hebrew language died out among the Jews in favor of Aramaic.[38]

The extant sources give little evidence to state with certainty that Aramaic was the Semitic vehicle of speech in the first century in

Lycaonian, to Paul's preaching in Greek.

[37] G. Mussies, "Greek as the Vehicle of Early Christianity." *New Testament Studies* (Cambridge: University Press, 1983) Vol. 29, 356–369.

[38] E. M. Cook, *Solving the Mysteries of the Dead Sea Scrolls* (Carlisle UK: The Paternoster Press, 1994) 54. "Perhaps the most surprising fact, at least to gentile scholars, was the prevalence of Hebrew in the scrolls."

the Jewish land. Jewish scholars always have maintained that in the first century, Hebrew was the language of the Jews.[39] They derived their argument from the fact that the Mishnah, the compilation of all Jewish religious knowledge about the time of the second temple, was written in (Mishnaic) Hebrew. However, the Mishnah was written at the end of the second century and, strictly speaking, does not represent the language of the first century. Nevertheless, there is so much information about the period of the second temple in the Mishnah that it is impossible to deny that the Mishnah represents the Hebrew language of this period. Finally, some have pled the case that a mixture of Hebrew and Aramaic was used in the first century by mutual influence of both languages.[40]

The opinion that Aramaic was the language of Jesus is not an invention of the last century. The idea arose only a few generations after the beginning of Christianity. After the Jewish wars in AD 70 and 135, the Romans decided to remove Israel from the map by incorporating the region into Syria, named Syria-Palestina. As Aramaic was the vehicle of speech in Syria, this language became the official language of Judea and Galilee. Moreover, a growing stream of Jewish immigrants from Babylon settled there. Many of them felt it a holy duty to refill the depopulated country with descendants of Abraham, Isaac, and Jacob. And so from the third and fourth century onward, Christian pilgrims heard Aramaic in the country where Jesus had lived, and many thus supposed that Aramaic was the vernacular of Jesus. This opinion obtained a foothold even among church fathers. The fact is that the flourishing Jewish state before AD 70 differed widely from the country that was made of it by the Romans after that time.

Of course, there are many Aramaic influences in the New Testament, such as Abba (my father), Rabboeni (my great master), Pascha (Easter), Korban (offering), Messiah, and so on. In fact, they are mostly Hebrew words with Aramaic modifications. The corresponding

---

[39] M. H. Segal, *A Grammar of Mishnaic Hebrew* (Oxford: Clarendon Press, 1927) 1, 3–6 "It is clear from the facts presented by its grammar and vocabulary that MH had an independent existence as a natural living speech." MH, Mishnaic Hebrew language from 400–300 BCE to about 400 CE in Israel.

[40] A. Merx, *Die Vier Kanonische Evangeliën* (Berlin: Reimer, 1911), 418.

Hebrew words of those just mentioned are Abbi (my father), Rabbi (my teacher), Pesach (Easter), Karban (offering), and Massiah. Only a few words are plain Aramaic, such as Cephas (rock), Talitha (girl), Se'bach (to leave), and others. A lot of names are combined with the Aramaic word Bar (son): Barabbas (son of my father), Bartholomeüs (son of Tolmai), Barjona (son of Jona), and so on. It is not difficult to understand where the Aramaic influence came from. After the exile in Aramaic-speaking Babylon, the Jews in Judea always remained in close touch with the Jews who lived in Babylon. And the name *Babylon* is to be taken quite elastically, for it could cover the whole of Mesopotamia on the other (north) side of the Euphrates. Mingling of Hebrew, the classic Jewish language, with Aramaic could be a natural process because the languages are so closely related to one another. Finally, it should not be forgotten that Aramaic had become the second holy language for the Jews, as substantial parts of the holy books were written in Aramaic: Daniel 2:4–7:1; Ezra 4:8–6:18; 7:12–26. After the exile it became a religious duty not to neglect the Aramaic language. Certainly also for that reason, many Aramaisms entered into classic Hebrew vernacular after the exile.

Several examples indicate that Hebrew was the main language in Judea before the year 70. In the Letter of Aristeas (dated between ca. 250 BC and AD 50), we have a discussion between Demetrius and the Egyptian king Ptolemaeus.

> "I am told that the laws of the Jews are worth transcribing and deserve a place in your library." "What is to prevent you from doing this?" replied the king. "Everything that is necessary has been placed at your disposal." "They need to be translated," answered Demetrius, "for in the country of the Jews they use a peculiar alphabet (just as the Egyptians, too, have a special form of letters) and speak a peculiar dialect. They are supposed to use the Syriac tongue, but this is not the case; their language is quite different." And the king, when he understood all the facts of the case, ordered a letter to be written to the Jewish High

Priest so that his purpose (which has already been described) might be accomplished.[41]

The issue was that the librarian Demetrius of Phaleron received from king Ptolomy II the task to collect the five books of the Torah for the royal library of Alexandria (ca. 275 BC). A translation had to be made from the Hebrew; that also was the language normally spoken at that moment in Judea—although there is no common view as to exactly when the Letter of Aristeas was written. It was cited by Flavius Josephus (who wrote after AD 70), and so the letter stands as a witness of the general lingual situation in Judea during the second temple.

Another example: Flavius Josephus tells that with the fall of Jerusalem in 70, a few sons of King Izates were captured by the Romans. These five princes were in Jerusalem "to learn accurately the language of our nation, together with our learning."[42] Of course, King Izates of Adiabene did not send his sons to Jerusalem to educate them in the Aramaic language because that was the language of Adiabene. They went to Jerusalem to learn Hebrew.

Finally, the Greek term for "in Aramaic" is *Suristi* or *Chaldaïsti*. If the apostle John had intended to make clear that Aramaic was one of the three languages of the epigraph on the cross, he surely would have used one of these words. But he used *Hebraïsti,* the expression for "in Hebrew." The New International Version (NIV) of the Bible translates this as "and the sign was written in Aramaic, Latin and Greek," but why don't we simply translate the words of the text? The Revised Standard Version translates this correctly as "and it was written in Hebrew, in Latin, and in Greek."[43] Anyway, it is not proper to simply say that Aramaic was the general vehicle of speech of the Semitic-speaking people in Judea and Galilee.

---

[41] Aristeas, *Epistula ad Philocratem* 11. Translation: R. H. Charles ed., *The Apocrypha and Pseudepigrapha of the Old Testament in English II* (Oxford: Clarendon Press, 1913), 95

[42] Flavius Josephus, *Antiquitates* 20:71. Translation: W. Whiston, *The Works of Flavius Josephus* (Peabody MA: Hendrickson Publishers, 1996), 529.

[43] John 19:20.

2.2 The Semitic Sayings of Jesus and the Aramaic Theory

The second argument for the position that Jesus spoke Aramaic is based on some Semitic sayings of Jesus that are delivered within the Greek text of the New Testament. The great German scholar Gustaf Dalman defended the view that Jesus spoke Aramaic, and he published many studies on this issue. He "believed that it was only in the Words of Jesus that we had the right to assume an ultimate Aramaic original."[44] A contemporary of Dalman, Theodor Zahn, confirmed this view: "We possess scriptural witnesses about the language of Jesus. These are not parts of sermons, but important words spoken on significant instances. ... That proves that Jesus preached to the people in this language [Aramaic] and also taught his disciples in it."[45]

The sayings under debate are as follows:

- *Talitha cum(i)!* Little girl, arise!
- *Ephphatha!* Be opened!
- *Eloi (Eli), Eloi (Eli), lama (lema) sabachthani?* My God, my God, why hast Thou forsaken me?[46]

Some key words are Aramaic—Talitha (little girl), lema (why), sebach (forsake). Referring to these words, one may finish the argument about Jesus's language by claiming that these sayings are Aramaic. There is no other reason for them than that he spoke in Aramaic, the customary language of the people among whom he

---

[44] M. Black, *An Aramaic Approach to the Gospels and Acts* (Oxford: University Press, 1946), 3. Black followed Dalman in this respect (p. 14, n. 1): "Jesus may have spoken Greek, but He certainly did speak and teach in Aramaic."

[45] T. Zahn, *Einleitung in das Neue Testament I* (Leipzig: Deichert'se Verlag, 1906), 2.

[46] Mark 5:41; 7:34; 15:34 (Matthew 27:46. Eli, Eli, lema sabachthani?). We may define Mark 15:34 (Eloi, Eloi, lama sabachthani?) and Matthew 27:46 (Eli, Eli, lema sabachthani?) as two exclamations of Jesus. The first was uttered "at the ninth hour" (three o'clock p.m.) and the second a moment earlier "about the ninth hour." So we may speak about four Semitic sayings of Jesus.

lived. And so one may argue that Aramaic was the Semitic *lingua franca* (vehicle of speech) in Judea in Jesus's time.

However, are the four Semitic sayings of Jesus really decisive for the Aramaic view? On the contrary, they are far from decisive. The Semitic sayings of Jesus are best explained by considering them as Hebrew sentences with "borrowed" Aramaic words (loan-words). There are words that can be designated as plain Hebrew—*Eli, Eloi* (my God)—and the verbs *cum* (to stand up) and *patach* (to open) are used in both languages. The word *sebach* (to leave, forsake) occurs indeed in Mishnaic Hebrew as a borrowed Aramaic word. In Jesus's time, it was probably more current than the old Hebrew word *'azab* (forsake).[47] *Lema* (Aramaic) and *lama* (Hebrew) are so similar that they certainly were interchangeable in daily speech. And it is very possible to consider *Talitha* as a borrowed Aramaic word in a Hebrew context. However, the solution cannot be based on loan-words only. For a definite conclusion, the inquiry must focus on the conjugations of the verbal forms. They are decisive because they are not interchangeable between languages as loan-words are.

The form *cum(i)* (arise) has equal conjugation in Aramaic and Hebrew, and therefore this form cannot be decisive for Aramaic. The form *sabachthani* (you have forsaken me) has the Aramaic verb *sebach*; with regard to the conjugation in both languages Hebrew and Aramaic, the form *sebachthani* is to be expected. The sound change *e* into *a*, however, is typical Hebrew: *sabachtha* (you have forsaken) without the suffix *-ni* (me). While in Aramaic, without the suffix it remains as *sebachtha*. In other words, the form *sabachthani* shows typical Hebrew influence and argues in favor of colloquial use of the Hebrew language.

Ephphatha (be opened!) is a typical Hebrew conjugation. *Hiphphatha* is the Hebrew imperative form (niphal): Be opened! The Hebrew sound *Hi* is rendered in Greek with the letter *E*, according to the rule. For instance, the word *Gehenna*,[48] which in Greek transliteration is *Geënna*, comes from Hebrew *Gehinna(-om)*. And so we see *hi* becomes *e* in Greek. The same is seen in the name of King Hezekia; in Hebrew, it is *Hizkia*, while in Greek transliteration, it is

---

[47] Psalm 22:2.
[48] Matthew 5:22, 29, 30.

Ezekia.[49] For comparison, some examples of names are given out of the Septuagint (Greek translation of the Old Testament, ca. 200 BC) with the same transliteration (*Hi* becomes *E*).

Examples of Transliteration		
Hebrew Bible	**Greek Bible (Septuagint)**	**References**
Hinnom	Ennom	Jeremiah 7:31, 32
Hizkia (Hezekiah)	Ezekia(s)	Isaiah 37:3
Hiddai	Eththi	2 Samuel 23:30
Hillel	Ellel	Judges 12:13
Hiddekel (Euphrates)	Eddekel	Genesis 2:14, Daniel 10:4
Hiphphatha (Hebr. Imperat. Niphal)	Ephphatha (New Testament)	Mark 7:34 (Be opened)

The Hebrew *Hiphphatha* has received the correct Greek transliteration, *Ephphatha.*

Is it possible to recognize an Aramaic form in *Ephphatha?* Gustaf Dalman, who strongly promoted the Aramaic view in the beginning of the twentieth century, got stuck on this form. According to him, *Ephphatha* (be opened) was a plural form, not the singular, as is plain from Mark's Greek translation of it (7:34).[50] Dalman interpreted it as spoken to the ears of the deaf-mute man instead of to the man himself.[51] Jesus used a singular, as he wanted the man to be open (i.e., sounds could enter and sounds could come out). Implicitly but not explicitly, he spoke to the ears to hear and to the mouth to speak; he spoke to the man to be open—that is the point here. Theodor Zahn, the orthodox and learned contemporary of Dalman, immediately recognized that Dalman had taken the wrong (plural) Aramaic form *Ephphetaha* for *Ephphatha.* Zahn chose a singular imperative. However, he did not explicitly say to which

---

[49] Matthew 1:10.

[50] Mark 7:34. Ephphatha; that is, Be opened.

[51] G. Dalman, *Grammatik des Jüdisch–Palästinischen Aramäisch* (Leipzig: Hinrichs Verlag, 1905), 278, n. 1. Unfortunately, he made a mistake in speaking about *eyes* (German: Augen) instead of *ears.*

form he objected.[52] He had two possibilities: *Ephphetha* or *Ephphaththa*.[53] But these forms differ clearly from *Ephphatha*, as used in Mark 7:34. If Zahn intended the first form of the two, he had the problem of an *e* instead of an *a*. On the other hand, if he intended the second form, he had to do with the duplication of the *th*. Zahn, pretending to arrive at the final solution of the case, in fact never did. Later on, Dalman accepted Zahn's criticism and accepted the form *Ephphaththa* as model for *Ephphatha* in Mark 7:34, without explanation of the duplication of the *th*.[54] Many Bible teachers followed this explanation; for instance, the great British scholar F. F. Bruce.[55]

Currently, both Aramaic variants, as discussed above, are in circulation. In the Vulgate, the Latin Bible, Jerome makes Jesus say *Ephphetha*. On the other hand, in the "Hebrew translation of the New Testament,"[56] Jesus says *Ephphaththa*. From antiquity to modern times, many have tried to make the case that Jesus spoke Aramaic, as these Bible translations show. Aramaic forms were used at the cost of the Hebrew expressions Jesus used. This confusion[57] does not provide serious proof that Jesus spoke Aramaic. Moreover, it clearly shows that *Ephphatha* is purely Hebrew.[58]

---

[52] T. Zahn, *Einleitung in das Neue Testament I*, 2, 9.

[53] Ephphetha (Itpe'el) or Ephphaththa (Itpa'al). It is still a matter of debate, as there is no convincing evidence from the sources that Itphetha and Itphaththa indeed contract in Ephphetha and Ephphaththa. This is an assumption that also weakens the Aramaic position, a problem that does not exist in Hebrew.

[54] G. Dalman, *Jesus–Jeschua* (Leipzig: Hinrichsche Buchhandlung,1922), 10.

[55] F. F. Bruce, *The Books and the Parchments*, 56. He saw Ephphatha as the rendering of Ithpattach (Itpa'al).

[56] *The New Testament in Hebrew and Dutch* (London: Trinitarian Bible Society, 1990)

[57] To make the confusion complete, the NIV Study Bible gives the comment at Mark 7:34, "*Ephphatha!* An Aramaic word that Mark translates for his Gentile readers." Zondervan NIV Study Bible (2002), 1540. The form Ephphatha does not occur in Aramaic at all.

[58] I. Rabbinowitz, "Did Jesus speak Hebrew?" *Zeitschrift für die Neutestamentliche Wissenschaft* (Berlin: De Gruyter, 1962) Vol. LIII, 229–238 has shown that *Ephphatha* is plain Hebrew (niphal) and definitely not Aramaic. Be Opened = Ephphatha (Mark 7:34). J. A. Emerton, "Maranatha an Ephphata," *The Journal of Theological Studies*. (Oxford: University Press,1967), Vol. 18, 427–431

Not one Semitic saying of Jesus contains the necessary evidence (in the verb forms) to be Aramaic. And so none of them can be used as evidence for the opinion that Jesus spoke Aramaic. It's quite disappointing. They are all Hebrew sayings containing Aramaic loanwords. So Jesus spoke Hebrew, and the meaning of *Hebraïs* is simply Hebrew. In the same way, *Hebraïsti* on the epigraph at the cross is to be translated as "in Hebrew" and not as "in Aramaic," as the NIV has done (John 19:20).

2.3 An Impossible Theory

It asks a great deal of us to maintain that Jesus spoke Aramaic in daily life. It is, therefore, remarkable that so much labor has been spent on the Aramaic theory, as even at first glance this view seems strange.

We have seen that Greek (Koinè) was the vehicle of speech in the eastern part of the Roman Empire—from Rome to Athens, from Athens to Antioch, from Antioch to Alexandria. The Jewish land from Caesarea to Jerusalem was no exception. Jesus did not speak to the people somewhere in a corner of the country; but he moved to the people in the centers of the Jewish provinces of Judea and Galilee.

The New Testament came to us in Greek, not in Aramaic. There is a stream of old Greek manuscripts behind the New Testament—papyri from the second century onward and parchments from the fourth century onward. In total, we're speaking of about five thousand old documents—books, parts of books, loose pages, and

---

reacted and had to admit "that the word cannot be used as evidence that Jesus spoke Aramaic." He proposed that "Jesus may occasionally have spoken it [Hebrew]." S. Morag, "Ephphatha (Mark VII. 34): Certainly Hebrew, Not Aramaic?" *Journal of Semitic Studies* (Oxford: University Press, 1972), Vol. 17, 198–202 also reacted and claimed *Ephphatha* to be an Aramaic liturgical form of the Samaritans of ca. 1900. However, it is not convincing to use a Samaritan form from about two millennia after Jesus, as evidence for his language. A. Millard, *Reading and Writing in the Time of Jesus*, 141 referred to these articles and still listed *Ephphatha* among his Aramaic examples (also p. 85), just as other plain Hebrew words as *Amen* (Psalm 106:48) and *Hosanna* (Psalm 118:25, defective 2 Samuel 14:4) are used as evidence for the Aramaic background of the Gospels (140, 142).

small fragments. Not the smallest piece, not even a scrap, has ever been found with Aramaic text on it earlier than the Greek text. We only know the Syrian translation of the New Testament, which is Aramaic. If the Greek Gospels were translations of Aramaic originals—either completely or partly—how is it then possible that not the smallest piece written in Aramaic text from those early Aramaic documents has ever been found? On the contrary, we would expect a stream of Aramaic texts beside and even before the Greek stream.

The content of the Gospels is not compatible with the Aramaic theory. For instance, the Pharisees were afraid that Jesus would visit the Greek Dispersion of the Jews: "Does he intend to go to the Dispersion among the Greeks and teach the Greeks?"[59] They were afraid that he would visit the great Jewish communities all over the Greek-speaking world, in Phoenicia (Lebanon), Asia (Turkey), Greece, and Egypt in the south. If Jesus spoke Aramaic, they would not have been afraid that he would go to these regions but that he would go to the Aramaic Dispersion of the Jews in Mesopotamia. The coherence is missing completely in John 7:35, if Jesus spoke Aramaic in public and not Greek.

In Acts 2:9 (description of Pentecost), we read how Galileans spoke languages they never were expected to speak. The native language of the residents of Mesopotamia is also mentioned among these languages: (Chaldaic) Aramaic, which was therefore not the language of these Galileans. Syriac and Palestinian Aramaic can also be excluded.

We should remember the grasp of the prologues of John's first letter and Luke's Gospel. John says that the apostles delivered what they had heard as they had heard it, without translation. Luke says that he worked like the many, and they did not translate, but they wrote down the traditions of the eyewitnesses (also being servants of the spoken word) in the accomplished state of the events. So Luke

---

[59] "Where does this man intend to go that we shall not find him? Does he intend to go to the Dispersion among the Greeks and teach the Greeks?" (John 7:35).

also did not translate when writing his Greek Gospel.[60] The many did not translate, neither did Luke, and neither did John.

Because of the great resemblance between the Gospels of Matthew, Mark, and Luke, no doubt the other Gospel writers worked just like Luke; they also did not translate. The Semitic sayings of Jesus underline this position. If the Gospels of Mark and Matthew were translations from Aramaic or Hebrew into Greek, these Semitic sayings of Jesus also would have been translated into Greek. Because this did not happen, the inevitable conclusion is that we possess the words of Jesus in the Gospels, just as he spoke them—almost everything in Greek, only four times in Hebrew.

When Mary Magdalene said to Jesus, "Rabboni!"[61] she used an Aramaic loan-word. Yet the Gospel writer John says that she spoke *Hebraïsti* (i.e., in Hebrew). If Jesus had the custom of sometimes speaking in Aramaic with his disciples or with others, then John certainly would have used *Suristi* or *Chaldaïsti* here instead of *Hebraïsti*. Again, we are confronted with the existence of a borrowed Aramaic word within the Hebrew language of Judea and Galilee in Jesus's time.

And last but not least. If Jesus would have spoken Aramaic, he would have cried out on the cross: "Elaï, Elaï!" (Aramaic). But it was: "Eli, Eli!" and "Eloï, Eloï!" (Hebrew).[62]

When we glance at the history of theology, we also see how strange the Aramaic theory is. This theory was brought forward in the time of the Enlightenment (ca. 1750). It was quite a revolutionary idea; during the time of Renaissance and Reformation, scholars had rediscovered Greek as the language of the New Testament and Hebrew as the original language of the Old Testament. These discoveries made a deep impression on protestant theologians. Suddenly, there was the suggestion that Jesus did not speak Greek but Aramaic. Protestant theology has been burdened by it ever since and has not been able

---

[60] See section 1.1–2.

[61] "Rabboni!" (meaning: my great master; Teacher, John 20:16 RSV).

[62] *Eloï* is in the Greek text *Elooï*. It is from the Hebrew form: *Elohai*, and transcribed in Greek as *Elooï*. Comp. G. Dalman, *Grammatik des Jüdisch-Palästinischen Aramäisch* (Darmstadt: Wissenschaftliche Buchgesellschaft, 1960), 156, n. 1. He acknowledged the Hebrew vocalization (origin) of the form.

to shake off this misconception. The Aramaic theory hit protestant theology right in the heart, as it has two pillars: belief in the Lord Jesus Christ and belief in his very words, and this implies the entire Word of God. The scholarly threat that we do not really possess the authentic sayings of Jesus brought a permanent doubt in Christian thinking. Protestant theologians appeared to not be able to safeguard the words of Jesus intellectually. In the twentieth century, the Aramaic theory developed into a theological topic. Theology made Jesus and his disciples into Aramaic-speaking people, which they never were. It is not strange that many Christians and non-Christians do not have much respect for the Gospels and for the holy scriptures in general, which is greatly due to the Aramaic theory.

2.4 Jesus Communicated in Greek

Of course the question remains: Does it make any difference if Jesus spoke Hebrew instead of Aramaic? In that case, his sayings would seem to have been translated from Hebrew into Greek with the same result—that we are no longer in possession of his authentic words. But this is not the case. In the Jewish land and beyond, Hebrew was spoken primarily to maintain the knowledge of the Torah. Families that wanted to live according to the guidelines of the Torah spoke Hebrew at home to keep the Torah vivid among them. Even where Hebrew disappeared in public, these families kept the custom to keep the old Hebrew language vivid within family life. This happened in Galilee and in many parts of Judea, where the colloquial language had become Greek.

In Acts, when we read of the history of the first Christian church in Jerusalem, we are confronted with two social classes in the population: a Greek-speaking group and a Hebrew-speaking group.[63] The Greek section was the poorer and the lower class. We may learn this from the information that welfare was lacking for the Greek-speaking aged people, the widows. The Hebrew part of the community did not have to deal with this problem; it seemed to be the well-to-do part of the community. The existence of the two social groups within the Christian community is to be taken as a reflection

---

[63] Acts 6:1.

of the population that lived at that time in Jerusalem. Apparently, the poor part of the population of Jerusalem, the crowd, was accustomed to speaking Greek. When Jesus visited the city, he spoke to the crowd, to the lost sheep of Israel. That means he taught the people in the Greek language, not in Hebrew or Aramaic.

The epigraph on the cross shows the same picture. Hebrew is the first language mentioned on it and Greek the last. Speaking Hebrew in Jerusalem was certainly the distinguishing mark of the Jewish upper class. That's why the Hebrew part of the epigraph stood first—a nice gesture by Pilate to the ruling priestly circles of the city.

With respect to the languages, the situation of Galilee in the north differed from Judea in the south. In Galilee, the masses also spoke Greek. Speaking Hebrew in public would have been unusual in Galilee in the first century. In Acts 2, in the description of Pentecost, we read that Galileans spoke languages they never were expected to speak. Hebrew is mentioned among these languages, the language of Judea.[64] The hearers considered it a miracle that those backward Galileans spoke Hebrew. That was certainly not their public language. As mentioned, it was a language that was in use at home in pious families to safeguard the knowledge of the Torah and keep it vivid. That was the reason that Jesus spoke Hebrew at times; for example, in the house of Jairus, supervisor of the synagogue, or at the cross, where Jesus prayed to his Father in the language he had learned to pray at home in his childhood.

---

[64] Acts 2:9.

3. Stenography in the Roman Empire

In chapter 1 we learned that the teachings of Jesus were written down by eyewitnesses while they listened to him. In chapter 2 we saw that their work was not subjected to translation into Aramaic or Hebrew. And so we possess Jesus's words in the vernacular in which he spoke— in Greek. For more insight into the trustworthiness of Jesus's sayings as they are delivered in the Gospels, we will turn to the question of how people in Jesus's time dealt with the spoken word in written texts.

First we will trace this within the context of *historical writing* and subsequently within the context of *administration and jurisdiction*. We will emphasize the period of the Roman Empire (30 BC–AD 395) because the Gospels were written in the beginning of this period.

3.1 The Spoken Word in Greek Historical Writing

The father of Greek historical writing, Thucydides (ca. 470–396 BC), wrote the history of the Peloponnesian War.[65] In the introduction of his work, he explains how he dealt with the spoken word. About the speeches, he said,

> As to the speeches that were made by different men, either when they were about to begin the war or when they were already engaged therein, it has been difficult to recall with strict accuracy the words actually spoken, both for me as regards that which I myself heard, and for those who from various other sources have brought me reports. Therefore the speeches are given in the language in which, as it seemed to me, the several speakers would express, on the subjects under consideration, the sentiments most befitting the occasion, though at the same time I have adhered as closely as possible to the general sense of what was actually said.[66]

---

[65] The war between the Greek cities of Athens and Sparta over a long period of time (431–404 BC).

[66] Thucydides, *De Bello Peleponnesiaco* 1:22.1 Transl. C. F. Smith, *History of the Peloponnesian War*. LCL 108 (London: W. Heinemann, and Cambridge MA: Harvard Univ. Press, 1919), 39

From his definition of his working method, it is obvious that Thucydides gave himself room to not present the speeches exactly as they were spoken. He was concerned to present the tenor of the speeches, at least. Modern researchers in classical history as well as contemporaries and historians who worked after Thucydides understood from his definition that he left some room to maneuver. The spoken word lay embedded in the march of events that formed the backbone of the story.

Thucydides's working method became the standard for classical Greek historical writing. The handicap is that it's not clear how much room a historian permitted himself in using his own imagination, instead of the once-spoken word. For instance, Polybius (ca. 150 BC) drew the sword against authors who trifled with the truth. He reproached the writer Timaeus for using his rich imagination to bring forth extensive speeches on each occasion. He called it "untrue, infantile and a waste of time" to dish up stories like that.[67]

Polybius himself strictly followed the rule set by Thucydides to describe many events and to be sober with speeches. Many hold that the speeches presented by Polybius are very truthful. But Thucydides's rule makes plain that there is no certainty in whether we have verbatim reports or not. This was and has remained the weakness of Greek historical writing, once the premises were accepted. Eventually, it became customary for an author to use speeches to vent his own ideas about all sort of subjects, from moral education to even entertainment. In doing so, authors tried to make their books fascinating for the ordinary readers—or, more correctly, hearers—because there existed a wide-spread custom in antiquity to read to an audience (family, housemates, friends, neighbors) for entertainment.

The above-discussed ambivalence in the presentation of the spoken word in texts is seen in the work of two Jewish authors who lived in the first century in the culture of Hellenism. Both, Philo (ca. 20 BC–ca. AD 50) and Flavius Josephus (37–ca. 100), wrote a lot about the history of old Israel, and both used the Old Testament as a primary source. Where Philo introduces speeches and discussions in his stories, he is sober and closely follows the Old Testament text. It is true that he introduced long treatises about Hellenistic philosophical

---

[67] Polybius, *Historiae* 12:25, 5.

topics in his expositions in trying to show how the biblical persons could compete with Greek philosophers of his time, but in doing so, he did not change the spoken language of the Old Testament persons he described.

The work of Flavius Josephus is quite different. The classical guideline of Thucydides is recognizable. Mostly, he describes sequences of events, and on a few occasions we hear people speak, but in these cases he sometimes goes far beyond his sources. Telling the story of Abraham, who is about to sacrifice his son Isaac, we hear Abraham say,[68] "O my son! I poured out a vast number of prayers that I might have you as my son and when you had been born, I did everything that I could to bring you up and I believed that nothing could make me happier than to see you growing up to be a man and to see how you would be the successor to my dominion at the end of my life."

Abraham then finishes with the words, "He [God] wants to receive your soul with prayers and holy ritual to place you near himself. And there you will be my patron and supporter in my old age. Certainly, for that reason I had to bring you up; and so you will make God to be my Comforter instead of yourself." We don't read any of it in the Abraham story in the book of Genesis. Josephus followed Greek custom in writing history by inserting a speech at the culmination of the occasion with his vision on the event.

The point is, did the gospel writers who were contemporaries of Philo and Flavius Josephus work in the same way as these Jewish historians? If so, we cannot rely on the spoken words in the Gospels with respect to their authenticity. Or did the Gospel writers have other standards in presenting speeches and discussions?

3.2 The Spoken Word in Hellenistic Administration and Jurisdiction

In antiquity the preservation of the spoken word was important in historical writing, but in the fields of *administration, jurisdiction,* and *commerce,* the safeguarding of the spoken word was even more essential—in promulgation of decrees, specific applications of laws,

---

[68] Flavius Josephus, *Antiquities* 1:13.3. Transl. W. Whiston, *The Works of Josephus*, 43.

verbatim records of political discussions, trials, judicial sentences, and in matters of negotiation. In Hellenistic time, the Greeks were well prepared for all these things—this would be the time after Alexander the Great (331 BC) in the eastern part of the Mediterranean.

From the Hellenistic culture of Alexandria, a striking testimony about specific writing activities at the royal court is the so-called letter of Aristeas. It gives a description of how accurately secretaries worked at the royal court in Egypt in the Greek-speaking culture of the Ptolemies. They took the minutes of the conversations between the kings and their dignitaries; they recorded the smallest details, as Aristeas remarked. They worked out their notes, and the next day everything was confirmed by reading. It reads as follows:

> For it is the custom, as you know, from the moment the king begins to transact business until the time when he retires to rest, for a record to be taken of all his sayings and doings—a most excellent and useful arrangement. For on the following day the minutes of the doings and sayings of the previous day are read over before business commences, and if there has been any irregularity, the matter is at once set right. I obtained therefore, as has been said, accurate information from the public records, and I have set forth the facts in proper order since I know how eager you are to obtain useful information.[69]

In the Letter of Aristeas, we are confronted with a comparable working method as in the prologue of Luke. Aristeas is telling about a legation from Jerusalem at the court of Ptolemy II (283–247 BC), and Aristeas, who was present at the audience with Ptolemy, tells about it in his letter to his friend Philocrates. But before he did so, he was able to consult the archives to be well informed through records, as he wished to avoid mistakes. In the prologue of Luke, many are informed by public records of eyewitnesses, who even recorded the spoken words of

---

[69] Letter of Aristeas, or: *Epistula ad Philocratem* 298–300. Transl. R. H. Charles ed., *The Apocrypha and Pseudepigrapha of the Old Testament in English II*, 120.

the events. That seemed to be a standard procedure in the Hellenistic environment of which both Egypt and the Jewish land were part.

For several reasons, scholars consider the Letter of Aristeas not trustworthy in everything. There is also an ongoing debate about the date of writing of the Letter of Aristeas, between circa 270 BC and circa AD 100, roughly the period from Ptolemy II Philadelphos up to Flavius Josephus, who quoted from the letter. How one may judge these particular questions is not of much value for our subject. Josephus certainly held the letter as authentic, and he largely quoted from it. This means that in Josephus's time (first century AD), the letter had met approval and acceptance. And so we have to deal with the reality that in the Hellenistic world, skilled writers were able to record events just as described in the Letter of Aristeas. It is far from an anomaly that Luke referred to a custom of this kind in regard to Jesus's work.

Another Greek testimony comes from Philo of Alexandria (ca. 20 BC–ca. AD 50). He tells us about a magistrate called Lampo, who enriched himself by manipulating legal documents:

> For standing by the rulers when they gave judgment, he took notes of all that took place at the trial as if he were a clerk; and then he designedly passed over or omitted such and such points, and interpolated other things which were not said. And at times, too, he made alterations, changing and altering, and perverting matters, and turning things upside down, aiming to get money by every syllable, or, I might rather say, by every letter, like a hunter after musty records, whom the whole people with one accord did often with great felicity and propriety of expression call a pen-murderer, as slaying numbers of persons by the things which he wrote.[70]

This story shows that there were clerks at work at royal courts and also at trials to record the spoken word. A certain Lampo behaved like such a clerk in governmental practice but in a terrible way,

---

[70] Philo, *Flaccus* 131. Transl. C. D. Yonge, *The Works of Philo* (Peabody MA: Hendrickson Publishers, 1993), 736.

by perverting what was said. The people called such a man a pen-murderer. As there was one rule for all in the Roman Empire—the eastern Greek- and the western Latin-speaking part of it—we can be sure that important matters such as legal processes everywhere in the empire—and also in the Jewish land—had been organized in the same way, with clerks to preserve the spoken word on behalf of fair trials.[71] It is, of course, of great value to know how secretaries were able to accurately record the spoken word in the Roman Empire.

3.3.1 Origin of Latin Stenography

There is an important testimony from Plutarch (ca. 46–120 AD) on the beginning of stenography in public life:

> And its preservation [of Cato's oration] was due to Cicero the consul, who had previously given to those clerks who excelled in rapid writing instruction in the use of signs, which, in small and short figures, comprised the force of many letters; these clerks he had then distributed in various parts of the senate-house. For up to that time the Romans [literal: *one* instead of *the Romans*] did not employ or even possess what are called shorthand writers, but then for the first time, we are told, the first steps toward the practice [literal: *toward the trail*] were taken. Be that as it may, Cato carried the day and changed the opinions of the senators, so that they condemned the men to death.[72]

This is the oldest documented case of stenography—the verbatim fixation of the oration of Cato the Younger against Catilina and his conspirators. It was held on the fifth of December in the year 63 BC before the Roman senate. Plutarch remarks that the writers made use

---

[71] It is said in the Mishnah (Sanhedrin 4:3) that two scribes were writing during a process in the Jewish high court (Sanhedrin). Rabbi Judah remarked, according to this passage, that it used three writers.
[72] Plutarch, *Cato Minor* 23.3. Transl. B. Perrin, *Plutarch's Lives VIII, Cato the Younger.* LCL 100 (London: W. Heinemann and New York: G. P. Putnam's Sons, 1919), 290–91.

of special signs instead of ordinary letters and that these signs did not represent one consonant or vowel each but several sounds or letters each. This was the first stage of stenography that was characterized by one sign per syllable.

Plutarch is telling about an assembly of the Roman senate with one issue under debate: the conduct of life of Catilina, a high-born Roman citizen. He was the leader of a group of conspirators purposing to bring down the government. He wanted to get into power, and for that purpose he brought together an army of ten thousand men. There could be no doubt about his destructive intentions. It was clear to every citizen of Rome that Catilina and his conspirators were traitors, and they deserved no other characterization than subversive betrayers of the state. But what happened in this difficult situation?

Catilina and his conspirators were Roman citizens. Did they have the right to be punished as Romans, according to Roman law? If so, they should have been punished with a sentence of exile. Or did they lose the privileges that were applicable to Roman citizens since they intended to oppose and stand against the Roman state and consequently against Roman law? In this case, they had put themselves outside of the law, and they could be sentenced to death without trial. The senate hesitated about which choice to make, as Catilina and his conspirators were Romans by birth and had the right by law of a fair trial at a Roman court. On the other hand, the city of Rome was in a state of tension; Catilina's hostile army wandered through the woods of Italy, ready to attack the city, and the eyes of the people were turned toward the senate. What would be the decision in this dangerous situation?

The senate's final session on the subject had come, and the senator who was ready to bring forward the final oration was Cato the Younger. Consul Cicero, who knew that Cato had a harsh point of view on the issue (with which he agreed), brought some stenographers into the senate hall to record Cato's oration. When he finished, the entire senate was convinced that a firm stand would be taken in this matter. That day, Catilina was sentenced, in his absence, to death, and his Roman conspirators, who earlier had been brought to prison, were also sentenced to death; the sentence was executed that same day. The use of stenography had contributed in no small way to the outcome; it had proven to be a political tool. The senators realized that their words were written down, and everybody in Rome could hear about their individual positions within a few hours. There was no room for mistakes or doubtful statements. Moreover, it would be impossible to change positions later on, as they were recorded by the stenographers. The moment was now.

This event has remained a moment of significance within Roman history. The Republic was saved, and so all the ins and outs of the affair could not fade from memory or disappear from the annals of history. It remained irrefutable forever that stenography had been part of the scene, and it had appeared to be decisive in politics. It was no coincidence that, four years later, the taking of minutes was permanently implemented in the senate and connected with the regular publication of official records (acta senatus). At the same time, a daily newspaper was introduced in Rome (acta diurna).[73] This was the time of circa 60 BC. Within a few years, stenography had settled as indispensable in public affairs. A continuing progression of shorthand writing in the Roman culture was the result of Cicero's introduction of the art—refinement of the system and intensification of the art in various parts of society.

Testimonies from the first century BC and from the first century AD confirm this picture. From several orations from this period, we know, through explicit mentioning, that they were recorded by stenographers—orations from Caesar, Cicero, Antonius, Tiberius, Claudius, and Quintilianus.[74]

According to Plutarch, Cicero gave instruction in the use of steno signs to writers, who already excelled in rapid writing.[75] These signs

---

[73] S. Lauffer, *Abriss der antiken Geschichte* (München: R. Oldenbourg, 1956). Transl. J. H. Schmitz, *De Klassieke Geschiedenis in Jaartallen* (Utrecht/ Antwerpen: Het Spectrum, 1964), 141.

[74] C. Johnen, *Geschichte der Stenographie I* (Berlin: Ferdinand Schrey, 1911), 168. See further: H. Boge, *Griechische Tachygraphie und Tironische Noten: Ein Handbuch der antiken und Mittelalterlichen Schnellschrift* (Berlin: Akademie Verlag, 1973), 221.

[75] It is a question whether Cicero was allowed to admit slaves as stenographers to the senate meeting. In the fourth Catilinarian oration, Cicero says (5 Dec. 63 BC) that clerks of state were gathered at the forum of Rome to assign, by lot, new quaestor secretaries who took charge of the public archives and the public treasury. They belonged to the *ordo honestus*, and Cicero himself

became known as Tironian notes. Tiro, a liberated slave of Cicero, was the designer of the Latin steno system, and in antiquity his name always has been connected with the origin of shorthand writing in the Roman Empire.

3.3.2 Latin Stenography in the First Century BC and AD

After the introduction of stenography, we hear only sporadic testimonies about the art. Yet it is possible to get a global image of it from the few remarks in the available literature.

The first period of stenography appeared to be rather silent, from 63 BC until circa AD 65. Bishop Isidor of Sevilla wrote about it as follows:

> At first Ennius used about eleven hundred customary signs [notae vulgares]. The use of these signs was to record the spoken word fully in cases of public meetings and legal proceedings. Several writers worked simultaneously, each doing his own part of the work, taking down in regular order as much of what was said as possible. In Rome Tullius Tiro, a liberated slave of Cicero, was the first to present signs [notas], but only for the first syllables. After him Vipsanius Filagrius and Aquila (a liberated slave of Maecenas) have given a variety of additions. Finally, it was Seneca who brought everything together; he arranged and completed a collection of five thousand notes.[76]

---

had been quaestor for some time. It is possible that he had the opportunity to instruct clerks of state in shorthand. It seems obvious that only they were allowed to be present at senate meetings for recording.

[76] Isidor of Sevilla, *Etymologiae* 1:22. Transl. present author. Isidor wrote this between 615 and 618. It is generally accepted that Isidor, with his résumé about shorthand writing, goes back to the author Suetonius (ca. AD 77–140). Latin text in: www.hs-augsburg.de/~harsch/Chronologia/Lspost07/Isidorus/isi_et01.html#c22. German transl. C. Johnen, *Geschichte der Stenographie I*, 164.

The so-called signs of Ennius consisted of common script letters and figures and for that reason were called *notae vulgares*—common notes (normal letters and abbreviations). Long before Tiro, the system of Ennius (239–169 BC) was used for recording sayings of political or legal value by omissions of vowels, contractions, and regular abbreviations of standard expressions. Tiro presented new signs, each representing more sounds (letters) at the same time, and that remained the basic principle of stenography forever. As Isidor said, many improvements were added to Tiro's system later on by men such as Vipsanius Filagrius and Aquila, who lived in the period of Caesar Augustus (30 BC–AD 14). Still later, it was Seneca who made collections of existing signs, halfway through the first century AD. For that reason, steno signs have also been called signs of Seneca (*notae Senecae*) instead of signs of Tiro.[77]

Seneca (ca. 4 BC–65 AD) was extremely rich and has become known as an author and philosopher. He has given a remarkable statement about stenography, which is important for understanding why there was such a long silent period since the beginning. He said:

> Or our signs for whole words, which enable us to take down a speech, however rapidly uttered, matching speed of tongue by speed of hand? All this sort of thing has been devised by the lowest grade of slaves. Wisdom's seat is higher; she trains not the hands, but is mistress of our minds.[78]

It is clear that in Seneca's time, stenography was still slaves' work. The human minds needed training in wisdom *more* than the hand of the stenographer. He continued, "The other arts, it is true, wisdom has under her control, for he whom life serves is also served by the things which equip life." Seneca's statement explains that the Romans admired the skill of the slaves who understood stenography, but it was not good for Romans to do. They needed all their time for training

---

[77] C. Johnen, *Geschichte der Stenographie*, 169. He gives AD 54–68 (the period of Nero).

[78] Seneca, *Ad Lucilium Epistolae* 90.25 (26–27) Transl. M. Gummere, *Epistles of Seneca II*. LCL 076 (London: W. Heinemann, and Cambridge MA: Harvard, Univ. Press, 1920), 415–17.

the minds and spirits of the people; certainly he meant "to rule the immense Roman Empire." Stenography was a welcome tool for the Romans, but as slaves' work, it remained in the dark, and little has been left of it from the first century—no notes and a minimum of remarks in the available literature.

The differences between the life of a free Roman and that of a slave were many. Daily life brought the necessity of contact between the two classes, but a modus vivendi existed, with a minimum of contact. That was the best for both groups—no warm contacts or even friendships, which only caused disappointments and tensions. Although Seneca gave the command to his slaves to collect all the signs and to classify them, one should not suppose that Seneca, as a free Roman, was personally involved in the project. That would be overstepping the mark. The Romans indeed greatly admired shorthand writing, as we may learn from a saying of Martiales, the poet who worked from AD 64 in the city of Rome. He said, "Albeit the words speed, the hand is swifter than they: not yet has the tongue, the hand has finished its work."[79]

Why do we know so little about the first period of stenography? The reasons are as follows:

1. The signs were written on wax tablets, which were cleaned after use. Consequently, we don't have steno signs from that period.
2. Stenography belonged almost entirely to the world of slavery. It was many years before the Roman youth were educated in stenography (end of the first century AD).
3. Writers and orators were famous for their fine and elegant use of language, but stenography was seen as a mechanical process, not worth mentioning.

Still, there have been examples of warm contacts between slaves who were fluent in shorthand writing and their Roman masters, and therefore, they are worth mentioning. It started already with Tiro and

---

[79] Martiales, *Epigrams* XIV, 208. Transl. W. C. A. Ker, *Martial Epigrams II.* LCL 095 (London: W. Heinemann, and New York: G. P. Putnam's Sons, 1920), 513.

Cicero. They grew up together, and their relationship was so good that Cicero gave Tiro his freedom (53 BC). Plinius Secundus (23–79 AD), who perished in the eruption of Mount Vesuvius, had the habit of bringing stenographers on his journeys.[80] Suetonius has related that Emperor Titus (79–81 AD) competed in stenography with his clerks (*amanuenses*).[81] These exceptions confirm that stenography was in use in the highest layers of society already.

At the end of the first century, the poet Martiales gave testimony that the number of teachers in stenography was about the number of customary teachers.[82] From the second century onward, shorthand writing became a free profession, and young people (not only slaves) were educated in the art. At the end of the period of the Roman emperors, stenography had become one of the regular subjects of schooling. Unfortunately, examples of Latin steno signs from the period of the Roman Empire do not exist. In spite of many changes over the centuries, however, the system was in use until the late Middle Ages. Signs preserved from the time of the Middle Ages still substantially show how shorthand writing looked in antiquity.

About Latin stenography, the historian C. Johnen remarked: "The young art has taken a deep root in the old Roman culture and it grew up luxuriantly. In that brilliant building of the Roman flowering time until the death of Marcus Aurelius (180), in this 'newest time' of Roman history this small but remarkable characteristic of a high culture could not be missed in any way."[83] Indeed, in this period stenographers were some of the various servants of the public authorities: imperial and royal courts, senate, local authorities, and courts of justice.

From this time, the persecutions of Christians also increased in the Roman Empire. Many trials against martyrs were recorded by stenographers (Latin as well as Greek), and Christians often could lay hands on the records later on to read them in memorial services. From the third and fourth centuries onward, stenographers served the church fathers; they recorded their public preaching, teaching, instructions, and debates, and stenographers particularly took care

---

[80] C. Johnen, *Geschichte der Stenographie*, 170.

[81] Suetonius, *Titus* 3.3.

[82] C. Johnen, *Geschichte der Stenographie*, 171.

[83] C. Johnen, *Geschichte der Stenographie*, 171.

of recording the acts of church conferences. It is well known that nearly all church fathers and church teachers had stenographers at their disposal.

Greek-speaking:

- Origen (ca. 250)
- Eusebius (ca. 325)
- Basil the Great (ca. 350)
- Athanasius of Alexandria (ca. 375)

Latin-speaking:

- Jerome (ca. 375)
- Augustine of Hippo (ca. 400)[84]

When one or more regular stenographers of Augustine were absent during a service, there were always enough volunteers among the people to fill the gap. The next quote is from Basil the Great who had been a steno teacher himself: "Who has learned the art of stenography, not only has the signs and the meanings of them engraved on his soul, but also the octads and tetrads ... Who could strip off his body, would find on his inner self the text of the Commentary [the teaching steno system]."[85]

3.4.1 Early Greek Stenography in the Roman State

We are as little informed about early Greek shorthand writing in the first century BC and AD as we are about the Latin variant; the testimonies also are not very numerous. Early Greek stenography had a silent period in the beginning, just as did the Latin variant. An old tradition among scholars held the view that the Greeks were the inventors of stenography in the fourth or third century BC.[86] From

---

[84] C. Johnen, *Geschichte der Stenographie*, 120–21; A. Mentz, *Geschichte der Kurzschrift* (Wolfenbüttel: Heckner, 1949), 24.

[85] Basilius, *De Virginitate*.

[86] The learned Lipsius wrote a letter in 1597 with the title *De Notis* about shorthand writing in antiquity. He defended the thesis that there existed

approximately 1850, a change of opinion began among German scholars. Before World War II there was a difference of opinion about this between the two decipherers, H. J. M. Milne and A. Mentz. Milne defended the priority of the old Greek invention.[87] Mentz, on the contrary, denied that there existed any Greek stenography before the introduction of the art by Cicero in the senate. Increasingly scholars defended the view that the Romans invented the art and that Tiro, with his signs, was the starting point. Milne and Mentz agreed that the Greek and the Latin variants of shorthand writing developed according to the same principles. Milne said, "For the systems are without doubt closely related. Their basic principles are identical, and the formal coincidences are too frequent and too striking to be fortuitous."[88]

It was the conviction of Mentz that the Roman and Greek culture was interwoven so closely that it seemed impossible that an important art as stenography could exist in only one of the two cultures and was lacking in the other. About the necessity of the coming together of the Latin and the Greek systems in antiquity, A. Mentz remarked, "As we may observe in our modern culture, an invention which the world needs, is made nearly simultaneously in different places. At present nobody knows with certainty who was the original inventor."[89]

---

a Greek system of shorthand writing that was older than the Latin variant. E. R. Richards, "The Secretary in the Letters of Paul." in *Wissenschaftliche Untersuchungen zum Neuen Testament*. Zweite Reihe – 42, begründet von J. Jeremias, O. Michel (Tübingen: J. C. B. Mohr / Paul Siebeck, 1991) follows this point of view that the Greeks invented real shorthand (tachygraphy).

[87] H. J. M. Milne, *Greek Shorthand Manuals, Syllabary and Commentary* (London: Egypt Exploration Society, 1934), 1. Diogenes Laertius (ca. 300 AD) delivered a custom of Xenophon (ca. 400 BC) "*huposèmeioosamenos*" (underwriting/signing) *the spoken words to people*. Milne supposed that this referred to stenography: making notes in private (meanwhile) of the spoken words of people. However, this Greek term was never a technical term for steno. It could also be: writing a personal "sign" under dictated letters (spoken words to people), as Paul did under his letters (2 Thessalonians 3:7). One or more clarifying remarks under (at the end) of an epistle to someone. The substantive *huposèmeioosis* is still "footnote" in modern Greek.

[88] Milne, idem, 2.

[89] A. Mentz, *Ein Schülerheft mit altgriechischer Kurzschrift* (Bayreuth: Gauverlag Bayerische Ostmark, 1940), 55.

There was indeed a practical need for the existence of both systems: the Romans became dependent on stenography for administration and jurisdiction. This required an implementation of the art as quickly as possible in the Greek-speaking eastern colonies of the state. Roman governors, who were in charge, were obliged to work according to Roman standards, especially in cases of jurisdiction and administration.

Moreover, as the Greek and the Latin steno system was built according to the same principles, it seems that similar adaptations have taken place side by side. This is so striking that on the basis of these similarities, Mentz has said, "The genesis of the Greek stenography in three phases finds its accurate parallel in the development of the Latin system."[90] As we saw earlier, the first step of the Latin system took place with the work of Tiro. New developments came, according to Isidorus, with Vipsanius Filagrius and Aquila in the time of Emperor Augustus, while the last important event was initiated by Seneca—collecting and arranging the existing signs (section 3.3.2).

Greek shorthand has three old and important testimonies. First, there is a papyrus from AD 155, found in the Egyptian sand. This document contains an arrangement between a rich Egyptian named Panechotes and a steno teacher named Appolonios. The agreement is that the Greek slave Chaerammon of Panechotes will follow a course in stenography for two years. The fee of 120 drachmas will be paid in three parts: (1) at the start of the course, (2) when the pupil has learned the signs, and (3) when the pupil can record a simple dictation and read it faultlessly. This message shows that in about 155, Greek stenography existed and was rooted in the Egyptian culture. Also striking in this document are technical terms, such as *sèmeia* (steno signs), *sèmeiography* (stenography), and *commentary* (steno lesson book). These Greek terms are all standard expressions in Greek literature from the second century onward.

Another old testimony with a reference to Greek shorthand is Plutarch's testimony (ca. AD 100) of Cicero's introduction of stenography in the Roman senate, which is mentioned earlier (see section 3.3.1). In it, we find typical Greek steno expressions: *sèmeia graphein* (writing steno) and *sèmeiographos* (stenographer). It means

---

[90] Mentz, *Ein Schülerheft*, 54.

that by approximately AD 100, these technical terms already existed in the Greek language area. It is generally accepted, then, that Greek shorthand existed and was widespread in approximately AD 100. Last but not least, there is a letter in which the orator Cicero, the introducer of Latin stenography, used a Greek expression of the new art of writing.

3.4.2 Cicero's Letter to Atticus, dia sèmei–oon

There is a much older testimony about Greek stenography that, unfortunately, most scholars tend to overlook—a letter from Cicero to his friend Atticus in the year 45 BC.[91] In this Latin letter, Cicero used the later Greek technical term: writing *dia sèmei-oon* (through signs): "You don't quite understand what I wrote to you about the ten Commissioners, no doubt because I wrote *dia sèmei-oon* (through signs)." The early use of the term *sèmeia* (later the Greek term for steno signs) exercised many minds in the first half of the twentieth century. Did Cicero mean "through steno signs" with the expression *dia sèmei-oon*? And if so, what then did he mean?

A serious difficulty is that the term *dia sèmei-oon* was a Greek technical term meaning "through steno signs" about 150 years later than Cicero. So the question was, is it appropriate to apply this meaning to the expression, as it was used 150 years earlier? Another point that has brought confusion about the passage is that scholars have used it to defend the thesis that Greek stenography existed earlier than the Latin. The use of the Greek term *dia sèmei-oon* in a Latin context would prove that. However, it is far too much to state, from Cicero's use of this expression, that Greek stenography was earlier and more authentic than the Latin. When he used the expression *dia sèmei-oon*, twenty years already had passed since the introduction of the art in the Roman senate by Cicero. How is it possible that Cicero's rather flippant remark could refer to Greek stenography as many years older than the Latin variant? That is not very likely.

The confusion among scholars over this passage in the past has

---

[91] Cicero, *Ad Atticum*, 305 (XIII. 32. 3); 29 May, AD 45; Transl. D. R. Shackleton Bailey ed., *Cicero's Letters to Atticus V* (Cambridge: University Press, 1966), 175–179.

resulted in modern researchers having lost interest in the text. And that is a pity because we may indeed learn important aspects of the origins of Greek stenography from it. What happens when a speaker or author uses an expression in a different language? That is the kernel of the matter. There may be several reasons for a change of language. The speaker or author may like to stress something, or he wants to make a point with a strange word that is more applicable, or he wants to use a more eloquent style. And so this expression certainly had a significant meaning and could not be misunderstood. With these aspects in mind, the use of Cicero's expression *dia sèmei-oon* in his letter to Atticus is quite understandable.

Shakleton Bailey's authoritative translation of Cicero has "abbreviations" for *dia sèmei-oon*.[92] That really is to the point, as in an earlier letter to Atticus, Cicero gave the figure fourteen, not written in letters but in Roman numerals: XIIII. This was an abbreviation of written text.[93] Cicero later wrote that Atticus had not correctly understood the number XIIII. "You don't quite understand what I wrote to you about the ten Commissioners, no doubt because I wrote *dia sèmei-oon* [through signs, through abbreviations]." The figure XIIII that Atticus did not understand well is indeed ambiguous in

---

[92] Shackleton Bailey, *Cicero's Letters to Atticus*, 179. The translation "stenographically" or "by stenographical signs" (Wattenbach, Preisigke, Von Gardthausen, Viereck) lacks proof. The translation "by indications" (Weinberger, Mentz, Boge) is untenable, as the meaning of *sèmeion* is a clear mark. If this last translation is correct, then Cicero has a contradiction, in his letter. "You *don't quite understand* what I wrote to you about the ten Commissioners, no doubt because I wrote *dia sèmei-oon* (by clear indications)." Mentz supposed that indications in Cicero's question are the *sèmei-oon* instead of the abbreviations XIIII that Cicero used. Cicero, who introduced stenography, could not mistakenly use this term as a terminus technicus for writing of abbreviations. The translation "by indications" or *en demi-mots* (Tyrell, Purser) is an unjustified mitigation. A synopsis of the translations is found in Boge, *Griechische Tachygraphie und Tironisch Noten*, 43–45.

[93] "One has understood for long that with *vulgares notae* are meant abbreviations of normal writing, which are *litterae singulares*, therefore also the abbreviations of figures by the first letters of them." *Paulys Real-Encyclopädie XI der Classischen Altertumswissenschaft* (1922), 2225/2226. Transl. present author.

a former letter.[94] It can refer to a yearbook, and then we may read "the fourteenth yearbook" or "yearbook fourteen," but it can also refer to a period of time, and then we may read "fourteen years."[95] Cicero meant the last option, because in his later letter, he explained, "How could he have been a Commissioner XIIII [fourteen] years before becoming Praetor?" Again in this later letter, he used the abbreviations XIIII, and he justified this use with the stylish Greek expression *dia sèmei-oon* (through abbreviations/signs), which reveals several things:

1. The expression *dia sèmei-oon* was undoubtedly used here as a technical term concerning abbreviations in writing (XIIII).[96]
2. As Cicero switched to the Greek expression, it is clear that it was a popular, commonly used term that didn't need any explanation for Atticus.
3. The use of the Greek term in a Latin text shows clearly that the abbreviation system for which it stood was no less valued than the Latin system of stenography, which had been in use for about twenty years at that time.
4. Remarkably, the expression *dia sèmei-oon* was used here for Roman numeral signs (XIIII) and is only explicable as follows: Tiro had adopted current numeral signs for figures in Latin stenography, and the Greek stenographers in turn also followed the same Roman numerals for figures in Greek stenography.
5. Cicero switched to the Greek expression *dia sèmei-oon*, as Greek steno was a preferred form of speedy writing, more so than the Latin variant in Italy at that time.[97] The extensiveness

---

[94] To Atticus 303 (13.30.2); 28 May, AD 45; Shackleton Bailey, *Cicero's Letters to Atticus*, 176.

[95] It is possible to read, "In Libo's year-book XIIII (fourteen/fourteenth) Tuditanus is years later praetor than consul Mummius." But also possible is "In Libo's year-book Tuditanus is XIIII (fourteen) years later praetor than consul Mummius."

[96] Fourteen—Latin: quattuordecim; Greek: tettares kai deka, dekatessares.

[97] Great Greek-speaking communities in Rome and in other Italian cities lived together with the Latin-speaking population. Many Romans were bilingual. Even in the first century, the apostle Paul wrote his letter to the

of the large Greek communities in Rome and Italy will have contributed to it.

Considering these points, the question whether a Greek stenography existed in about 45 BC can be answered affirmatively. Cicero's letter to Atticus shows that a Greek steno system existed shortly after the beginning of the Latin system and also that the systems developed together. And there is more!

3.4.3 Origin of Greek Stenography

To answer the question when Greek stenography came into being, we have to return to the testimony of Plutarch (in full, section 3.3.1). The final remark of it is noteworthy and decisive (own translation in basic words): "For one did not yet train nor possess the so called stenographers, but then at first one descended onto a trail, one says."[98] The preclause says that one (the people; impersonal or general plural) did not yet possess the so-called *sèmeiográphous* (Greek for stenographers).[99].

Romans in Greek. The Romans admired the Greek culture and tried to duplicate it in many ways, which gave a positive interaction between the two populations in Italy (Greco-Roman culture).

[98] Plutarch uses the Greek here for "track, trail." He also uses the expression "enter into a trail," "stepping into a trail" in other instances. Meaning of *kathistèmi* put down (act.), go down (refl.) in combination with *eis íchnos*: make someone go (act.) on a trail, or: go (refl.) on a trail (trace, track, path). Examples of Plutarch, translations by B. Perrin: *Plutarch's Lives VII, Alexander.* LCL 099 (London: W. Heinemann, and New York: G. P. Putnam's Sons, 1919), 304 "They had *set* them *in the track* of the march" (27.3); *Plutarch's Lives X, Agis and Cleomenes.* LCL 102 (London: W. Heinemann, and New York: G. P. Putnam's Sons, 1921) 90 "and re-*entered the track* of their famous discipline" (18.4). Translation by W. C. Helmbold, *Plutarch's Moralia VI, Can virtue be taught?* LCL 337 (London: W. Heinemann, and Cambridge MA: Harvard Univ. Press, 1939) 8 "to *take a first step*, as it were, *on the path* of virtue." (439. F)

[99] There is no grammatical constituent for the third-person plural in the closing sentence to refer to, so there is no other option than an *impersonal* or *general* plural: *one* instead of *they*. The entire paragraph is a *one* message.

Who did Plutarch have in mind in the preclause with "one"? There are a few options:

1. He is speaking about the lack of Greek stenographers.
2. He is speaking about the lack of Latin stenographers.
3. He is speaking about the lack of stenographers in general, both Greeks and Romans.

From the perspective of the Greek language in which he is writing, the word *sèmeiográphous* (stenographers) might be applicable to Greek stenographers or of any other language area; in this case, of the Roman world. In the past, translators chose the Romans, but it is not in the text. Moreover, it seems that in the Greek expression "the so called *sèmeiográphous*," the Greek stenographers are included. In any way "one in general" refers to both Romans and Greeks together.[100]

In the preclause, Plutarch states that *in general,* no stenographers existed before 63 BC, neither among the Romans nor among the Greeks. The few men who were trained by Cicero on his personal initiative are to be excluded from the general state of affairs regarding the lack of Latin stenography in Italy in 63 BC, according to Plutarch's description here. Then, in the postclause (again a general plural), he affirms that in both languages (contrasting context, antithesis), one began to follow the steno signs "but *then for the first time* one descended (stepped) on a trail as one says."[101] In short, the institution of the

---

It starts with *one* (general plural): "This is the only speech of Cato which has been preserved, *one* says."

[100] Examples of the impersonal or indefinite (general) plural in the New Testament are given by Turner, *A Grammar of New Testament Greek*, 292–93. Mark 3:21; 14:2—for one (they) said; Mark 10:13—And one (they) brought children to him. A. Mentz emphasized the meaning of *one* (German: *man*) as a general plural in Plutarch's testimony, in: *Geschichte und Systeme der griechischen Tachygraphy* (Berlin: Verlag von Gerdes & Hödel, 1907) 15. However he failed to see the restrictive meaning of the indefinite pronoun *one: Greeks and Romans*. The term *so called* in the preclause refers to the type of craftsmen in Plutarchs time known as "stenographers", that is among: *Greeks and Romans*. And this is therefore the meaning for *one* (they) in pre- and postclause.

[101] TDNT III, 402. "*Ichnos* means 'footprint,' and may be used either for an individual impression on the ground or for a continuous line of such

so-called stenographers (Roman as well as Greek) in the Greco-Roman culture of Plutarch's time started following the track right from the introduction of the art in the Roman senate.

The most interesting aspect of Plutarch's final remark is that an accurate year can be given for the beginning of Roman and Greek stenography in history: 63 BC. After Cicero's introduction of it, Romans and many people of the Greek communities in Italy looked for intelligent slaves to learn the new signs of writing or to develop them (for the Greek part).

Why did Plutarch speak of "a (sort of/certain) trail" and not of "the trail" to his Greek readers? After the first application of stenography in public, many improvements of the art followed for the Latin as well as for the Greek variant. In both languages, they elaborated on the first principles of stenography, as given by Tiro. In particular, the Greek stenographers could copy many—but not all—Roman signs of stenography. Once it was created for Latin, the principles could be applied to the Greek language immediately. The signs of Tiro were created from fragments of ordinary letters, capitals, and script letters, and the Greeks did the same. Mentz remarked about the Greek signs, "In everything one is reminded to the work of Tiro."[102] That was certainly the reason that Plutarch spoke about *a* trail instead of *the* trail.

The old assumption that stenography was a Greek invention from the time of the great Greek authors in approximately 500 BC caused scholars, before World War II, to think that Plutarch was writing only about the breakthrough of Roman stenography, according to the supposed old Greek example. However, the lack of stenographic technical terms over the period of 500–63 BC in Greek makes this view impossible. This was Mentz's main argument for the priority of Latin stenography. And he was right, but he gave only a vague suggestion in answering the question of when the Greeks began with the new art of writing. He supposed it was approximately 50 BC.[103]

---

impressions, i.e., a trail."

[102] Mentz, *Geschichte der Kurzschrift*, 20.

[103] Mentz's vague suggestion (*Ein Schülerheft*, 53, 55) about the beginning of Greek stenography in 50 BC gave a foothold for the current assumption that the Greeks followed the Roman invention late, only in the second

It is worth noting the Greek background that must have influenced the wording of stenography in the Roman world. Ennius was born (239 BC) in the Greek-speaking community of Rudiae in the neighborhood of Tarente in Italy. He introduced many Greek elements into Latin literature, and he taught Greek language in Rome. He introduced eleven hundred notes into Latin (*notae vulgares*, abbreviations by normal letters). It is hard to believe that this was his own invention; rather, he followed Greek practice. At that time, *oksugraphy* already existed in Greek. This technical term referred to a form of speedy writing by omitting letters, particularly vowels (Greek: *oksus*, fast; *graphy*, writing). We know that because in the Greek translation of the Old Testament, the Septuagint from the third/second century BC, the word *oksugraphos* is used in Psalm 45:2. As the Hebrew writing system worked without vowels, it is clear that the Greek word *oksugraphos* has the meaning in the Septuagint of a writer who wrote quickly by omitting letters. This one Greek word, *oksugraphos,* for two Hebrew words (sopheer mahir—ready scribe, speedy writer) is convincing evidence that the Greeks already knew a system for speedy writing in the third/second century BC, but it was not yet stenography.

In the Letter of Aristeas, we read about royal secretaries at the court in Alexandria (third/second century BC) who recorded everything that was done and said, no doubt by using *oksugraphy* (see section 3.4.3); that was certainly the Greek fashion at that time. When Tiro introduced improvements into the Latin system by steno signs, it was a natural consequence that the Greek-speaking community in Italy enthusiastically would apply Tiro's invention instead of the old system of oksugraphy. This state of affairs fully explains Cicero's easy switch to the Greek term *dia sèmei-oon*.[104] The Greeks set the fashion for the Romans in Cicero's time, even in the art of shorthand writing that Tiro had invented.

---

century AD (Boge, *Griechische Tachygraphie und Tironische Noten*). See section 3.5 Contra Boge-Millard.

[104] Oksugraphy was compelled to disappear after Tiro's introduction of stenography. In Latin, however, many notae vulgares remained extant later on as fixed forms; for example, abbreviations of figures (Roman numerals), PR (Populus Romanus: People of Rome), SPQR (Senatus PopulusQue Romanus: Senate and People of Rome).

3.4.4 Developments of Stenography under Caesar Augustus

The decipherers Milne and Mentz have pointed out that in Latin and in Greek stenography similar improvements were applied. It's worth mentioning that Bishop Isidor of Sevilla also made reference to improvements (section 3.3.2): "In Rome Tullius Tiro, a liberated slave of Cicero, was the first to present signs [notas], but only for the first syllables.[105] After him Vipsanius Filagrius and Aquila (a freed slave of Maecenas) provided a variety of additions. Finally, it was Seneca who brought everything together; he arranged and completed a collection of five thousand notes." Mentz supposed that improvements deviating from the Tironian syllables were made for the Latin: word endings (declinations).[106] Case endings of words appeared in Latin steno later than Tiro's signs and were also adapted for the Greek system; they are, in fact, tiny scraps at four fixed places around the sign of a last syllable of a word-stem.

Vipsanius Filagrius was probably of Greek origin, as his name shows, while the name Aquila is linked to Latin.[107] C. Johnen has demonstrated that these freed slaves lived within the entourage of Caesar Augustus.[108] And so it looks as though these men worked together in preparing and implementing their improvements. It may be the case that Vipsanius and Aquila worked out the new additions for Latin and Greek stenography to standardize steno for the west and the east of the Roman Empire. If so, it was a brilliant initiative, and who could better take this initiative to organize government, jurisdiction, and trading than Caesar Augustus, who ruled during the most successful period of the empire (golden age)? If we are

---

[105] Tiro started with the presentation in steno of the first syllables of a word; that is, without declinations (declensions) of the words. Some have supposed only the first syllable of a word, but that's unlikely, as it would imply too much confusion.

[106] Mentz, *Ein Schülerheft*, 28; *Geschichte der Kurzschrift*, 16–17, 20.

[107] Vipsanius Filagrius: (Greek: Philargyros, who loves silver, money?). Aquila: (Latin: eagle), the Greek variant is Akulos.

[108] Johnen, *Geschichte der Stenographie*, 169. Vipsanius Filagrius probably was a liberated slave of Marcus Vipsanius Agrippa, a general and nephew of Augustus. Aquila was a liberated slave of Maecenas, an adviser and friend of Augustus for a long time.

right in pointing to Vipsanius Filagrius and Aquila for the latter improvements in Latin and Greek stenography, we have a realistic explanation for the approximately five thousand notes in Seneca's collection (testimony of Isidor; see section 3.3.2). Let us assume for the notae vulgares about fifteen hundred abbreviations each for the Greek and the Latin system. That would leave about two thousand steno signs; or about a thousand steno signs for each system (Greek and Latin). Included in each system were then Tiro's old steno signs, the improvements by Vipsanius Filagrius and Aquila, and changes of individual stenographers before and after them.[109] Then we are dealing with realistic figures that underline the theory that Latin and Greek stenography originated in Italy and that the Romans promoted both systems as valuable tools in society.

According to a more accurate grammatical analysis of Plutarch's testimony it is possible to give a different picture for the beginning of Greek stenography, based on better historical evidence. In 63 BC, Greek stenography began, together with the Latin variant, with the signs for syllables, according to Tiro's principles (Tironian notes). From the outset, it was an adequate tool to record speeches, as was the Latin variant, with which one picked up the speeches of Cato and, later, Cicero and Caesar.[110] There is no reason to suppose there was a divergence when the improvements of Vipsanius Filagrius and Aquila were implemented in the Latin system in the time of Caesar Augustus, at the beginning of the era. They were immediately followed in the Greek system to standardize the important tool of stenography in administration, jurisdiction, and commerce in the Roman Empire.

3.5 Contra Boge-Millard

A. Millard showed that reading and writing were integral parts of the Jewish culture in which Jesus lived and worked. He claimed, however, that Greek stenography originated in the second century AD.[111] He relied on a study by H. Boge for his opinion: "The most extensive study of

---

[109] After Tiro, early and late, there have been stenographers who elaborated with their own improvements on the standardized systems, as is certain from steno documents and steno messages in books and on tombs.

[110] Mentz, *Geschichte der Kurzschrift*, 16.

[111] Millard, *Reading and Writing in the Time of Jesus*, 175–76.

the topic concluded there was no true Greek shorthand until the second century AD when it was borrowed from the Latin."[112] Millard does not say why he regards this study of Boge as so reliable, neither does he give any argument from the work supporting this view, and so he keeps his readers in the dark concerning the evidence for his opinion.[113] Why should one attach so much value to an author (Boge) who lived two thousand years after the events? Why not listen to the testimonies of Cicero and Plutarch, skilled authors, who lived then? Before seeking to unravel this, we have to remark on the quality of Boge's work.

Boge was a student of Arthur Mentz, one of the decipherers of Greek stenography in the twentieth century. Boge brought together all the evidence about stenography in classical times, including discussions of older scholars. Among that was the work of his teacher Mentz, who had emphasized continuously that the Romans were the inventors of stenography and not the Greeks, with reference to Plutarch's testimony. Mentz's argument for the priority of the Latin system has been generally accepted. Only one point remained weak in Mentz's position: When did Greek stenography appear in history?[114] He believed that the Greeks started with stenography around 50 BC.[115] As an argument for its rather rapid development, he recalled the close interaction of the two cultures (Roman and Greek), where neither could accept being left behind. In this respect, Boge followed a different path: he pointed to the second century AD for the beginning of Greek stenography.

Boge completely ignored the argument that Greek stenography followed the Latin system rather quickly due to the connection of the two cultures, as Mentz had argued. Boge does not give any explanation for the gap of about 150 years between the origins of the two systems, neither does he give any historical impetus for the supposed beginning

---

[112] Boge, *Griechische Tachygraphie und Tironisch Noten*.

[113] Millard, *Reading and Writing in the Time of Jesus*, 175.

[114] Mentz missed the point of Plutarch's hint to the beginning of Greek shorthand, as he incorrectly translated the final clause of Plutarch's Testimony (see sections 3.3.1, 3.4.3), speaking about "the first trail" (die erste Spur; Mentz, *Ein Schülerheft*, 41), which he connected with the beginning of Roman stenography. However, *prooton* is not an adjective but adverbial: "but then *at first* they went on a trail, they say."

[115] Mentz, *Ein Schülerheft*, 55, 53; Boge, *Griechische Tachygraphie und Tironisch Noten*, 147.

of Greek stenography in the second century AD. It is just a lost historical detail to him. Of course, this is inadequate concerning an art of writing that played an important role in public life during the Roman state and the beginning of the empire (tunnel vision).

Boge's theory about Plutarch's testimony is based on assumptions. He first gives as his supposition (German: Ich vermute; I suppose) that Plutarch invented the Greek term *sèmeiographos* by translating the Latin term *notarius* (stenographer). This made it easy for Boge to suppose that the Greek term had no history prior to the end of the first century AD. Of course, this belies Plutarch's fine remark to his readers, speaking about the "so-called sèmeiographous," which refers to common knowledge of the term at the time of writing and to a significant tradition of the expression. Further, he seeks to confirm his view with five parallels of the phrase "so-called"[116] He claims that this usually refers to Roman matters, which is not the case. For example, Aemilius Paulus 27.1: the prison, which is called "karkare"—*among them.* Why use the addition *among them* (Romans) if the expression already indicated this? No, with the closing remark of his "Testimony on Stenography," Plutarch made a statement about stenography *in general*—that one did not train or possess the so-called *sèmeiographoi,* but then at the historic momentum of the introduction in the Roman senate, the starting point was given for the training of Roman as well as Greek stenographers.

Unfortunately, Boge and Millard failed to see the consistency of the oldest testimonies by Cicero and Plutarch. Boge claimed a historical critical judgment concerning the matter, but historical criticism that is a reduction of evidence is undesirable. Such a judgment is only legitimate if the minor details of a passage have received a proper place. This is not the case in the Boge–Millard construction, how much they may have contributed to our knowledge of reading and writing in Jesus's time.

3.6 The Fullness of Time

Now that we have painted the picture of Greek and Latin stenography in the first century BC and the first century AD by putting together the historic essentials, it is time to turn to the implications of this

---

[116] Boge, *Griechische Tachygraphie und Tironisch Noten,* 89.

picture for the New Testament. In Luke's prologue, we do not find any technical term about stenography; nevertheless, the description of what has been done by the eyewitnesses who were servants of the spoken word was exactly the work of stenographers at that time. To deliver the spoken word of Jesus to the many during the events, being in fulfilled states, was made possible at that time by stenography, especially with long speeches and dialogues. It is not necessary to suppose that everything in the Gospels has been handed down through stenography. Of course, there were other ways to preserve the spoken word in writing, as in the case of short sayings. Luke did not need to explain this, as it was common knowledge for everyone involved in reading and writing at that time. Listening to the teachings in the Gospel of Luke, the hearers were supposed to understand how it was possible that they heard Jesus's own words. Stenography was a normal part of their culture.

Matthew followed the same method. The Gospel of Matthew is distinguished from the other Gospels by the presentation of large orations by Jesus. In three cases, Matthew gives the important phrase at the end that shows the professionalism of the original writers. After the Sermon on the Mount (7:28), the Discourse on the Kingdom (19:1) and the Eschatological Discourse (26:1) we read, "when Jesus (had) finished (all) these sayings (words)." This is not a theological reference to the foregoing, or a literary ornamentation, or a transition formula but a confirmation of the original writers that they had documented (reported) the words of Jesus. Matthew presupposed that his readers understood the professional background (i.e., stenography) necessary for correctly (verbatim) presenting an extensive oration.

Luke was an educated man. From the book of Acts, we know that he was perfectly acquainted with the culture in Asia Minor and Greece, where the apostle Paul worked. The functions and titles of the Roman and autochthon authorities he mentions in Acts are accurate and correct, as has appeared from archaeological findings.[117] It was Luke who brought the public life of Jesus onto the map of the world.

---

[117] F. F. Bruce, *De Betrouwbaarheid van de Geschriften van het Nieuwe Testament* (Amersfoort: Internationale Bijbelbond, Telos Nederland, 1977), 75. Translation of: *The New Testaments Documents. Are They Reliable?* (Downers Grove IL: Inter-Varsity Press)

"In the fifteenth year of the reign of Tiberius Caesar, Pontius Pilate being governor of Judea, and Herod being tetrarch of Galilee, and his brother Philip tetrarch of the region of Ituraea and Trachonitis, and Lysanias tetrarch of Abilene, in the high–priesthood of Annas and Caiaphas, the word of God came to John the son of Zechariah in the wilderness."[118]

Luke knew what was what about his time and the Greek and Roman cultures. Without any doubt, he was acquainted with the existence, the use, and the results of stenography in his time. And it was certainly such a widespread art that he could presuppose the same knowledge among his readers and listeners. About ninety years after the introduction of stenography in the Roman senate, with which Cicero saved the state, neither Luke nor his hearers could be ignorant about it. It was no question for Luke and his readers how it was possible that they met a formula more than six hundred times, such as, "Jesus said" or "He answered and said." It was not only uncustomary to give an explanation about stenography but also not necessary. The prologue of Luke's Gospel presupposes a general knowledge about the possibilities of writing in the time of Jesus's appearance. In a quite natural way, Luke made use of that knowledge, speaking about the eyewitnesses who were delivering during the spoken word of the events.

The Romans used two armies to maintain their power. The first was formed by their soldiers, armed with swords and spears; the second by their civil servants, armed with pen and paper. The first army enabled them to conquer new areas, and with their second army, they remodeled new regions to Roman fashion. We read in the Christmas story about a decree from Caesar Augustus "that all the world should be enrolled."[119] Certainly this was an immense writing operation from the desert of Judea to the Atlantic Ocean. Only the second army of writing officers made this operation possible for Caesar Augustus. Of course, many people were not able to read or write in the Roman Empire; nevertheless, writing was such an important part of society that W. V. Harris has remarked, "The Roman Empire depended on writing. The affairs of magistrates and

---

[118] Luke 3:1–2.
[119] Luke 2:1.

later of the imperial court, the taxation of citizens and provinces, the affairs of innumerable city governments, the maintenance of armed forces—for all these writing was indispensable. Many people were thus more or less deeply involved in the writing and also in the delivery, storing, and retrieving of the resulting texts—an aspect of Roman life which historians have greatly neglected."[120]

Christianity came into being in the Jewish land that was part of that huge Roman Empire, in which stenography reached perfection. The Jewish country was not a backward area but a rich and prosperous part of the empire. Stenography, the Latin as well as the Greek variant, was an indispensable skill in administration and in jurisdiction in this area. The Gospels of Jesus Christ originated in a society where stenography enjoyed reputation and application. He came in "the fullness of time." Everything was ready to preserve his teaching and to make him known to the world.

---

[120] W. V. Harris, *Ancient Literacy* (Cambridge/London: Harvard University Press,1989), 206.

Part II

Sources

4. From Writing Tablets to the Gospels

In chapter 3, we saw how one dealt with the rendering of the spoken word in historical writing, jurisdiction, government, and administration in the Roman Empire. We also saw that an enormous amount of writing activity existed at that time in the Middle East and that the use of stenography already had increased in the century before our era. Everything we know about the origins of the Gospels—from Luke's prologue, the letter to the Hebrews, and the first letter of John—fits perfectly into the developments within the Roman Empire. An oral tradition preceding the Gospels must be excluded. Indeed, Jesus came in "the fullness of time."[121]

4.1 The Spoken Word in the Gospels

The spoken word forms an important part of the contents of the Gospels. It is explicitly remarked no fewer than 604 times that Jesus said something (he said, he answered and said, etc.). Luke did not speak about the work of shorthand writers. He only felt the need to define the work of Jesus's writers who served the spoken word. That may seem strange to us, but in Luke's culture, it was not the rule to speak about stenographers. Authors and orators were held in great respect, but recording and shorthand writing was seen as a mere mechanical activity; it was important but not worth mentioning in books or official documents. According to the custom of a good historian, however, he explained accurately from where he got his information. He did it so precisely that his hearers could directly link his words to the art of stenography. Speaking of "just as delivered to us the eyewitnesses ... also being servants of the spoken word (of the events)," Luke made very clear to his readers that in most cases, stenography was the way of note-taking for these servants of the spoken word.[122]

Unfortunately, orthodox theologians have repeatedly maintained

---

[121] Galatians 4:4.

[122] In the Dutch Parliament, stenographers are not in the forefront, but after the discussions, the members of Parliament often take a run to the shorthand writers to receive copies of the reports.

that the Gospels and Acts were written according the rule of Thucydides.[123] In that case, the presentations of the speeches would not be verbatim records at all; instead, they would represent the meaning of what had been said once but not the very words. This was supposed to justify the reliability of the Gospels and Acts because these books then would have been written just like the finest specimens of classical Greek historical writing. These theologians, however, did not properly realize that this approach created more problems than solutions. Because in this case, it is obvious that we can no longer see whether we are reading the words of the original speakers or the words of the authors. Therefore, this position is not very profitable concerning the Gospels.

Of course, the Gospels and Acts are not to be measured with the rule of Thucydides but with the rule of Luke, which he formulated at the beginning of his Gospel. It is most interesting that Luke, as did Thucydides, only told how the material he used came into being and how he worked with that material. And so it is up to the readers and hearers to draw their conclusions.[124] Many followers of the Lord used the completed state of an event to copy a story about what had happened. After an event, a new story could be added, and for that they used a written transmission that was handed down to them by eyewitnesses of the events, who also had been servants of the spoken word. Just as the many worked, so did Luke in writing his Gospel, he says. He also used the first apostolic transmission of the eyewitnesses. The miracle they did not see was that their work would stand for centuries to come.

It is out of the question to measure the Gospels and Acts according to the rules for Greek historical writing at that time.

4.2 Three Manners of Recording the Spoken Word

Jesus preached in Galilee, which had an important Jewish population. Still, Galilee had not been influenced only by the Jewish but also by the Greco-Roman culture. The Hellenistic or Greek culture dominated

---

[123] S. E. Porter, "Thucidydes 1.22.1 and Speeches in Acts: Is There a Thucididean View?" In *Novum Testamentum* (Leiden: Brill, 1990), Vol. 32, 121–142.

[124] Luke 1:1–4.

the Middle East since the time of Alexander the Great (circa 300 BC). The Greeks introduced into the eastern part of the Middle East not only the Greek vernacular as common (Koinè) language but also Greek philosophy and science; in short, the Greek culture and way of life. The Romans who inherited this huge area made a very effective use of this Hellenistic culture by building their Roman culture on it. Therefore, it is possible to define more properly the origins of the Gospels.

Why didn't Luke speak of stenographers in his prologue? It was not only because it was usually the work of slaves, as we have seen earlier. There was another reason for Luke to define the first writers only as "servants of the (spoken) word." It implies a greater group than just stenographers because there were several possibilities to record the spoken word.

It was possible that impressive statements were jotted down shortly afterward. And so the spoken word could be established by two or three witnesses, just like the habit in the practice of stenography that several writers worked together to avoid mistakes. This was also the rule of Deuteronomy in Jewish jurisdiction in establishing a case.[125] But what about a situation like a storm on the Lake of Galilee? It was not possible to write during a storm, but such impressive things happened there that it would have been a great loss to not deliver what happened. When the disciples went ashore, the writers among them could start collecting testimonies and make stories based on them.

It was also possible for those who were trained in writing to quickly jot down the words of the Lord in many situations, especially in cases of short sayings and teachings. Also, the rule of several writers working together and making notes applied to them. These writers are to be distinguished from those who worked as pure stenographers.

The last group that was covered by Luke's expression—"servants of the (spoken) word"—were, of course, the stenographers. They were sufficiently skilled to write down the greater parts of Jesus's teaching—the speeches and the long dialogues. As earlier brought forward, they worked in the Roman Empire, often in pairs or more,

---

[125] Deuteronomy 19:15.

to guarantee the quality of the results. This already was the case when Cicero introduced stenographers in the Roman senate in 63 BC. Certainly Jesus's stenographers would have worked in the same way.

It is evident that all of these possible ways of recording the spoken word were used by the writers of Jesus, one of whom said, "A great prophet has arisen among us!" and "God has visited his people!" And this report concerning Jesus spread through the whole of Judea and the surrounding country.[126]

4.3 Jesus's Stenographers

After the introduction in the Roman senate, the art of stenography could not be stopped. Also, in the eastern Greek-speaking part of the empire, it became the way to preserve the spoken word in public—politics, jurisdiction, the army, and commerce. We know from Seneca that it was practiced in the first period by slaves, who had invented the art, which certainly implied that in lower social classes, more individuals were skilled in stenography. Jesus himself belonged to the lower class of society, just as the masses he set in motion. It is not an anachronism that stenographers were active in Jesus's ministry. But who were Jesus's stenographers? Although they are never mentioned explicitly in the Gospels, it may be possible to trace some of them.

Of the twelve closest disciples of Jesus, we have to think of the two brothers, James and John. The event of the transfiguration may be a good illustration in this regard.[127] Jesus went up on a mountain to pray, and three of his disciples—Peter, James, and John—went with him. Up there, the disciples immediately fell asleep, as they were tired, but Jesus started to pray. Two persons appeared to him: Moses and Elijah. And they spoke of "his departure which he was to accomplish at Jerusalem." Suddenly they were interrupted by Peter, who had become awake and suggested they build three tents for them. He repeated it several times (as is clear from the dissimilarities between his sayings in the Gospels). With his words, he brought the revelation to an abrupt ending. A cloud overshadowed them, and a voice came out saying, "This is my Son, my Chosen, listen to

---

[126] Luke 1:16–17.
[127] Matthew 17:1–13.

Him!" (again, several times with small differences), and the heavenly persons disappeared.

Who were the writers? Peter can be excluded, as he was involved in the event. James and/or John remained to record what was said and done. Like Peter, they were awake, but instead of trying to become partners in the talking, they took a wax tablet. Unfortunately, Peter's interruption put an end to the attempt; only the words of Peter and of the voice from the cloud could be preserved. Later on, when they descended with Jesus, they had a short discussion about a certain opinion of the scribes, that Elijah would appear before the coming of the Messiah. It was again James and John recording this. Jesus charged them not to talk to others about what they had seen and heard on the mountain, and so they kept their notes to reveal them later. It is not possible to determine whether James and John used true shorthand or if they only wrote fast. But there are other indications that point to both disciples as writers and even as stenographers.

During some other events, it appeared that James and John were only eyewitnesses. The first instance was the resurrection of Jairus's daughter. They went into the room of the dead child, together with Peter and her parents. In the second instance, they were present together with Peter at Jesus's prayer time in Gethsemane. It was night, but they could write short notes of Jesus's loudly spoken words by the light of their lanterns, or recall them to mind later. James and John were among Jesus's first disciples. From the very beginning of Jesus's ministry, they could fulfill their writing task. Zebedee, the father of James and John, was a well-to-do man with a well-patronized fisherman's trade in Capernaum, with day laborers at his service. No doubt he had sufficient financial resources to permit James and John to become experienced stenographers. It seems that they wanted to establish their proven importance as clerks when they asked to sit with Jesus in his kingdom at his right and left sides, because it was the clerks who normally had standard positions nearest the leader of a discourse.

One of Jesus's eschatological orations was spoken to Peter, James, John, and Andrew. This longer speech, Mark 13:5–37, certainly required more than accurate writing. We have to reckon with stenography in this case. Also, the long dialogues in the Gospel of John are only understandable as having been recorded by John as

71

one of the stenographers. Maybe Andrew belonged to the circle of Jesus's writers, as he too was a disciple from the very beginning. There must have been more stenographers among Jesus's disciples. Apart from James and John, there was also Matthew. As a tax official, he was in direct touch with the Roman public authorities, and therefore he had plenty of opportunities to meet stenographers and to see the effectiveness of their work. He had the opportunity to learn the art, and by doing so he could make himself valuable in public service. The existence of his name on the Gospel of Matthew is decisive. This can be explained only by the fact that after the resurrection of Jesus and the Pentecost event, John and Matthew continued their scriptural work. In Jesus's ministry, the two already had proven their professionalism and trustworthiness. Within the inner circle of Jesus's followers, we may conclusively point to James, John, Matthew, and maybe Andrew as the eyewitnesses from the beginning, who were also the servants of the spoken word—stenographers. It is not impossible that some other disciples of the twelve were in charge of the writing task, but we simply have too little information to be conclusive in this respect.

It is also possible to point to men outside the peer group of the twelve, as with Luke and Mark as professional steno writers, who may have served Jesus very early; they could fill the gap of writing when the twelve were on their mission journey (Matthew 10–13). The primary role of Luke and Mark was as secretaries (see sections 6.3.1–3). In this role, they could offer their skill in writing the reports arranged by the note-takers and settle their ability to replace them, if necessary, and to cooperate with them in writing Gospel books later on.

Shorthand writers also were at work in the wider circle of Jesus's disciples. We may mention Joseph of Arimathea and Nicodemus, members of the Sanhedrin, the highest Jewish Council. They must have played an important role in recording what happened during the trial of Jesus. The condemnation by the Jewish Council after an inquiry during the night was unanimous.[128] Joseph, however, who belonged to the council, did not give his vote.[129] Obviously, he belonged to the clerks who recorded the ins and outs of the process and who therefore did not vote. Joseph must have been one of the

---

[128] Luke 22:66–23:1.
[129] Luke 23:51.

stenographers of the council. To hear the testimonies of common people against Jesus, it was necessary that important parts of the process were spoken in ordinary Greek. It seems that Nicodemus, who was also a member of the council,[130] was in the same position as Joseph, and so he also was one of Jesus's stenographers.[131]

Last but not least, we have to realize that there also must have been women who worked as stenographers. We are able to trace only one: Salome, who was also known by the name Joanna.[132] It has always been an insoluble riddle as to why Mark and Luke referred to three women near the tomb who saw the angels and the Lord, while Matthew referred only to two women who worshipped Jesus.[133] Salome, who was also present, did not worship; as a reporter, she took her writing tools and, as usual, wrote down what she saw and heard. She was the unknown but accurate worker who noted the words of the angels and of Jesus.[134] Salome did not work in concert with other writers at that moment. And that probably was the reason that the disciples were not willing to believe the reports of the women about Jesus's resurrection. Later on, her work would still be accepted as holy scripture as she shared an extraordinary revelation, for which she and her work became sanctified. In the same way, Moses spoke with God on Sinai, as a friend.

4.4 Revelation and Writing

Was it possible to write during special revelations? Were those who received a revelation (e.g., an angel) shocked, overpowered, and paralyzed with fear? Certainly not; they were made partners in God's work, spiritually prepared and well instructed. On the contrary, all their qualities necessary for the task were enabled. Also, writing abilities belonged to these qualities at the very moment. The greatest example might be Moses, who was instructed by the Lord on Mount Sinai.

We should realize that writing was a daily practice. Many had a

---

[130] John 7:50.
[131] About their task of writing, see also Appendix 1. Confrontation at night.
[132] Mark 16:1; Luke 8:3; 24:10.
[133] Luke 24:10; Mark 16:2; Matthew 28:1, 9.
[134] About her task of writing, see also Appendix 4, Jesus's resurrection.

wax tablet and stylus at hand, and therefore writing could occur in situations with the highest spiritual experiences. Zechariah likely was permitted to have a wax tablet in his clothes with the prayers he had to say in the temple house. He was old and had to fulfill his duty carefully to say the right words. Having done his duty, he received the revelation of an angel, who brought him the message about the birth of a son named John. When the angel reassured him, he only needed to open the wax tablet and put the words of the angel's message on it. It is possible that he wrote the name of his son John on the same wax tablet later, when the neighbors wanted to know the name of the child.[135]

When Gabriel visited Mary, he acted as a customary visitor, and when he announced that he had a message for her, she could quite naturally take her writing materials to make notes of his words. In a dream, Joseph heard the voice of an angel telling him to accept Mary as his wife and to give her baby the name Jesus.[136] After he awoke and was overwhelmed by the impact of the words, he only needed to take his writing tablet and write down what he had heard. Through the power of the revelation, the words he had heard still echoed in his mind and heart. Later on, when the shepherds came to the stable, again it must have been Joseph who recorded their testimonies. They also were certainly overwhelmed by the spirit of God and still had echoes of the message and the song of the angels in their ears.

Years later, when Peter was set free from prison by an angel, he remembered the short instructions that were given to him by the angel, and when Peter told the brothers about the story, he asked them to bring the message of his liberation to James. Certainly there were enough writers to make a report for James, containing the things Peter had said.[137]

When Saul was on his way to Damascus to persecute Christians there, it happened that Jesus appeared to him. The time was about noon;[138] that was the time when Pharisees took a break to say their prayers.[139] No doubt Saul was in prayer when Jesus revealed himself

---

[135] Luke 1:63.

[136] Matthew 1:20-21.

[137] Acts 12:7–9, 17.

[138] Acts 22:6; 26:13.

[139] Acts 3:1; 10:3, 30.

to him. Probably he was in great despair, unsatisfied with persecuting Christians and calling to heaven for an answer. Jesus himself was the answer.

The information in Acts about the occurrence suggests that there are three perspectives:

1. Those who remained on the road near the horses and equipment (Acts 9:7, those who traveled with him). They heard the sound of the voice without understanding the content.
2. Those who did their devotions in a different place than Saul, fellow believers of Saul (Acts 22:9, *who were with me* is an expression of close connection). From their viewpoint, they saw the light but did not hear the voice.
3. Saul's point of view and that of some who remained with him to say their prayers. The light was shining "round me and those who accompanied me" (Acts 26:13). Only this little group is supposed to have heard what was actually said by the voice.

Probably one of the last was also a scribe, a personal secretary of Saul. After saying his prayers, he sat waiting with his tablet for instructions. Despite the heavy revelation (they fell on the ground), maybe he or someone else was able to record the spoken words to Saul.[140] It is possible that this scribe and others became Saul's disciples later in Damascus.[141] It is also possible that the words to Saul were so terribly impressive that he could not erase them from his mind. Three times he asked "Who are you Lord?" Three times he got a short and heavy answer. Three days he had to wrestle with them in darkness.

Is it going too far to suppose that people in such unusual situations recorded the spoken word? To answer this question, realize that the number of such occasions was rather small in relation to the period of time over which they occurred. But above all, the art of recording the spoken word was not at all a legalistic

---

[140] Acts 9:4–6; 22:7–8,10; and 26:14–18.
[141] Acts 9:25.

way of life. Just as we like photographs in modern times as personal references of the past, in those times the recording of the spoken word might have fulfilled a similar function. When reports were read to the people, it certainly caused exclamations of recognition. For that reason, we have to consider that although stenography started within the circle of slavery, the art broke through in many other circles of society after some time. Those who were able to record the spoken word possessed a unique skill of which many others could be envious, and of course they managed their lives to get the most out of their skill.

4.5.1 Are the Gospels Interdependent? Two–Source Theory

Two paintings with nearly the same images will evoke the thought that at least one of them is a copy. When the name of a famous painter is on the canvas, we treat it as a very expensive painting, on the understanding that we indeed have the authentic work in front of us. On the contrary, if it can be proven that the painting is a copy, it is nearly worthless, no matter how famous the name on it may be. The question is, which one is the copy, and which one is the original? Experts start an investigation, and they examine the paint. Maybe in some places the paint is not yet dry; that may indicate a recent artifact. They investigate the canvas. How old is it, and does its age match with the time that the painter lived? How are the strokes of the brush? Does this correspond with other works of the master? By answering all of these questions, the experts are able, in most cases, to determine the original.

We have a comparable case in the phenomenon of the Gospels, especially in the synoptic Gospels—Matthew, Mark, and Luke. There are so many similarities with regard to content, structure, style, and linguistics that the most plausible inference is that the Gospels are *interdependent*. The main questions in New Testament research are, therefore, which Gospel writer has copied (with modifications) his book or parts of it from another?

Firmly established is the so-called *two-source theory*. It says that Mark was the first to write his Gospel in about AD 65; Matthew wrote his in about AD 75 by using the Gospel of Mark and an unknown Gospel, indicated with the letter Q (German: Quelle, meaning *source*).

Later on, Luke would have written in the same way in about AD 80, also using Mark and Q.

Common material in Matthew and Luke is attributed to Q, but both also have new specific material not in Mark or in Q. In this view, there are two original main sources: Mark and Q.[142] Obviously, if we accept this theory, we have to deal with many unanswered questions. For instance, why was it important for Matthew and Luke to repeat the same stories described in Mark? Wouldn't it have been more convenient for Matthew and Luke to collect new stories (not in Mark) and bring them out in one or two new books? And when they redacted Mark's work, why did they also redact (or change) the direct speeches of Jesus? This is incomprehensible when we keep in mind that in Israel, changing the words of the prophets in copies was simply not done.[143] On the contrary, they were always copied scrupulously.

Following the two-source theory, there is another question: Is the Gospel of Mark the most valuable of the three because the others (Matthew and Luke) are only copies? Of course, there are theologians who will reply, oh no, Matthew and Luke have brought forward their own specific theologies, and therefore they are as important as Mark and Q. These theologians, however, are missing the point, because the question is whether or not the Gospels present the original sayings of the Lord, leaving aside specific theologies of the authors.

The two-source theory has been accepted widely, but many do so with restrictions because of the penetrating questions connected with it. Generally speaking, it is *impossible* to deny the implication of the

---

[142] The Gospel of Mark has 661 verses, and six hundred of them are also (nearly the same) found in the Gospel of Matthew, while Luke's Gospel has only 350 verses that are comparable with Mark. The material of Q that is common in Matthew and Luke would cover about 250–300 verses.

[143] It was accepted practice to quote prophetical texts with all sort of variations, on the condition that one spoke in the spirit of the prophet, or that one remained within the standards of Jewish religion of old. It is not difficult to show that Jesus also followed this custom, but we should not forget that prophetical texts (of the Old Testament) that were to be read in the synagogues met the highest standards of accurate copying. In the same way, the Gospels were meant to function as holy texts from the beginning (Acts 2:42).

two-source theory that the Gospel writers would have manipulated the texts for their own purposes—that they would have introduced alterations, "corrections," and beautifications into the Gospels, copying and redacting the work of former writers.

4.5.2 Are the Gospels Independent? Memorization Theory

There is another approach to the Gospels other than the two-source theory. Many scholars who defended the complete trustworthiness of the Gospels took the view that the four Gospels are not interdependent. This would imply that the authors did not use of the work of another Gospel writer and that they all have the same value and divine authority.[144] This *theory of independence* is fully in contrast with the two-source theory. The similarities between the Gospels in language and style are explained by the common events, which are expected to have brought forward the same words, expression, and style in a natural way. It cannot be denied that this may be so in some cases, but is it plausible to suppose that this phenomenon happened chapter after chapter? To give this theory more credibility, some have combined it with the theory that the followers of Jesus trained themselves to memorize the teachings of Jesus from a very early stage—the *memorization theory*.[145]

According to this view, the sayings of the Lord would have been preserved in the Gospels. The memorization theory also says that Jesus would have used all sorts of linguistic techniques in word choice, rhythm, and so on to activate the memories of his disciples. Advocates of the theory also state that memory was much better trained at that time, as memorization was the standard method of education and a common practice. But how conclusive are these arguments? In the surrounding world of the Greeks and the Romans, higher education

---

[144] For instance, Linnemann, *Is There a Synoptic Problem?* 1992.

[145] Two scholars who standardized the memorization theory were H. Riesenfeld and B. Gerhardsson in the period after World War II. They supposed that rabbinical teaching in Jesus's time fundamentally was oral and not scriptural, and so would be Jesus's teaching.

was practiced through conversation (*diatribe*) and by note-taking as it was necessary in academic life.[146]

Despite some positive elements of the memorization theory, it is untenable. This theory functions merely as a philosophy to explain similarities in the Gospels, but it does not result in a serious working method to deal with the many dissimilarities. In fact, these dissimilarities contradict the memorization theory, as they are in complete contrast with it. Furthermore, we do not have any testimony that Jesus's disciples actually memorized his words. On the contrary, we have the information from Luke and John that the disciples *wrote down* what the Master said. It is an untenable opinion that those who wanted to learn and who were able to write did not exploit their writing skills for this purpose. It is much more realistic to hold that disciples who were trained in reading and writing also were involved in the scriptural recording of what Jesus said.[147] When he sent out his disciples, they had at their disposal accurate written copies of his sayings and doings. That was the scriptural message they could read to their hearers about the kingdom of heaven.[148]

Proponents of the memorization theory defend the oral tradition as preceding the Gospels. No matter how intelligent one may be or how easily one may learn to repeat passages by heart, the law of the oral tradition rules with an iron rod and is relentless; oral tradition does not operate without mistakes. The memorization theory is only a specific form of oral tradition and is therefore hostile to the classical view on the holy scripture, saying that "All scripture is inspired by God"[149] and is therefore trustworthy in everything. Proponents of the memorization theory embrace the theory of the oral tradition

---

[146] About Hellenistic time, John Wenham, *Redating*, 113 refers to L. C. A. Alexander: "in connection with the training of professional men in the Greek-speaking world that note-taking was 'necessary in academic life.'" L. C. A. Alexander, *Luke—Acts in its Contemporary Setting* (Oxford: D. Phil. Diss, 1977), 146.

[147] The description of Peter and John as "uneducated common men" in Acts 4:13 has been recognized for a long time as signifying their lack of higher education and not that they were illiterate.

[148] Matthew 10:5–7, 1 John 1:1-4.

[149] 2 Timothy 3:16.

with accompanying changes—omissions and embellishments—in the ultimate text.

Finally, there are a great number of scholars who reckon with the possibility of note-taking during Jesus's teachings. John Wenham listed a number of them.[150] He referred to E. J. Goodspeed[151] in agreeing that Matthew, as a tax collector, had a lifelong habit of noting things down and preserving what he had written. He also defended the view that the world of Jesus's day was highly literate and that it is altogether likely that there were people who made notes of what Jesus said. Jesus made a tremendous impact on a wide variety of listeners, and therefore it is unlikely that no one attempted to make a record of what he taught. Wenham referred also to others who brought forward the aspect of literalness among Jesus's first disciples, such as W. M. Ramsay (1907) and G. Salmon (1907) but also by later ones, such as H. Schürmann (1961), R. H. Grundry (1967), R. Riesner (1981), D. A. Carson (1983), and E. E. Ellis (1987).

Literalness of Jesus's disciples is an important aspect with regard to the Gospels, but does it suffice? That is highly unlikely. With this point of view, we must reckon with written transmissions as well as with oral traditions from Jesus's ministry onward. So it would still not be possible to say "The Lord has said," because it would not then be conclusive as to what parts of the Gospels were transmitted scripturally or orally. (In subsequent chapters, we will see that the documentation theory does not wrestle with all these peculiarities.)

4.6 Grammatical Criticism

Concerning the Gospels, New Testament theology never has established the theory of oral transmission in a pure, grammatical-critical way. It has brought forward only historical-critical philosophies as a foundation for it, the shortcomings being that they did not and do not result in sound working methods to explain details. Traditionally, we read Luke 1:1–2 as proof for the theory of oral transmission, but it contains the strongest proof for the opposite: note-taking during

---

[150] John Wenham, *Redating*, 112–114.

[151] E. J. Goodspeed, *Matthew, Apostle and Evangelist* (Philadelphia: J.C. Winston, 1959).

the spoken word. The customary exegesis of this passage contains in no way evidence for a massive theory of an oral tradition. This theory is nothing more than an unproven prejudice, and it is really disconcerting to say so. We should no longer hide the reality of the Christian faith within a defective theological concept. We do possess the words of Jesus; this truth is critical to the essence of the faith, and no one can measure the spiritual damage, past and present, caused by the undermining theory of the oral tradition. Gospel research should be liberated from that trap.

Oral tradition is also the old explanation for how the Mishnah would have come into being—the collection of sayings of the rabbis who lived in the period of the second temple.[152] The Mishnah is dated at about AD 200, and it contains the lessons of the rabbis that would have been transmitted orally by their students. However romantic it may sound and however often it has been stated, grammatical-critical evidence from the sources is lacking. Moreover, it is not probable. In a culture where the words of the prophets were preserved literally with painstaking care, it is hard to understand that the words of the rabbis remained oral during their deliverance. Of course, the practice of memorizing sayings of the rabbis did exist among their disciples for practical application in ordinary life, but this certainly did not happen for the purpose of preserving these sayings for the future. There existed better tools for that. The Mishnah contains the collected notes of the rabbis made by their disciples during their

---

[152] The Mishnah is called oral law, not because it was delivered orally but to make clear that it will never be a competitor of the written law of Israel, given by Moses (Torah). Nevertheless, one has always felt the necessity to discuss (oral law) the written law to help understand it and apply it in daily life. From this point of view, it is customary in Judaism to say that discussion (the oral law) also was a necessity and given by Moses (on Sinai). Jesus accepted this and spoke freely about all matters of the law, when he spoke with the teachers as a boy in the temple and, later on, with the scribes and Pharisees. He was against putting the harsh conclusions and duties on the people, deduced from the law of Moses, which obscured the divine light of the Torah.

conversations. M. Lowe and D. Flusser wrote, "It was common practice for the disciples of rabbis to make notes of their sayings."[153]

If we want to explain the great similarities between the Gospels and the many dissimilarities, we have to turn to a different paradigm of Gospel writing. The solution is much nearer than one generally assumes. It was the same writers—skilled in speedy writing and stenography—who produced the reports that later constituted the Gospels. And for that reason, all these reports are of equal quality and value. The most important aspect may be that they were written under and through the inspiring activity of the Holy Spirit, who worked in the described events as well as in the hearts and minds of the writers who were present. In the following chapters, we will deal with a tidal wave of questions about the similarities and the dissimilarities in the Gospels and how they are explicable from this point of view.

---

[153] John Wenham, *Redating*, 113 citing: M. Lowe, D. Flusser, "A Modified Proto-Matthean Synoptic Theory." *New Testament Studies* 29 (Cambridge: University Press, 1983) 47.

5. Four in a Row

In chapter 4 we saw how it is possible for the Gospels to have many agreements; they sprang from the same source. The question now is, why four Gospels? Why did the apostles give us four books instead of one single Gospel, with all the details together? The existence and the form of the four Gospels has everything to do with Jesus's writers.

5.1 Why Four Gospels?

It has always been a riddle as to why the Christians use four Gospels among their holy books. Nobody asks why, since this was the accepted state of affairs from antiquity onward. Yet when we start thinking about this issue, we can't avoid questions such as, why are three gospels amazingly the same (Matthew, Mark, and Luke)? And, consequently, why is one (John) so different from the others? Why did the apostles not leave one complete autobiography of Jesus? Wouldn't that have been more convenient? Instead, we have four books containing many nearly identical stories. Why the waste of materials, time, and energy? Moreover, didn't the apostles run a great risk in building the church on these four books with so many undeniable differences?

Of course, many good reasons have been brought forward to answer these questions; for example, each gospel writer gave a special picture or characteristic of Jesus. Matthew showed him as King (of the kingdom of heaven), Luke as the Savior, and John as the Son of God, while Mark painted his human character as the Son of Man. Of course there is some logic in these definitions, but we should not forget that all of these characteristics—his kingship, his humanity, his saving work, and his relationship with the Father—are found in each Gospel. It is no secret that the synoptic Gospels (Matthew, Mark, and Luke) contain many agreements, not only in style and wording but also in structure, as we see in the outline of the subjects, below:

Content of the Synoptic Gospels			
	Matthew	Mark	Luke
Birth and childhood	1, 2	–	1,2
John the Baptist	3	1	3
Jesus in Galilee	4–18	1–10	4–9
Journey to Jerusalem	–	–	10–19
Last days in Jerusalem	19–25	11–13	19–21
Passion, death, resurrection	26–28	14–16	22–24

In each Gospel, a chapter about John the Baptist precedes the public life of Jesus. The synoptic Gospels each have three divisions with, generally speaking, the same contents. The first division gives a description of Jesus's ministry in Galilee. The second division describes the last days of Jesus in Jerusalem. And the last division describes Jesus's death and resurrection. Additions in Matthew and Luke are the introductory chapters about Jesus's birth and childhood. Only Luke has a long insertion containing Jesus's last journey from Galilee to Jerusalem.

The style of the synoptic Gospels represents a remarkable consistency. The majesty of the events is in great contrast to the simplicity and brevity of the reports. Usually, a few indications about place and/or time are followed by an extremely short description of the action, including the results. Then the story continues with a new report with the same characteristics.

The Gospel of John differs in structure and style from the synoptic Gospels. This Gospel says only a few things about Jesus's public ministry in Galilee. The book informs about Jesus's visits to Judea and Jerusalem, particularly. With respect to the character of the book, there are short reports but especially long dialogues in it. The differences from the other Gospels are so striking that we get the feeling of dealing with different content. John's Gospel seems more intimate, more spiritual than the synoptic Gospels. And the question is, of course, how do we explain the differences between the Gospel of John and the other Gospels?

5.2 The Teaching Records of Matthew

Let's turn first to the Gospel of Matthew. The educational aspect of the book is striking indeed. It contains six lengthy discourses in which Jesus's disciples are taught how to live in the kingdom of heaven:

- Sermon on the Mount
- Mission of the Twelve
- Parabolic Discourse
- Discourse on the Church
- Against Scribes and Pharisees
- Eschatological Discourse[154]

Also scattered throughout the book are a lot of short teachings, as compared to Mark and Luke. For example, in Matthew's version of the "Cure of the Centurion's Servant," he gives the information that many from all over the world will enter the kingdom of heaven. This teaching is lacking in the parallel passage of Luke's Gospel.[155] Moreover, there are many references to the Old Testament and direct quotations from it. A standard formula in Matthew is, "This was to fulfill what was spoken by the prophet." In this way, Matthew teaches that in the past, it was prophesied what Jesus would do and who he was—the Messiah.

Last but not least, Matthew's frequent use of the term *kingdom of heaven* (instead of kingdom of God) is significant.[156] The summary below shows the differences when compared with the other Gospels.

Jesus's Message: The Kingdom				
	Matthew	**Mark**	**Luke**	**John**
Kingdom of heaven	34 times	absent	absent	absent
Kingdom of God	4 times	14 times	32 times	2 times

Matthew's use of this term is an important observation, especially from a teaching standpoint. Obviously, Jesus showed his disciples that

---

[154] Matthew 5–7, 10, 13, 18, 23, 24–25.

[155] Matthew 8:11–12; Luke 7:1–10.

[156] In Matthew, the term *kingdom of God* was used once to the disciples (19:24) and three times to Pharisees (12:28; 21:31, 43).

his kingdom was not an earthly but a heavenly kingdom. He forced them to put out of their heads the idea that his kingdom would work on the basis of all sorts of human trickery—jealousy, intimidation, manipulation, boasting, gossip, and all the other things people do to appear better than another. All of that does not belong to the kingdom of heaven at all. This term also warned against exaggerated expectations of an earthly kingdom of God at that time. Many people had an unreal image of the kingdom of God, that of a restored throne of David in Jerusalem, with a Messiah on it as a ruler of the world. Parts of this dream were at least the liberation of Judea by a well-trained army and of course an exultant nation of Israel at the Messiah's feet.

Out of all these characteristics, the conclusion must be that the Gospel of Matthew is a specific teacher's book. R. T. France rightly opens a review on Matthew as follows: "Matthew has been called 'the Teacher's Gospel' because its material is so presented that it is very suitable for use in teaching. It was probably for this reason that this gospel was the most widely used of the four in the early Church."[157]

This teaching character of Matthew is not strange, considering that Jesus chose twelve disciples specifically to teach them. The writers that followed Jesus not only produced public records (for public usage; see section 1.2), but they also made records with more specific teachings for the inner circle of disciples, especially for the twelve. After Jesus's departure, the twelve had the task of continuing the work, and they were equipped for the task by specific teachings, which came to be very important later on. Jesus revealed himself a priori as a spiritual teacher. That was also what his disciples believed, as Peter said, "Lord, to whom shall we go? You have the words of eternal life!"[158] The words of Jesus are important for the here and now and for the hereafter. "If you continue in my word, you are truly my disciples, and you will know the truth, and the truth will make you free." And "Why do you call me 'Lord, Lord.' and not do what I tell you?" And finally, "He who has my commandments and keeps them, he it is who loves me; and he who loves me, will be loved by my Father, and I will love him and manifest myself to him."[159]

---

[157] Carson a. o., *New Bible Commentary. 21th Century*, 904.

[158] John 6:68.

[159] John 8:31–32; Luke 6:46; John 14:21.

After Jesus's departure, the time came that the twelve had to teach others in turn. "Go therefore and make disciples of all nations ... teaching them to observe that I have commanded you."[160] This is the mandate Jesus gave his disciples, which is reflected in the second part of the apostolic manifesto (1 John 1:3–4). There is nothing wrong with doing Jesus's words, especially now that *we know* we have them on the table. A turn in Christian experience is possible—not only believing Jesus's words, but also knowing, with the intrinsic right to live according to them (James 1:22).

To preserve Jesus's special teachings to the inner circle of his disciples, the writers produced *teaching* records for them. These records contained information that was especially interesting for those who followed Jesus as their Master. The inner circle grew from twelve to seventy and finally reached 120 in number.[161]

5.3 The Public Records of Luke

From the prologue of Luke's Gospel, we see there were several writing activities around Jesus. All of these reporting activities included, first of all, writing by eyewitnesses of the spoken word and what happened during the events. Second, after an event, teaching records were made for the inner circle and public records for the wider circle of followers. Third, public records were copied by many people of the wider circle (Luke 1:1). Luke also used the public records for his Gospel at a later point.[162]

After an event, many copied a public record that was at their disposal from the writing eyewitnesses. The public records informed the people about Jesus and his work, for a great prophet had risen among them. His name became well known in the Jewish land, as well as outside.[163] The apostles later on presumed that Jesus's reputation was all over the country. Peter said to the Roman Cornelius, "You know the word which He (God) sent to Israel, preaching good news of peace by Jesus Christ." To King Agrippa, Paul referred to the suffering and resurrection of Jesus: "For the king knows about these things, and to

---

[160] Matthew 28:19–20.
[161] Luke 10:1; Acts 1:15.
[162] Luke 1:3.
[163] Luke 6:17; 7:16.

him I speak freely; for I am persuaded that none of these things has escaped his notice, for this was not done in a corner."[164]

In the past, scholars have noticed that in Luke's Gospel, he gives striking details that are lacking in the other synoptic Gospels and which are most interesting for publication. In the story of the healing of the centurion's slave, Luke remarks that first a delegation of Jewish elders came up to Jesus for help. They emphasized their message with the remark that the centurion had helped to build their synagogue. After the elders, also friends of the centurion were sent to Jesus for help, with the message that Jesus did not need to enter the house of the centurion, as the centurion felt himself unworthy to receive Jesus. These were remarkable details for the public: a Roman who had good contacts with Jewish elders, with a heart for the Jewish religion, and who humbled himself before a Jewish teacher. In the record of the parallel story in Matthew, these details of the elders and his friends are missing. Matthew's teaching record limits his message to the great faith of the centurion and his personal contact with Jesus. Luke continually presents background information about people and circumstances to show the human side of Jesus—how he associated with sinners, the poor, the rich, women, and children.

L. Morris put this together in his comment on the Gospel of Luke as follows: "An important part of God's concern for people is that it is manifested towards groups not highly esteemed in first–century society: women, children, the poor, the disreputable."[165] The human character of Jesus is also stressed by Luke's repeated remark that Jesus was praying. As a result of the public records, the Gospel of Luke became a detailed account that shows Jesus's concerned and humane character.

5.4 The Remnant Records of Mark

Careful consideration shows that speedy writers and shorthand writers were also responsible for the structure and nature of the Gospel of Mark. Unused material often remained after the composing of a teaching and/or public record—notes of circumstances and of sayings. The writers did not throw away this material; they brought it together

---

[164] Acts 10:37; 26:26.
[165] Morris, *Luke, An Introduction and Commentary*, 44–45.

in the right sequence. In fact, new records resulted from it. These remnant records, containing words and works of the Master, also were preserved and found their place later on in the Gospel of Mark.

It has been recognized for a long time that in the narrative parts of Mark's descriptions—not in the direct speeches—he excels in a direct style and vivid vernacular. The "Marcan" way of speaking may be defined as a *primary* use of language, and it is easy to explain, as he used the remnant records, the unornamented notes of the writers. Teaching and public records received cultivation (editing) in the narrative parts, as they were written with specific purposes: teaching and information. It is still most interesting that Mark often presents the first notes with respect to circumstances and what happened. The result is that Mark, in some way, seems more vivid than Matthew and Luke. A few examples follow:

Resurrection of Jairus's Daughter		
Matthew 9:23	**Mark 5:38–39**	**Luke 8:51–52**
23 And when Jesus came to the ruler's house, and saw the flute players, and the crowd making tumult, he said: ...	38 When [And] they came to the house of the ruler of the synagogue, [And] he saw a tumult, and people weeping and wailing loudly. 39 And when he had entered, he said to them: ...	51 And when he came to the house, he permitted no one to enter with him, except Peter and John and James, and the father and mother of the child. 52 And all were weeping and bewailing her; but he said: ...

Mark often said the same things twice, sometimes in different ways:

1. The ruler of the synagogue (verse 38). In verses 22, 35, and 36, Mark already mentioned that Jairus was a ruler of the synagogue.
2. Tumult (verse 38). This is repeated in the words "people weeping and wailing loudly." In Matthew, only *tumult* is used for the behavior of the people. In Luke, we read only weeping and bewailing, while *tumult* is lacking.

Twice, Mark gives repeated information in a small passage. It shows that he used a remnant record containing simple observations. Mathew and Luke used records with nearly the same words, painting the same picture, but without repeated information. They used records that had been edited properly by Jesus's writers.

Another striking detail in the Gospel of Mark is the overuse of "And/and-sentences". This is when a new sentence begins with *And*, or clauses inside with *and*. In the example above, it happens three times. In the Revised Standard Version of the Bible, this phenomenon is not visible, as it is in the King James Version. And so in the example, the word *And* has been placed in brackets [] in the text. The simplest way for the writers was to put the remaining observations together in the remnant records by using And/and-sentences. Mark copied everything as he found it in his source; he did not change records that were compiled under the inspiration of the Holy Spirit in the completed state of the events.[166]

Before looking at the second example, let's first look at the words of an older exegete (B. H. Streeter) about the language and style of the Gospel of Mark in contrast with Matthew and Luke:

> But the difference between the style of Mark and of the other two is not merely that they both write better Greek. It is the difference which always exists between the spoken and the written language. Mark reads like a shorthand account of a story by an impromptu speaker—with all the repetitions, redundancies, and digressions which are characteristic of living speech. And it seems to me most probable that his gospel, like the Epistles of Paul, was taken down from rapid dictation by word of mouth. (...) Matthew and Luke use the more succinct and carefully chosen language of one who writes and then revises an article for publication.[167]

---

[166] Only a few additions have been made by the Gospel writers; for example: "Now it came to pass on a certain day" (Luke 8:22); "who became a traitor" (Luke 6:16). This information could be recognized as results from the past at the moment of writing the Gospels.

[167] B. H. Streeter, *The Four Gospels, A Study of Origins* (London: MacMillan and Co., 1930 rev.), 163.

It is interesting that the author explains the style of Mark as spoken language reported by shorthand writing, and we can agree with that. The difference between Streeter's model and the present approach is that Streeter believed that Mark wrote his Gospel from records based on shorthand notes of Peter's preaching, instead of Jesus's preaching.[168]

The second example of Mark's style is in the ministry of John the Baptist.

John the Baptist		
Matthew 3:1, 4	**Mark 1:4, 6**	**Luke 3:3**
[1] In those days came John the Baptist, preaching in the wilderness of Judea ... [4] Now John wore a garment of camel's hair, and a leather girdle around his waist; {and} his food was locusts and wild honey.	[4] John the baptizer appeared in the wilderness, preaching a baptism of repentance for the forgiveness of sins... [6] Now [And] John was clothed with camel's hair, and had a leather girdle around his waist, and ate locusts and wild honey.	[3] and he went into all the region about the Jordan, preaching a baptism of repentance for the forgiveness of sins.

Reading the verses of Mark, we see the repeated information *baptizer* and *baptism* in verse 4. Moreover, questions likely enter our minds with regard to baptizing in the wilderness—how did that work? You need water for baptizing, don't you? How exactly did John dress himself? Did he wind camel's hair around his body? And what about those locusts? Did he eat them alive or dead?

---

[168] Streeter and many theologians believed the apostle Peter was the source from which Mark composed his Gospel. Their idea is that Peter, later on in Rome, worked with Mark as his servant and interpreter. At that time they had learned enough Greek that, as a result, Mark could write down his Gospel from Peter's own lips. Streeter and his fellow theologians were not able to release themselves from the stranglehold of the Aramaic theory. They believed that Jesus spoke Aramaic, and therefore, it was impossible for them to suppose that the Gospels originated directly from the real source, Jesus Christ.

The narrative part of Mark's message is not wrong; it's simply unrefined. Later on, he explains that the people were baptized in the River Jordan. For most people, it was clear that the expression "clothed with camel's hair" related to clothes made of camel's hair. And of course, "eating biscuits baked of ground up locusts" is, in fact, eating locusts.

In reading Matthew's message, we see Mark's unrefined diction is replaced with a more eloquent style. He "preached" in the wilderness instead of "baptized" in the wilderness. He says neatly that "his garment" was of camel's hair. And the addition of "food" shows that the locusts had been transformed properly into food before eating. These details in Matthew's description were important, as they formed the substance of a teaching report about John the Baptist to show that he was a true prophet, not only in words but also in behavior. He wore the mantle of a prophet (i.e., made of camel's hair, the cheapest material for clothes). He also ate the cheapest possible food, made of locust meal. In other words, there was reason for the writers of this teaching report to give an instructive description of John the Baptist as a prophet of old.

Reading Luke's message, we see that a styling took the place of Mark's diction. For those who didn't know the situation in the Judean desert with the River Jordan, the writers used the expression "in the region about the Jordan," instead of "in the wilderness." Luke says "preaching a baptism"; that means a baptism in the River Jordan he mentioned. John is here only the messenger of the coming Messiah, and therefore the typical details about a prophet (food and clothes) are missing. This record is a proper description without double information.

It's important that in the ministries of John the Baptist and of Jesus, the same way of reporting was used. It suggests that a standard way of reporting existed already, which was not limited to Jesus's writers.

The public records, teaching records, and remnant records, which Luke, Matthew, and Mark, respectively, used, all originate from the completed state of the events. Certainly it was the same writers who wrote these records and who worked under the guidance and inspiration of the same Holy Spirit, as it was the Lord himself they heard and who spoke to them through the Spirit. Therefore, the synoptic Gospels, representing these records, have always been of equal value.

5.5 A Shorthand Diary of John

The Gospel of John differs widely from the synoptic Gospels. It seems more intimate and more spiritual. The Gospel of John often has the level of a heavenly drama. A great difference from the other Gospels is that John particularly has Judea and Jerusalem as the scene of action, whereas the others have Galilee as the environment of Jesus's work.[169] These characteristics are interrelated with one another, as we will see.

Sometimes Jesus forbade his disciples to pass on to others their experiences with him; for example, when Peter confessed Jesus to be the Christ, or when Moses and Elijah appeared to him.[170] After his resurrection, they were allowed to speak about it.[171] In other words, some public records remained hidden from the public during Jesus's ministry. Particularly, the records that were made in Judea and Jerusalem seem be banned from publication in an early stage.[172] In that area, it seems that neither public reports nor teaching reports were made by Jesus's writers. There were too many conflicts, too many clashes during Jesus's visits to the southern region. There were too many dangerous quarrels with religious fanatics among Pharisees, Sadducees, elders, scribes, and priests. The results were hostile discourses, instead of moments of peaceful teaching. Publication of these quarrels would create only confusion among the crowd and could even provoke revolts against the leadership of the nation.

Ordinary life in Judea had been steeped in religion in all of its forms—sometimes spiritually but often rigidly, through religious strictness and through laws and rules. Religious leaders saw themselves as the truthful keepers and teachers of the Law of Moses, which they once received from Ezra. Through the possession of the authorized

---

[169] In John, only four passages deal with the region of Galilee: 2:1–12; 4:43–54; 6:1–7, 9; 21:1–23.

[170] Matthew 16:20; 17:9.

[171] Luke 9:28–36.

[172] Exceptions: Jesus's journey to Jerusalem (Luke 10–19) and the last week of Jesus in Jerusalem, as written in Matthew, Mark, and Luke.

law, the tribe of Judah could determine and dominate civil life in all its aspects—politically, spiritually, ethically, and, not unimportant, economically. The religious pressure in this region was so strong that Jesus had left Judea in an early stage of his work to form his disciples in the northern region of Galilee.[173] In this part of the Jewish land, people felt much freer because they lived far from Judea and because they could not boast of the possession of a heritage that originated from Ezra. They were no scrupulous bearers of the old traditions. Of course, there were strict synagogues in Galilee, following the Judean religious standards in all details, but that could not remove the great freedom the Galileans generally allowed themselves. Jesus acknowledged that the Judeans indeed possessed God's revelation in the law and prophets—the holy books safely stowed in the holy temple. He was ready to defend them literally, but he opposed an inhuman and rigid misapplication of the books, by which the common man was kept ignorant of the spiritual richness of the law and the prophets.[174] We recognize this gap when we hear a few fanatic Pharisees say, "But this crowd, who do not know the law, are accursed."[175]

On his visits to Jerusalem, Jesus met with religious intolerance regularly, and the clashes with opponents were so serious that he was threatened with death repeatedly. Because of these dangerous conditions, the dialogues were kept in full by the writers in, without editorial elaboration for publishing in teaching, public, and remnant records. Only a few remarks were added at the beginnings and endings of the dialogues to describe the circumstances. Complete dialogues later on entered into the Gospel of John—the discourse with Nicodemus, the Samaritan woman, the many religious debates in public, and the long conversations with his disciples in private. Already mentioned is the

---

[173] John 4:1–3, 43–44.

[174] John 4:22.

[175] John 7:49. This blunt expression "the crowd who don't know the law" is certainly related to the fact that the lower social class of the Jewish people did not speak Hebrew anymore but Greek. The greater part of the Jewish nation had lost the true knowledge of the law, as a great many of them were unable to read the Torah in Hebrew. This was the painful grief of the religious leaders of Jerusalem, but as a result of a rigid application of the law, many of them had lost sight of the spiritual intentions of the law.

personal and spiritual style of John's Gospel. Certainly, this is also due to the long and complete dialogues of the book.

The Gospel of John is not a dramatic tragedy about the life of Jesus, as Jesus does not die in a desperate effort to work out his high ideals. He stands above this all, and across the events we hear his voice, he who shows his disciples the higher plan of God. This voice prepared them for all the events to come. And in this way, no victory of death emerged; rather, it was a victory over death as the final work of God.

5.6 Distribution of the Word: Note-Takers, Secretaries and Sources

When comparing parallel passages in the Gospels, one often finds sayings of Jesus with similar words and word order, but very often there are small differences. Not only do the sayings of Jesus have these "shortcomings," but the utterances of other people have them as well. For instance, Jesus's questioning of to his disciples on their opinions of him, we read Peter's answer in Luke: "The Christ of God." In Mark, it's "You are the Christ," and in Matthew, "You are the Christ, the Son of the living God." Certainly these three answers agree in meaning but not in the rendering of the words (for the solution, see section 7.1). The magnitude of this phenomenon becomes apparent as follows: On a superficial view, Mark has 661 verses, of which about 600 are found in Matthew and about 350 in Luke. Apart from that, Matthew and Luke together also have about 250 to 300 verses in common (and are not in Mark). The parallel passages of these verses swarm with Jesus's sayings with comparable meanings, but they usually have small differences in wording and/ or word order. It is striking that the number of Jesus's sayings in the Gospels that are given verbatim are only ten (and with variants, about fifteen).[176] What is the explanation for this strange phenomenon? The answer has to do with Jesus's writers working according to an

---

[176] Identical sayings are Mark 1:11 and Luke 3:22; Mark 1:24 and Luke 4:34; Mark 2:14 and Luke 5:27; Matthew 14:26 and Mark 6:49; Matthew 14:27 and Mark 6:50; Matthew 16:15, Mark 8:29a, and Luke 9:20a; Matthew 22:20–21a and Mark 12:16b; Matthew 27:29 and Mark 15:18; Mark10:14–15 (var.) and Luke 18:16–17; Mark 15:2a and Luke 23:3a. Possibly identical are Mark 1:25 and Luke 4:35 (var.); Matthew 8:2 and Luke 5:12; Matthew 8:3, Mark 1:41,

established practice or concept, but first, let's look at the materials the writers used at that time.

For recording the spoken word, the note-takers generally worked on a writing tablet covered with a thin layer of wax. As the wax was dark, the inscriptions in it became light through the light color of the wooden tablet. By heating the wax, it could be poured out over the surface of the tablet between the edges, that raised a few millimeters. After cooling, it was ready for use. It was possible to bind more tablets together into a codex, a sort of booklet, which could be closed with an iron clip. The speedy writers and shorthand writers used a stylus (Latin: *stilus*) in the wax of the tablets. The stylus had one sharp end and one flat end. With the flat end, the writer could smooth the wax if he wanted to correct something. By this means, a writer had the ability to write and to improve his style. The many words incorporating the words *style* or *styling* (hairstyling, for example) in modern languages are derived from this usage of the classic stylus.

Now let's look at the many comparable sayings of Jesus with slight differences. Some framing of a theory is necessary to imagine how Jesus's writers made their records. After an event, they worked out their (shorthand) notes, discussed, and marked the parts of the spoken word they needed for a teaching record and a public one. Their choices often implied a reduction, as reiterations were avoided. For the purpose of short reports to be copied after a Jesus event, it was important to write as directly as possible. Repetition did not add to the aim of spiritual teaching or information in any way. From the Mishnah, we also learn that the rabbis' scholarly discussions remained preserved, usually in rather essential sayings.

For the teaching report after an event, the note-takers discussed and chose the appropriate parts of what had happened, together with the relevant sayings. One of the note-takers or a secretary wrote the story that came into being on a slice of papyrus, with an introduction to the beginning of the story and an ending with a result or conclusion. When the teaching record was ready, it was read back to be sure that everything was done correctly.

Subsequently, a public report was created in the same way. They

and Luke 5:13; Mark 3:5 (var.) and Luke 6:10; Matthew 11:3 and Luke 7:19 (20 var.); Matthew 26:26b and Mark 14:22b (var.).

marked a few parts of the discourse that were suitable on their wax tablets. Sayings that had been avoided as reiterations in the former teaching report now could be used, and with a proper beginning and ending, the marked sayings together formed the public record.

If there was more interesting material of the discourse on their wax tablets that had not yet been used, it was put together for a remnant record. Sayings not used already could be combined with the first annotations of observations for the narrative part. With the and-style, everything could be enumerated effectively, which resulted in a remnant record. Remnant records could not be made on all occasions, as often the best material had been used already for the teaching and public records.

Thereafter, the reports were published among those who attended, and many made use of them for copying public reports and teaching reports for the closer disciples. Because the people were able to make copies from each other, the reports could spread quickly among those who wanted to take home a shorter or longer story about the rabbi of Nazareth. When everything was done, the new reports were put together with older records for conservation.

The custom of making several types of short reports caused a strange phenomenon: distribution of the spoken word to teaching, public, and remnant records. The writers of Jesus followed a standard concept with respect to the division or distribution of the spoken word. And this had a strange consequence for the Gospels, which were composed later from these records. As a rule, the parallel passages of the Gospels do not contain precisely the same sayings of Jesus and his interlocutors—the same events but *not* the same sayings.

In general, Jesus does not seem to give the same pronouncements in separate descriptions of the same events, yet the descriptions constantly show the same type of words or expressions. For this phenomenon, Bible scholars usually follow the explanation that an oral tradition preceding the Gospels was responsible for these discrepancies. In the best case, they state that these discrepancies do not contradict each other through the providence of the Holy Spirit. Nevertheless, many Bible scholars suppose that through mistakes resulting from the oral tradition, pious embellishments and even pure lies have penetrated the Gospels. The tragedy of the oral tradition is, of course, that according to most theologians—including evangelical theologians—it is not possible anymore to speak proudly about Jesus's *original sayings* in the four Gospels.

However the distribution of the spoken word shows that in the Gospels, we are still confronted with the original teachings of Jesus in his very words. Through the painstaking work of Jesus's writers, we are enabled to hear the voice of the Lord Jesus Christ. The Holy Spirit certainly has given them the inspiration to work with the greatest care. All the sayings in the Gospels can be accepted as authentic. This is the clear result of the documentation theory. To my knowledge, it is impossible to come to the same outcome via any other theological concept. It should be observed that this is a basic concept. Sometimes a teaching or a public record is missing in Matthew and Luke, or a teaching or a remnant record is lacking in Matthew and Mark. Many variants are possible. During Jesus's ministry, four sources emerged under the authorization of Jesus's writers, note-takers (e.g., stenographers), and secretaries:

1. Teaching records
2. Public records
3. Remnant records
4. Unpublished dialogues

In chapter 7 and onward, we will face many consequences of the distribution of the spoken word, but first we have to deal with the questions of where and when the Gospels were written.

6. Redating the Gospels

Currently, several theories about the origins of the Gospels are available. For the most part, they attempt to answer the following questions: Who wrote them? Why were they written? Where, when, and to whom were they written? In all of the current theories, an oral transmission preceding the Gospels is assumed, which results in a rather late edition of the Gospels—in general, during the second part of the first century between the years 65 and 95 (late dating). A few scholars, however, have maintained—with strong evidence—that these figures are too high. They maintain some earlier dating, between the years 40 and 65 (early dating). In the first case, we have a gap of approximately thirty-five to sixty-five years, and in the other case, the gap is about ten to thirty-five years between the events and the edition of the Gospels. This gap of at least one decade is a result of the assumption of an oral tradition between events and Gospels. In fact, the dating of the Gospels and the theories about their origins affects the question of the reliability of the books. According to the principle of the oral tradition, it is inevitable that the longer the oral tradition endured, the more untrustworthy the Gospels are.

In the approach to the origins of the Gospels, in which stenography and speedy writing play an important role, the question of the dating of the Gospels does not seem to be important in relation to their reliability. The records of Jesus's writers have simply been copied in the Gospels, and therefore they are just as reliable as firsthand reports. However, the late dating and early dating have to do with our subject. The dates resulting from these theories invariably confirm the assumption of the oral tradition. Now that we know there never was an oral tradition preceding the Gospels, it seems possible and desirable to reevaluate the current theories about the origins of the Gospels.

6.1 Premises for Gospel Dating

To solve dating problems, scholars search in the Gospels for arguments. As a clear statement about the subject is nowhere to be found in the Gospels, however, scholars have made all sorts of analyses to come to final conclusions. The nature of these analyses is that scholars have been forced to involve numerous premises in their work, which are sometimes only suppositions. Let's look at the premises usually followed in Gospel dating.

The Inheritance Theory: After a shorter or longer oral transmission of their message, the apostles, feeling that the end of their lives was near, decided to put their remembrances on record. As earlier presented, this point of view will bring the dates of the Gospels to the period of approximately AD 65–95.[177]

The Two-Source Theory: The Gospels of Matthew and Luke were based on two sources. These sources were the Gospel of Mark and an unknown Gospel, Q, and the contents of these two sources were then modeled according to the insights of Matthew and Luke when they wrote their Gospels. Unfortunately, the document named Q has been lost. This point of view makes the Gospel of Mark the oldest one.

Mix Theory: General practice is to use a mix theory built on the former premises. The philosophy is then that an oral tradition started, and later on it brought forward a written tradition, which finally resulted in a period of Gospel writing. The possibility is kept open, in some variants, that a few documents may have originated directly from Jesus's ministry and were incorporated into the Gospels. The problem of this option is that nobody is able to define which part of the Gospels may belong to this stock of early documents, the result being that nobody really reckons with them in scholarly discussions.

Current Dates of the Gospels				
	Matthew	**Mark**	**Luke**	**John**
Traditional	ca. 75	ca. 65	ca. 80	ca. 95
J. A. T. Robinson[178]	40–60	45–60	57–60	40–65
John Wenham[179]	ca. 40	ca. 45	ca. 54	

---

[177] A great deal of modern Gospel research of Protestant and Roman Catholic scholars focuses on the supposed history of oral and written forms within form criticism and redaction criticism.

[178] J. A. T. Robinson, *Redating the New Testament* (London: SCM Press LTD, 1976), 352.

[179] John Wenham, *Redating*, XXV

The summary above presents three dating possibilities—first, the traditional and generally followed dates (late dating), and then two dating possibilities that result from more recent research (early dating).

It is obvious that the approach to the Gospels presented in this book opens new premises for Gospel dating. Let's remember what the apostle John said in the apostolic manifesto (1 John 1:1–4). The proclamation of the Gospel has been based on "that which we have seen and heard," and written documents were involved in their preaching from the very beginning. From the prologue of John's first letter, we arrive at two important conclusions:

1. The apostolic proclamation of the Gospel always contained an oral and a written announcement of the public life of Jesus, to make him known among the people. The written part of the proclamation, therefore, contained documents of Jesus's public appearances, from his baptism to his death and resurrection. That meant real Gospel books.

2. As the proclamation of the Gospel after Jesus's departure started with the occurrence of the outpouring of the Holy Spirit at Pentecost, we may say that from that moment on, a complete written picture of Jesus was needed. In other words, immediately after this great event, the writing of the Gospel books took place.

Several times Jesus had forbidden his disciples to make known everything they had experienced or what they had seen and heard. This ban was in force with respect to Petrus's confession of Jesus as the Messiah and the occurrence of Jesus having spoken with Moses and Elijah (Matthew 16:20; Mark 9:9). Jesus had even prophesied about the moment to break this silence: "until the Son of man is raised from the dead."[180] Fifty days after Jesus's resurrection, the outpouring of the Holy Spirit took place; this became the starting point to make everything known to the world.

In theology, one thing has been terribly disregarded. After the Pentecost event, an eruption of scriptural documents started. Real Gospel books started to flow throughout the world. Pentecost

---

[180] Matthew 17:9.

appeared to be a volcano that came to life to give new power and also true knowledge of the Lord. Immediately there was a great demand for the teachings of the apostles: "And they devoted themselves to the apostles' teaching" (Acts 2:42). The apostles only needed to bring out the teaching records and public records that they had made during Jesus's ministry. This was precisely what Jesus had said to them before his departure, "teaching them to observe all that I have commanded you; and lo, I am with you always, to the close of the age."[181] At last, the moment had come to edit all the records into books; the Gospels were to be born.

The four Gospels appeared under apostolic supervision—it's quite easy to see that. The titles of the four Gospels are rather strange, even by antiquity standards. Above the gospels, we read, "According to," followed by the name of the author—Matthew, Mark, Luke, and John. They did not write these titles above their books, but the apostles did. In this way, they gave their support and authority to the books. These titles were in use from the beginning, as we can see from the prologue of Luke's Gospel. In verse 3 of the prologue, Luke introduces himself with *me* without any explanation: "It seemed good to me also ... to write an orderly account for you, most excellent Theophilus." That was a rather unusual move, as in books of that time, an author normally gave an introduction about his own person and the reason for writing his book. With the use of *me* in verse 3, Luke linked himself with the title "According to Luke." The organic connection between title and prologue through the word *me* shows convincingly that the words "According to Luke" were part of this Gospel from the moment of its appearance. No doubt the other Gospels also bore their titles from the moment of their appearance in the same way. Of course, the apostles understood immediately that they could not work for a period of years with all sorts of longer or shorter text units to serve the people; chaos would be the inevitable result. The decision to present authoritative materials was the only logical step for the apostles to serve the thousands who had come to the faith after Pentecost. The question, rather, is this: What was their plan of action?

---

[181] Matthew 28:20.

6.2.1 The Matthew–John Project

Two apostles—Matthew and John—were appointed to produce books. The Gospel of Matthew describes the life of Jesus in Galilee, while the Gospel of John describes Jesus's visits to Judea and Jerusalem. Either of these books alone would not give a complete picture of Jesus, but together they do. The conclusion drawn from this observation is that Matthew and John worked together, or at least there was a work plan for them to follow. John writes in his apostolic manifesto (1 John 1:1–4) that a written image of Jesus was part of the apostolic proclamation, so it is clear that John's Gospel and that of Matthew are to be dated in the first year of the Christian community in Jerusalem—circa AD 30.[182] It is difficult to decide which of the two Gospels appeared earlier, John's or Matthew's, but it doesn't seem to make much sense to attempt to resolve this question.

Concerning the *very early dating* of these Gospels, it's important to see that specific motives in these books more often reflect the first part (the thirties) of the first century than the second part, as is usually assumed. Full attention will be given to these aspects in the presentation that follows.

6.2.2 The Gospel of Matthew

As seen earlier (section 5.2), the Gospel of Matthew is a real "teacher's Gospel," and many sayings of Jesus in it have a teaching content. After Jesus's departure, the apostles had the task of teaching the new Christians who had joined them. What did they teach? They taught the teaching records that they'd made when Jesus was with them. Why would they wait to edit these records properly into a book, while a lot of public records circulated among the people as a heritage out

---

[182] For the chronology, we take as a starting point that Jesus began his work in the fifteenth year of Tiberius, (Luke 3:1, 23), in the beginning of that year before Pesach. In John's Gospel, Pesach follows a short time after Jesus's baptism. The year AD 28 is generally accepted as the fifteenth year of Tiberius. We reckon two years for Jesus's public ministry according to the three feasts of Pesach, of which John makes mention (2:32, start of Jesus's work; 6:24 halfway; 11:55, the end of Jesus's work). The Christian Church began with Pentecost in AD 30.

of Jesus's ministry, particularly when there was good reason to bring out the teaching records as soon as possible in Jerusalem?

Matthew copied his material without adding embellishments. This is a reasonable conclusion when we observe the so-called formula quotations in his Gospel. The formula—"This was to fulfill (or "then was fulfilled") what was spoken by the prophet saying"—is found about ten times, followed by a quotation from an Old Testament prophet (or, in one case, the Psalms).[183] Even during Jesus's ministry, the disciples already understood that Jesus was the fulfiller of Old Testament prophecies. From the outset, they were convinced that he was the long-expected Messiah (John 1:35–2:11). Concerning the Messianic fulfillments, they saw direct fulfillments of prophetical predictions, and they often saw fulfillments in occurrences that showed only great comparison with great Old Testament events.[184] The writers of the first records already had added the fulfillment quotations; thus, it was not the work of Matthew when he wrote his Gospel. This is clear from the Passion history in which almost no fulfillment quotations are found.[185] The explanation is that the disciples did not see any prophetic fulfillment in Jesus's suffering and death: "But they understood none of these things; this saying was hid from them, and they did not grasp what was said."[186] Only after Jesus's resurrection did they begin to understand the meaning of Jesus's Passion: "For as yet they did not

---

[183] Matthew 1:22–23; 2:15; 2:17–18; 2:23; 4:14–16; 8:17; 12:17–21; 21:4–5; 27:9–10. Only 2:5–6 has the formula, "For so it is written by the prophet."

[184] Example of the first type of fulfillment: Matthew 8:17 refers to Isaiah: "He took our infirmities and bore our diseases." Nobody in Old Testament history had ever healed the sick as Jesus did. Example of the second type of fulfillment: Matthew 1:23 refers to a word of Isaiah: "and his name shall be called Emmanuel (God with us)." Isaiah had prophesied about a prince in his own time who would be born, and his name would be a sign that he (Isaiah) spoke the truth (7:14). With the birth of Jesus, a new Prince of Truth would come, and he would show the meaning of Emmanuel (God with us) as no one had before.

[185] There is one quotation of Jesus himself (Matthew 26:54, 56) and one from recognizable later time: Matthew 27:8–9. It is obvious that this passage did not belong to the first record. It is an addition after Pentecost, which is made clear by the words "to this day." (Therefore, that field has been called the Field of Blood to this day.)

[186] Luke 19:34.

know the scripture, that he must rise from the dead" (John 20:9).[187] This state of affairs is the explanation of the absence of fulfillment quotations in the Passion history. The point is that Matthew, when writing his Gospel, did not add any reference to the Old Testament in this part of his book. It is possible to deduce many prophecies from Isaiah 53, with respect to the Passion and resurrection of Jesus. Not one of them was used by Matthew as a fulfillment quotation to make clear to the reader that this was all according to a divine plan. Matthew's reserve makes it possible for us to speak of an indicator of authenticity on behalf of the Gospels. For certainly the other Gospel writers worked just as Matthew did. They copied the original records of Jesus's writers; only in a few cases did they add something from the completed state, which is still recognizable as an addition from later time (e.g., "who betrayed him").[188]

During the same period that Matthew worked on his Gospel, the apostle John worked on his book also, and, as mentioned, they worked out a clear-cut plan. John described Jesus's visits to Judea and Jerusalem, while Matthew left out these parts of Jesus's public life, except his last visit to Jerusalem. Matthew's Gospel dealt with presenting Jesus as the Messiah and his teaching with regard to discipleship and the normal Christian life. John's Gospel provided the knowledge of the Messiah's divine descent, because during his visits to Jerusalem, his religious opponents put his person and origin in the center of their confrontations with Jesus.

6.2.3. Judeans and Galileans in the Gospel of John

The Gospel of John also served historical and practical purposes. To understand the historical impact of John's Gospel, it is necessary to describe the historical relationship between the regions of Judea and Galilee. In Galilee, the old tribe unity, as they had functioned in ages past, had disappeared. In this region, a mixed population of Israelites lived, while in Judea, the tribe of Judah still dominated public life. In Galilee, the old Hebrew language of Israel had disappeared; it was

---

[187] The story of the Emmaus men (Luke 24:13–35) is also a striking example. Jesus himself had to explain to them that his suffering was all part of God's plan.
[188] Matthew 10:4; Mark 3:19; Luke 6:16.

still in vogue only in the synagogues and among pious families. That was the reason why Judeans considered the Galileans as backward and looked down on them. We meet this negative feeling about Galilee in the Gospel of John: "Can anything good come out of Nazareth?" "Is the Christ to come from Galilee?" "Are you from Galilee too? Search and see that no prophet is to rise from Galilee."[189] These statements taken from the Gospel of John show how the Judeans disregarded Galilee and the Galileans.

Judeans called the tune in the Jewish land in the social and religious respect. They exercised their influence even in Galilee, often to the displeasure of the Galileans. From indirect remarks in the Gospel of John, we may learn also that the differences in daily behavior and religious traditions were great.[190] Sometimes John creates the impression that he is rather negative about "the Jews." But this is not the case. Where John uses the word *Jews*, we should simply read *Judeans*, as distinct from Galileans. He is certainly not speaking about "all the Jews," including the Galileans, as we might suppose, had we no knowledge of the circumstances at the time of his writing. This insinuation might be correct, if we could accept that the edition of John's Gospel dates from about AD 95, as the majority of scholars do. In that case, the meaning of *Jews* cannot be understood in any other way than as all the Jews, because the political situation of the Jews in the Roman Empire at that time changed completely after the Jewish war of AD 70. The difference between Judeans and Galileans had ceased to exist; they were all Jews then.

John admired the Judeans and accepted their religious leadership, but on the other hand, he was surprised that the sharpest criticism of Jesus came from the part of the nation that seemed to be most blessed. How was it possible that those who seemed to be more chosen than the other Israelites so often rejected the signs Jesus did? This perplexity is found often throughout the entire book.

---

[189] John 1:46; 7:41; 7:52.

[190] John 2:6 speaks of "the Jewish (i.e., Judean) rites of purification." John 2:13; 6:4, 11:55 speaks about "the Passover of the Jews (i.e., the Judeans)." A great difference was that in Galilee, the meal was held without the flesh of a lamb, as only in the temple of Jerusalem were lambs to be slaughtered for Passover.

In the prologue of his Gospel, John says, "He came to his own home, and his own people received him not."[191] His home was Judea, with Jerusalem, the temple, and of course his tribesmen, the Judeans (as Jesus was also from the tribe of Judah). John does not generalize; immediately after this statement, he says, "But to all who received him, who believed in his name, he gave power to become children of God." John also saw how a majority of Judeans followed Jesus, often in secret (John 11:45, 12:19, 42). In the Gospel of John, there is no total rejection of the Jews, as is often argued, although it is undeniable that the widespread theological misconception of a late date of John's Gospel has given rise in history to serious anti-Semitic feelings.[192] The mere thought of this should give theologians motivation to reevaluate the traditional late dates of the Gospels.

John also speaks about Galileans in his prologue: "And the Word became flesh and dwelt among us, full of grace and truth; we have beheld his glory."[193] Jesus had lived among the disdained Galileans. They had seen him, they had heard him, and they did not have problems with him, as did many of their fellow citizens in Judea. They had seen his glory. The words *us* and *we* in his prologue certainly refer to the Galileans, and it makes clear that this Gospel was not only written for the Christian community in Jerusalem but also for the Galileans, who believed in Jesus as the Messiah and still lived in Galilee, and who had many urgent questions after Jesus's departure.

---

[191] John 1:11.

[192] We have to reckon with two meanings of the word 'Ioudaios'. Outside the Jewish land it certainly had the meaning of: (1) 'Jew', a member of the Jewish nation and of the Jewish religion. Inside the Jewish land it had often the meaning of: (2) 'Judean', 'member of the tribe Judah', 'inhabitant of the region of Judea' in contrast with 'Galilean', 'inhabitant of Galilee' and without general religious reference. After the fall of Jerusalem in 70 AD the second meaning disappeared and one began to read the Gospel of John with the first inappropriate meaning. If John wrote his gospel in ca. 95 AD he colored the Jews in a negative way as a result of the religious meaning of 'Ioudaios'. Certainly he loved his people too much to ever have done that.

[193] John 1:14.

6.2.4 The Gospel of John

After Jesus's unexpected death, a new historical situation existed in Galilee. It's not difficult to understand that questions arose among the Galileans. Why was Jesus crucified? Why had their religious leaders played a central role in this event? What was the Roman part of the story? What was the meaning of Pentecost for them, while a new community of Messianic believers was growing in the city of Jerusalem? And most of all, was Jesus indeed the Messiah in whom they had believed, or should they expect another one to come? Who was he? All of these questions cried out for answers, not only for the Christian community in Jerusalem but also for the multitudes in Galilee who had believed in Jesus. The Gospel of John answered all of these questions, and for that reason, it was as important as Matthew's Gospel. Both books were needed at the start of the Christian Church.

The content of John's Gospel made clear to the people that the relationship between Jesus and the religious leaders and teachers of the nation did not collapse due to a sudden clash. Chapter after chapter reveals a deep-rooted and nagging conflict between Jesus and a rather small but influential elite of rigid fellow Judeans. These Judeans felt it their duty to defend the traditional religion that was centered around the belief in one God (strict monotheism). From the beginning, they felt that Jesus did not act or speak as a normal person. He was different. He forgave people he had never seen before; others fell on their knees in front of him, and he never interrupted them by saying (as Peter once did[194]), "Stand up; I too am a man." Moreover, he spoke with an authority that was completely unusual; in fact, they were not able to overcome him in their confrontations with him. Their conclusion was this: "It is not for a good work that we [want to] stone you but for blasphemy; because you, being a man, make yourself God."[195] They could not grasp that Jesus was truly divine and truly human (truly God and truly man)—the Messiah.

John starts his Gospel with a description of Jesus's peculiar Messianic position: "The Word was God." And "The Word became flesh and dwelt among us." Before Jesus's coming on earth, he was the speaking and working Word of God, and as such, he was part of

---

[194] Acts 10:26.
[195] John 11:33.

God (being God). In the same way, Paul would say about this Word, "and all drank the same supernatural drink. For they drank from the supernatural Rock which followed them, and the Rock was the Christ (the Messiah)" (1 Corinthians 10:4). In Old Testament times, the people of Israel already experienced the Messiah, but at that time, he had not yet become man; he was still "the Word."

John and the twelve had the privilege of beholding this new revelation of the Word as God and man. Of course, it was difficult for these men from Galilee to understand this. They had grown up with a deep respect for the one single God of Israel. And certainly, John did not write his prologue as a result of his own theological reflection. That being the case, he would not have dared to write the first sentence of his Gospel: "In the beginning was the Word, and the Word was with God, and the Word was God." Only by revelation was he able to write this. One of the issues certainly must have been that in the forty days after Jesus's resurrection, he revealed himself to his disciples, speaking with them about the kingdom of God. Jesus must have patiently spoken about it, because after Thomas's exclamation to Jesus—"My Lord and my God!"—there was a lot to explain.[196]

The Matthew–John project resulted in two books. The Gospel of Matthew answered the questions on how to live the Christian life. The Gospel of John answered the questions on how to think about Jesus, as well as how to experience him (i.e., to believe in him).[197] This last important aspect of John's Gospel has to do with the revelation of the Holy Spirit. Of course, in the first Christian community in Jerusalem, the work of the Holy Spirit was part of daily life, and there was no urgent reason for Matthew to say much about it in his Gospel. However, John also had the people of Galilee in mind. How could they continue with their faith in Jesus after his abrupt departure? That was the second great question of the Galileans who believed in Jesus. John was concerned with this question, and he reckoned with it by the choice of his material. And

---

[196] John 20:28. In the New Testament, the two aspects of Jesus's personality—his human and his divine nature—are not always equally discussed. Sometimes his divine nature is stressed, sometimes his human nature. But most often, neither of them is hidden as a result of his titles and names: Son (human) of God (divine), Jesus (human) Christ (divine), etc.

[197] John 20:31.

the Holy Spirit, writing through John, included information that we, many years later, need to have also.

During his ministry, Jesus spoke about a new revelation that was near: the coming of the Holy Spirit. In John 7:37–39, we read, "On the last day of the feast, the great day, Jesus stood up and proclaimed, 'If anyone thirst, let him come to me and drink. He who believes in me, as the scripture has said: Out of his heart shall flow rivers of living water.' Now this he said about the Spirit, which those who believed in him were to receive; for as yet the Spirit had not been given, because Jesus was not yet glorified." The person and work of the Holy Spirit was of vital importance for the first Christian community in Jerusalem; the same was applicable for the countless followers of Jesus who had remained in Galilee. The believers in Galilee had come to the same point to which the apostles had come, when Jesus said to them, "Receive the Holy Spirit."[198] Saying this, Jesus had breathed on his disciples, which certainly was a sign of what he meant with this word. They had already received the Holy Spirit in them but not *over* (on) them. Just as Jesus had been born of the Spirit (and the Spirit lived in him), still he received the Spirit over (on) him at once, immediately after his baptism by John the Baptist. And now Jesus had promised that all who believed in him would, by drinking from him, experience a new working of the Holy Spirit, as flowing rivers of living water. With this message of John's Gospel, the great center of Messiah believers in Galilee could continue. They again had to concentrate on Jesus's words in this new situation, just as they had heard them before, and the Holy Spirit was willing to confirm them.

6.2.5 Dates of the Gospels of Matthew and John

John's Gospel has two endings. The first was written by John himself. "Now Jesus did many other signs in the presence of the disciples, which are not written in this book, but these are written that you may believe that Jesus is the Christ, the Son of God, and that believing you may have life in his name" (John 20:30–31). John's Gospel had come to this point organically by Jesus's revelation to Thomas, to whom he said, "Have you believed because you have seen me? Blessed are those

---

[198] John 20:22.

110

who have not seen and yet believe" (John 20:29). Believe what? That Jesus is the Messiah, the Son of God (God and man), according to verse 31. This first ending of John's Gospel sets the objectives of the book (belief in Jesus and a new life through this belief).

The second ending contains an authorization of the Gospel: "This is the disciple who is bearing witness to these things, and who has written these things; *and we know that his testimony is true.* But there are also many other things which Jesus did." Who wrote the words in italics? Who are *we* who know that this Gospel is true? Several suggestions have been offered in the past, and they need not be repeated here. For our subject, it is sufficient to concentrate on the matter of concern. That is, who was able and qualified to pass the judgment, "and we know that his testimony is true." This judgment includes the reliability of the described events and sayings in John's Gospel. Of course, only the other apostles were able and qualified to give this judgment. The *we*, by the nature of the case, are the other apostles, and one of them wrote this phrase to authorize the book in their name.[199]

John was the author of this Gospel. He wrote on behalf of the apostles of the first Christian community in Jerusalem, who were the publishers of the book. The Gospels of Matthew and of John are to be dated in the first year of the Christian Church in Jerusalem, as the books were necessary for the proclamation of the Gospel from its beginning; that sets the date at about AD 30.

6.3.1 The Secretary Gospels

It is quite remarkable that two men, Luke and Mark, emerged to also write Gospel books. Matthew and John were real apostles, chosen by Jesus for the peer group of the twelve who were appointed to be his witnesses. He taught these twelve men all they needed for their task, and at the end he authorized them. "You are witnesses of these things" (Luke 24:48). Or as Peter said later, "And we are witnesses to all that He did both in the country of the Jews and in Jerusalem" (Acts

---

[199] It was accepted custom for the Gospel writers to make an insertion in their narratives, if they made clear in the context that the insertion did not belong to the original they copied. The insertion of the apostles in John 21:24 is to be taken in this way.

10:39). Indeed, it is remarkable that two individuals outside the group of the twelve became gospel writers. How is that possible?

First we have to admit that it was not only disciples of the twelve who were appointed for note-taking. During the missionary journey of the twelve, Jesus continued to teach the people and a new inside group of disciples.[200] A large part of this teaching material has been preserved only in the Gospel of Matthew (11–14). Who were the stenographers? To answer this question, it is important to see that there were also secretaries among Jesus's writers.

The role of a secretary was important later in the lives of the apostles. Peter wrote his first letter (5:12) through Silvanus; Paul once made use of Tertius to write down the letter to the Romans (16:22). It seems that all Paul's letters were written by secretaries, as it was Paul's custom to write a greeting and blessing in his own handwriting only at the end of his letters.[201]

Just as the apostles made use of secretaries, so did the note-takers of Jesus. When they discussed their notes to make their threefold reports, they could make use of the services of other skilled writers, secretaries who wrote down the final wording of the stories. As usual for secretaries, of course, was the reading back of the final text for the note-takers, who had the first notes before them on their tablets. Only secretaries who had proved their skill and trustworthiness earlier could be set in to fill the gap of note-taking during the missionary journey of the twelve. The same was true for them when they were invited to write Gospel books for the early apostolic church in Jerusalem, to fully inform about Jesus and his deeds. It was secretaries, Luke and Mark, who worked together with Matthew and John to fulfill this important task.

6.3.2 The Gospel of Luke

After the Pentecost event, a great demand for public records remained. It was time to bring them together, to arrange and to collect them into one volume. From the point of view of the apostles, it was important to bring structure to the mass of public records that went around. Just as they did with the Matthew–John project,

---

[200] Matthew 12:1; 13:10, 36.
[201] 2 Thessalonians 3:17–18.

which resulted in authorized books, they must have felt the need for authorized public records. It was Luke who accepted the job. Luke certainly belonged to the larger circle of Jesus's disciples, for which the public records originally were made. As showed earlier Luke followed the example of the many who, during Jesus's ministry, had arranged longer stories by copying records, one after another.

Luke had the opportunity to use original public records that were the property of the apostles. So he was able to add stories that had been kept secret, according to Jesus's wishes (e.g., the resurrection of Jairus's daughter and Jesus's glorification on the mount, 8:56, 9:36). In Luke's Gospel, they also received a proper place.

Luke could simply follow the order of the Gospel of Matthew, as most public records had been produced parallel to the teaching records. Luke also gave information about Jesus's last journey to Jerusalem in about ten chapters, which are completely absent in Matthew's Gospel. Apparently, Matthew considered Jesus's teaching to have ended when he decided to leave Galilee and to travel to Jerusalem. He continued his story at the moment that Jesus entered into Judea (19:1), crossing the River Jordan in the south. According to Matthew, the Passion story began from that moment.

Luke ends his book with the messages of Jesus's resurrection and appearances, just as the evangelists John and Matthew did. This is the first indication that Luke wrote his Gospel in Jerusalem, not long after these events occurred; it seems that they lay fresh in the memories and hearts and minds of the people. He did not need to write about the work and experiences of the Holy Spirit in Jerusalem. He felt it was outside his purpose, as his goal was to present the life and work of Jesus, but he also felt his readers lived in a context in which the Holy Spirit was experienced daily. His readers knew everything about that: "You have filled Jerusalem with your teaching," as the council members reproached the apostles (Acts 5:28).

A second indication that supports this early publication of the Gospel of Luke may be seen in the first chapters of the announcement, birth, and youth of Jesus. True enough, Matthew also gave some information about this period of Jesus's life, but the specific information from Luke about this period could not wait for years.

It is possible to demonstrate that the Gospel of Luke was written almost simultaneously with the Gospels of Matthew and John. It seems possible to establish this view according to the following argument: Luke says that he had followed all things closely before writing "that you may know the truth concerning the things [Greek: spoken words] of which you have been informed."[202] Undoubtedly, Luke referred in this phrase to the public records that were already going around before Pentecost. Theophilus had already heard a lot through the public records, but through the work of Luke, he got structure and order in all these records, which resulted for him in "that you may know the truth ... of which you have been informed." In Greek, the word *asphaleia* has been used for the truth; that is, firmness, stability, certainty (firm coherence). If Theophilus had already known the Gospels of Matthew and John for a time, it would seem that Luke wanted to give certainty about those Gospels. In that case, Luke would have been giving his Gospel a superior place, above the other Gospels. And, of course, that could never have been his intention. This leads us to the conclusion that Luke's Gospel was brought out at about the same time as the Gospels of Matthew and John, in the year 30.

Many have theorized that Luke was a Christian living in the region of Antioch (Syria) and that he was of Gentile origin. One expects to find confirmation of the latter in Paul's description of Colossians 4:10–14, where Luke is not reckoned among Paul's Jewish coworkers who were circumcised and who were an encouragement to him. Indeed, it is reasonable to assume that at that time, Luke also was a coworker of Paul's (Philemon 24). However, one must proceed here with caution, for even Timothy (Colossians 1:1), who was circumcised, is not mentioned in Colossians 4:10–14. Timothy did not receive a firm Jewish education, as he was circumcised late; he was by then a young man (Acts 16:1–3). It is therefore realistic that Luke, too, was of Jewish origin but had not grown up in accordance with all the rules of the Law.

Therefore, there is no reason to suppose that Luke was of Gentile origin and no member of the first Christian community in Jerusalem. On the contrary, we have good reason to conclude that Luke was the Gospel writer who wrote his Gospel in the year 30 in Jerusalem, together with the apostles Matthew and John.

---

[202] Luke 1:4.

6.3.3 The Gospel of Mark

The Gospels of Matthew, John, and Luke have been arranged inside the context of the first Christian community of Jerusalem. What about the Gospel of Mark? This book finishes with the words, "And they went forth and preached everywhere, while the Lord worked with them and confirmed the message by the signs that attended it." It gives the impression that the apostles went out of Jerusalem and preached the Gospel everywhere.[203] However, this is again a typical Greek sentence that deserves special attention because of the indefinite pronoun it contains (everywhere—where exactly?). Moreover, the verb forms are more correctly rendered as "And going forth they preached everywhere." The intention is more that where the apostles came, there they preached. This may perfectly refer to the first preaching activities of the apostles in Jerusalem already. This last sentence of the Gospel of Mark is not a hint that they left Jerusalem and "preached in the whole world."

This observation makes it possible to take the date of the Gospel of Mark very early, just as with the other three canonical Gospels, according to John's apostolic manifesto, that they made known their apostolic knowledge about Jesus right from the source as one testament (section 1.5.2): "That which we have seen and heard we *proclaim (from the source)* also to you ... and we are writing this (these things) that our joy may be complete." In the same way, Hebrews 2:3 says, "How shall we escape if we neglect so great a salvation; which beginning to be spoken by the Lord, was confirmed (established) in behalf of us by those who were hearing." Here also it's spoken to the early Christians concerning the complete written tradition about Jesus for their benefit. Moreover, Hebrews 9:17 makes mention of a testament that becomes effective after the death of the testator. Certainly the author refers to Jesus and suggests that the same is at stake with the testament of Jesus. His words needed to be opened after his death to make them known to the people. In short, it was fitting that the four Gospels were brought out together, including Mark's Gospel. That brings us to the date of the Gospel of Mark,

---

[203] This view was brought forward in the first edition of this book with the date of the Gospel of Mark in AD 34. This view has been left in this edition.

contemporary with the other canonical Gospels in the year 30 AD, and to the place of publication, the city of Jerusalem.

The Gospel of Mark was intended as a practical document inside and outside Jerusalem. Many disciples who had followed Jesus in Judea, Samaria, and Galilee did not have the opportunity to show a flourishing Christian community in their environment, where everything they believed was visible. In this Gospel, they received a document by which the Gospel could become a living context by reading and hearing it. Therefore, it starts with the words "The beginning of the Gospel of Jesus Christ, the Son of God." This opening sentence makes directly clear that this is the book of the Messiah, the one who is God and man. The ending of the book also refers to that living context—institutions of the community and even apostolic miracles are laid down in the hands of common believers (16:16–18).[204]

The features of the Gospel of Mark seem to best fit the characteristics of the earliest period of the church. The book presupposes knowledge of the Jewish land. Mark does not explain details of the Jewish land. Moreover, geographic details are assumed to be well known among the readers. Of the desert (1:4, 12), we may ask, "Which part of it?" And of the mountains (3:13; 6:46; 9:2), no specific identifications were given. On the other hand, Mark gives striking reader explanations about Jewish words and customs within the text. Where Matthew only has three "that is" explanations, Mark has ten.[205] Words that Mark explains are, for instance, Corban; that is, "given to God" (7:11); the day of Preparation; that is, "the day

---

[204] The expressions in it as 'pick up serpents' and 'drink any deadly thing' have symbolic meanings which refer to false teachers who would try to diminish the power of the Gospel and spread their own destructive teachings. John the Baptist called some Pharisees who came to him 'serpents, brood of vipers'. (Matthew 3:7, Luke 3:7)

[205] Matthew 27:33 (Golgotha; that is, the place of a skull); 27:46 ("Eli, Eli" etc.; that is, "My God, my God, why hast thou forsaken me?"); 27:62 (Next day; that is, after the day of preparation); Mark 3:17 (Boanerges; that is, sons of thunder); 5:41 ("Talitha cumi"; that is, "Little girl, I say to you, arise"); 7:2 (hands defiled; that is, unwashed); 7:11 (Corban; that is, given to God); 7:43 ("Ephphatha"; that is, "Be opened"); 12:42 (two copper coins; that is, a penny); 15:16 (the palace; that is, the praetorium); 15:22 (Golgotha; that is, the place of a skull); 15:34 ("Eloi, Eloi ..."; that is, "My God, my God, why

before the Sabbath" (15:42). Mark also had readers in mind who were less acquainted with typical Judean practices and expressions.[206] Indeed, in the early church in Jerusalem, there were many Judean believers who were not acquainted with the old Hebrew language and religious practices (Acts 6:1). And certainly Mark also had Galileans and Samaritans in mind, who always had received Jesus's special attention. The unelaborated style of the remnant records made the Gospel of Mark a dynamic and challenging report of Jesus's public life. In Jerusalem, around the year 30, the apostles provided four important books:

1. The Gospel of Matthew—the church Gospel
2. The Gospel of John—the personal Gospel
3. The Gospel of Luke—the Gospel history
4. The Gospel of Mark—the common Gospel

The apostles marked and authorized these books as undeniable theirs with titles such as "Gospel according to …," together with the forever incomparable content of the books. These books have remained a unity of four in the canon lists in the history of the church.

In traditional Gospel research, scholars assume that the Gospels were written between the years 65 and 95 as a result of an oral tradition. Unfortunately, this does not take into account the enormous influence of reading and writing in the first century among Romans, Greeks, and Jews. In this traditional framing, it seems as if Jesus worked in a sort of prehistoric time, in which people were not supposed to write. We may like, then, to deal with the Gospels as "history" after the "prehistoric era," because it is undeniable that the Gospels are documents. Are there really convincing arguments, however, for this unsatisfactory picture? No, the evidence speaks for a totally different paradigm. Speedy writers and stenographers followed Jesus to pick

---

hast thou forsaken me?"); 15:42 (Preparation; that is, the day before the Sabbath).

[206] It is not clear whether the "that is" explanations are from the first writers (of the remnant sources) or from Mark (also 7:3–4; 14:51–52; 16:9–13; 19–20). If they are from the first writers, it is possible that the remnant records also were used in Jesus's ministry for publication, for those who preferred narratives with a less eloquent style.

up and document his sayings accurately. The records they produced, under the inspiration and guidance of the Holy Spirit, were able to provide an explosion of Gospel books that started to flow throughout the world as an inheritance of the first Christian Church of Jerusalem until the present day, as Isaiah foretold:[207]

> Listen to me, my people,
> and give ear to me, my nation;
> for a law will go forth from me,
> and my justice for a light to the peoples.
> My deliverance draws near speedily,
> my salvation has gone forth,
> and my arms will rule the peoples,
> the coastlands wait for me,
> and for my arm they hope.

6.4.1 The Longer Mark Ending

In the evaluation of the Gospel of Mark, a starting point is the authenticity of the longer ending of this Gospel (16:9–20). It is called the longer Mark ending, as there also exists a shorter ending, which generally is seen as of a later date.[208] Many respectable scholars, however, consider the longer ending as not original.[209] The arguments are as follows: (1) external evidence—it is missing in the oldest and best Greek documents (fourth century); (2) internal evidence—the wording and style of the passage are not Marcan; and (3) it seems to be a composition from other Gospels (Luke and John). Before dealing with these arguments, we must notice that

---

[207] Isaiah 51:4–5.

[208] The so-called shorter ending: "But they reported briefly to Peter and those with him all that had been told. And after this, Jesus himself sent out by means of them, from east to west, the sacred and imperishable proclamation of eternal salvation." This shorter ending is clearly an attempt to solve the problem of verse 8 as an improper ending of Mark ("for they were afraid"), the problem that is created by the rejection of the longer ending.

[209] Th. Zahn, D. Guthry, A.F.J. Klijn, R.A. Cole, J.R.W. Stott, S. Motyer, H. Baarlink, I. Broer etc.

the longer ending of Mark occurs in an overwhelming majority of Greek documents, from the fifth century onward. Moreover, it is old and certainly not of a late date because Irenaeus cited it (ca. AD 180).

"It is missing in the oldest and best manuscripts"—this is generally felt to be an impressive argument against the longer Mark ending. The older a document, the higher its value because the risk of copy errors is the least. But the above argument is misleading because the omission of the longer Mark ending is not a copy error at all. Only two important manuscripts—Codex Sinaiticus and Codex Vaticanus—omit the longer Mark ending, and this was a knowing choice.[210] Before the canon acceptance of the twenty-seven books of the New Testament at the end of the fourth century, churches could decide to exclude books or portions of them. That is the background for which that old witnesses, such as Sinaiticus and Vaticanus, omit the longer Marcan ending. It has nothing to do with scribal errors. After the canon decisions of the fourth century, the practice of omitting portions from scripture soon ended. During the canon discussions in the fourth century, the longer Mark ending was not a serious issue of debate—conclusive evidence that the omission of the longer Mark ending was only a marginal phenomenon in the church, in the period before the canon had been accepted generally.

If the longer ending is not authentic, then the end of this Gospel is Mark 16:8, where we read, "For they were afraid." It is a serious problem, in that exegetes don't have a realistic explanation for this "last and least verse" of the Mark Gospel. Is that how a Gospel, a joyful message, should end? Of course not; all exegetes who support the rejection of Mark 16:9–20 are tongue-tied when they have to explain this strange ending. In fact, they all admit that it is strange. The idea that the last page of this Gospel has disappeared by accident has been rejected as a realistic argument for a long time. A missing last page in one or a few books could in no way influence the complete stream of delivering the entire Gospel of Mark. We

---

[210] In Codex Vaticanus, it was probably an economic choice. There is enough room left in the document to insert the longer ending. It seems that the seller of the manuscript kept his sales potential as wide as possible. Who wanted the longer ending, could get it.

may finish this point with a saying of the apostle Paul: The gospels were not written "in a corner" (Acts 26:26). This argument is even more weighty with regard to the *very early* dating of Mark (AD 30). It is impossible that during the decades while the apostles still were alive, the last page of this book could disappear without anyone discovering that.

There are enough positive arguments for the unusual style of the longer ending. Within the documentation theory, the different style is not an obstacle because Mark wrote remnant records that were made by different writers. Besides, after Jesus's resurrection, the entire scene changed, as well as the relationship between Jesus and his disciples. A shift within the discourses between Jesus and his disciples seems inevitable. He certainly had things to discuss with them that were new and were in a totally new perspective for them. Before Jesus's death, he had said to them, "I have yet many things to say to you, but you cannot bear them now. When the Spirit of truth comes, he will guide you into all truth."[211] When he met them after his resurrection, he immediately started speaking to them from where he had left off, speaking about the kingdom of God. They had to be prepared for many things, so we should not be surprised to see new issues and new words in the longer ending of Mark.

Some scholars have drawn attention to the fact that several aspects of the longer ending are seemingly not in accordance with the other resurrection stories. Before dealing with these problems, we will first present the text under discussion.

> [9] Now when he rose early on the first day of the week, he appeared first to Mary Magdalene, from whom he had cast out seven demons.
> [10] She went out and told those who had been with him, as they mourned and wept.
> [11] But when they heard that he was alive and had been seen by her, they would not believe it.
> [12] After this he appeared in another form to two of them, as they were walking into the country.

---

[211] John 16:12–13.

¹³ And they went back and told the rest, but they did not believe them.

¹⁴ Afterward he appeared to the eleven themselves as they sat at table; and he upbraided them for their unbelief and hardness of heart, because they had not believed those who saw him after he had risen.

¹⁵ And he said to them, "Go into all the world ..."

Problem 1: The two men (verse 12) seem to be the men from Emmaus (Luke 24:13), but when they returned to Jerusalem and said that they had seen the Lord, the reaction seems in contrast with verse13—positive: "The Lord has risen indeed, and has appeared to Simon."

Problem 2: The moment of Jesus's appearance to his disciples seems to be the evening that followed on the first day. However, the first time that Jesus appeared to his disciples—we know from John's Gospel—Thomas was not with them. Still, in Mark we read "he appeared to the eleven" (verse 14). This seems contradictory.

The solution to these problems lies in a good understanding of what Mark has done in these verses. He possessed a short remnant record with verses 14–19. This record contained a short description of the situation (verse 14), followed by Jesus's sayings to go out into the world. To make the disciples' negative behavior of unbelief understandable for his readers, Mark first had to write about the details of that unbelief. From the Gospels of John and Luke, which already existed, he could take verses 9–11 about Mary Magdalene and 12–13 about the two men of Emmaus, respectively. But through the two examples of unbelief on the first day of Jesus's resurrection, it gives the impression that the record (14–19) also deals with the evening following that first day. That, however, is not the case. Verse 15 is an and-sentence, which means (interruption of events, section 7.2). It is of a much later date, at least eight days later, because the eleven disciples were present, including Thomas, who had been absent the first time Jesus met the disciples (John 20:24). One tends to suppose that this occurrence took place at the evening after resurrection day because Jesus exhorted them about their unbelief on that day.[212] It should not be forgotten, however, that Peter was not confronted with his threefold denial at his first meeting with Jesus after his resurrection. Jesus confronted him later (John 21:15–17). With this in mind, it is possible to solve the two problems.

Problem 1. When the two men of Emmaus returned to Jerusalem, we read, "And they found the eleven gathered together and those who were with them, who said, 'The Lord has risen indeed, and has appeared to Simon!'" It is obvious that "those who were with them" believed in Jesus's resurrection (Luke 24:34–35) and said, "The Lord has risen." The eleven did not say that, and certainly Thomas could not stand this enthusiasm any longer and left, while the men of Emmaus told their story. The Gospel of Mark underlines the fact that the eleven disciples could not believe in Jesus's resurrection; even the appearance of Jesus to Peter that first day did not change the hearts of the others.

Problem 2. From the available evidence we get the following:

- Jesus appeared to Mary Magdalene on resurrection morning (John 20:14–17).
- Jesus appeared to the Emmaus men late in the afternoon, toward evening (Luke 24:13–31).
- Jesus appeared to Peter before the Emmaus men entered Jerusalem (Luke 24:34).
- Late in the evening after resurrection day, Jesus appeared to the disciples without Thomas, who had left a little earlier (John 20:19–23; Luke 24:36–48).
- Jesus appeared eight days later to the disciples, with Thomas (John 20:26–29). It is reasonable to take Mark 16:14–18 as part of this appearance. By now, Thomas had come to believe, and Jesus could indeed exhort them all.

---

[212] The translation "Afterward" in verse 14 may indicate "After these events"; the Greek word *husteron* means later (in the future).

Conclusions:

1. The longer ending of Mark is in accordance with all the ins and outs of Jesus's first appearances, as we know them from the other Gospels.
2. The longer ending differs in style and wording with regard to the discourse. The discourse contains elements of new things as a result of the resurrection.
3. The longer ending differs in style and wording with regard to the narrative part, because two passages are in Mark's hand: 9–12 and 19–20. The bulk of this Gospel represents the wording and style of Jesus's speedy writers and stenographers.
4. There is no serious reason to deny the authentic character of the longer ending of the Gospel of Mark. The larger ending is a hundred times more convincing than Mark 16:8 as a closing formula.
5. The longer ending of Mark shows, in an impressive way, the purpose of the Gospel of Mark: the transference of the Gospel and all its implications to common believers and common churches.

6.4.2 And What about Papias?

From the beginning of the second century, there are a few testimonies of Bishop Papias about the origins of the Gospels. And because of the lack of other early material, Papias's vision on the Gospels is often accepted, even in our time. Papias worked as a bishop in Hierapolis in the beginning of the second century, until approximately AD 130.

According to Papias, Mark wrote in his Gospel what he had heard from Peter when they were in Rome, many years after Jesus's public appearance. Therefore, according to Papias's view, Mark's Gospel is basically Peter's Gospel. It is obvious that Papias presupposed an oral tradition—the preaching activity of Peter. It is also obvious that Papias did not build his opinion on scripture but on what had come to him by hearsay.

A few decades after the destruction of Jerusalem, the Christians in the other parts of the Roman Empire could not imagine how refined and prosperous the old Jewish culture had been. With both biblical and historical lack in his knowledge on this subject, it is understandable that Papias reverted to rumors. Unfortunately, many after him have followed Papias's view, even until today, because he was an early witness of the postapostolic church.[213]

The problem with Papias's statements is that it is difficult to evaluate them. For some time, Mark was indeed a servant of Peter (1 Peter 5:13), but was he also his interpreter? Most probably Papias connected personal views about the origin of Mark's Gospel with the single idea that Mark once had been Peter's servant.

Papias also made a statement about the apostle Matthew: "With regard to Matthew he (Papias) has said: 'Matthew collected the oracles in the Hebrew language and each [Mark, Luke and John] interpreted them as best he could.'"[214] There would have been a Hebrew source with sayings of the Lord (nowadays mostly interpreted as Aramaic). One assumes that Matthew collected these sayings from the oral tradition and maybe from older documents for this source. According to Papias, the other Gospel writers made translations of the Hebrew sayings into Greek.

Just as Papias's theory that Mark's Gospel was Peter's Gospel, this theory about Matthew has remained attractive until today. The similarities in the Gospels could be explained as originating from a common Hebrew source, the dissimilarities between the Gospels could be explained as translation differences. Moreover, the authority of the source could be traced back to the apostle Matthew. Papias's statement, in fact, contained an overall theory of how the Gospels were compiled, and this theory has stood for centuries as a confirmation of the oral tradition preceding the Gospels. Despite the modern modification that not Matthew but Mark is the oldest Gospel, this theory has not lost its attractiveness; the general opinion of the oral tradition preceding the Gospels seems to be confirmed by an early respected bishop.

However, Papias's statements about the compilation of the Gospels do not have any serious biblical foundation. The supposition that Matthew translated his Gospel from Hebrew is not tenable.

---

[213] Many commentators (e.g., T. Zahn, B. H. Streeter, D. Guthrie, R.A. Cole, J. R. W. Stott, E. Linnemann, John Wenham).

[214] Eusebius, *Ecclesiastical History* III, 39, 16.

Matthew's style does not give the impression of a translation; the style is smooth and does not represent translation language. D. Guthrie has remarked, "Almost all scholars are agreed that Matthew's gospel was written in Greek, not in Hebrew or Aramaic (as Papias probably supposed)."[215] The model of Papias seems to be a speculation of his own, instead of a theory soundly based on facts and arguments. What really counts is this: The biblical sources are enough to come to solid convictions. There was no reason at all for the Gospel writers to translate. Neither an oral tradition nor translation played a role in the compilation of the Gospels.

6.4.3 The Imaginary Gospel Q

Finally, a few remarks are needed about the so-called Gospel Q. It's all about a set of sayings (of Jesus) in the Gospels of Matthew and Luke that are nearly identical, at least in meaning.

In New Testament theology, it is widely accepted that there once existed an unknown Gospel, and many call it the lost Gospel Q; it would have been written between AD 50 and 60. Together with the Gospel of Mark, this Gospel Q was supposedly used by Matthew and Luke to compose their Gospels. The idea is that common parts in Matthew and Luke show evidence of a common source, and that hypothetical source has received the name Q (German: Quelle = source). For many theologians, it is an attractive idea that apart from Mark there also existed an older (read: better) Gospel than the great Gospels of Matthew and Luke.[216] And therefore, one supposes that Mark and Q are more reliable than Matthew and Luke. Of course, this is not relevant for the documentation theory, as one has to admit that Q also would be a result of the oral tradition. It would mean that Q is burdened with all the negative consequences of the oral tradition. Additionally, there has never been found a historical Gospel Q! In the history of the early church, there is no mention of it. Up to the nineteenth century, nobody had ever heard about

---

[215] Guthrie, *New Testament Introduction*, 37.

[216] About 235 verses in Matthew and also in Luke, so A. Wikenhauser, *Einleitung in das Neue Testament* (Freiburg in Breisgau: Herder, 1963), 176, circa 18 percent of Matthew and 16 percent of Luke; or 221 verses, H. Baarlink, *Inleiding tot het Nieuwe Testament* (Kampen: Kok, 1989), 91.

it. Historical evidence does not exist for Q, but it is a theoretical concept. To the contents of Q, one reckons specific sayings, of which the most important are in the overview below.

Ascribed to Q	
Sayings in Matthew	**Sayings in Luke**
John the Baptist, baptism of Jesus (3:7, etc.)	Idem (3:1, etc.)
Temptation (4:11 etc.)	Idem (4:1, etc.)
Sermon on the Mount (5:1 etc.)	Sermon in the field (6:20, etc.)
Centurion's servant (8:5, etc.)	Idem (7:1, etc.)
After Mission of Twelve (11:1, etc.)	Journey to Jerusalem (9:51, etc.)
Second Coming (24:3, etc.)	Idem (17:20, etc.)
Parable of the talents (25:14, etc.)	Parable of the pounds (19:12, etc.)

The order determined for the sayings in Q corresponds with the order of the sayings in Luke. About 65 percent of the teachings in Q are found in Luke's "Journey to Jerusalem" (10–18:14). The teachings in Matthew that correspond with them are roughly during the "Mission of the Twelve." When the twelve had left him, Jesus continued to teach to a new group of close disciples and the crowds. Matthew also has new reports. Many sayings of the reports are parallel with sayings of the last Journey to Jerusalem by Luke. This makes clear why Matthew had no compelling reason to incorporate the story of Jesus's last journey to Jerusalem. Matthew had already presented a lot of Jesus's teachings of the same character.

According to many modern exegetes, the Gospel Q belongs to the most authentic information about Jesus. One supposes that without the Passion and resurrection, one would find in Q a picture of Jesus in its purest form. All in all, the conclusion must be that Q cannot play a significant role in the documentation theory of the Gospels, which says the complete content of the Gospels is the presentation of the original reports of speedy writers and stenographers. In the subsequent chapters, we will see how fruitful this approach is for exegesis and for a better understanding of the Gospels.

6.4.4 Failing Gospel Theories

After the exposition of the documentation theory concerning the foundations, sources, and dates of the Gospels it is time to give a short overview of main Gospel theories that have been developed in the last two hundred years and which do not sufficiently respect the self-testimony of the New Testament about the preservation of Jesus's words. The following theories should be mentioned:

The theory of the oral tradition. Clearly, wherever they went, the apostles announced the Gospel by word of mouth, but it is halfway to supposing that they or others wrote their full stories about Jesus after a period of decades. The consequence would be all sorts of shortcomings in the presentation of Jesus's sayings and deeds. The many dissimilarities in the Gospels—notwithstanding the similarities—seem to contradict the integrity of the Gospels, especially in the comparison of the direct speeches in the Gospels. However, documentation of the spoken word is the testimony of the New Testament (chapter 1).

The Aramaic theory. It is a widely accepted view that Jesus spoke Aramaic, and somewhere in the process of oral delivery, a translation in Greek would have taken place, with the consequent loss of the original words of Jesus. Evidence would be the Semitic sayings of Jesus. However, the verb form *Ephphatha* (Be opened!) is a perfect Hebrew form and not Aramaic. This is a clear falsification of the Aramaic theory. The other verb forms cannot be defined exclusively as Aramaic, while good Hebrew explanations are available. And so the assertion that Jesus's Semitic sayings would be "clear evidence that Jesus spoke Aramaic" is definitely false. Jesus's note-takers did not translate in Greek; they only delivered (Luke 1:2). The many (Luke 1:1) wrote the narratives *just as* the eyewitnesses, also being servants of the spoken word, delivered, and Luke, in turn, acted *just as* the many did. In this chain, there is no place for a translation from Aramaic into the Greek language. Jesus spoke Greek in his teachings to the people (chapter 2).

The form-historical method. Also known as form criticism, this method studies the forms of sayings and narratives that would have changed or developed in the oral tradition and in the supposed written interdependence of the Gospels. However, the oral tradition was no source for the Gospels: *Es gab nie eine Formgeschichte.* There has never been a history of changing forms (sections 7.1–3).

Community theology (Gemeindetheologie). The Gospels supposedly written at the end of the oral tradition period would most likely contain all sorts of theological elements belonging to the hopes and fears of the Christian communities, where these books would have come into being. The teachings of Jesus, especially, would reflect these elements, as the authors would lay them on his lips. The community elements should be separated from the Gospels to uncover the original intentions of the Christian belief. Redaction criticism is the appropriate method for this field of research, but the Gospels are not products of the community but of Jesus's speedy writers (section 6.3.3 and 8.4).

The same event/saying theory. This theory refers to parallel descriptions, defined as relating to the same event or saying. It is standard procedure in the comparison of the four Gospels to define parallel sayings or narratives (i.e., with nearly similar content, despite small differences) as *identical* sayings or narratives.[217] The consequence of this working method is that the historical sequence of events is hopelessly frustrated in modern Gospel research, as there are so many parallels (but never exactly identical) scattered all over the Gospels (section 8.4).

Late dates. The dates of the Gospels usually are set around or after the year 70—the fall of Jerusalem. However, according to the documentation theory, we know that the Gospels were written very early, as it was the mandate of Jesus to his disciples, "teaching them to observe all that I have commanded you."[218] This could not wait decades but was taken up immediately after Jesus left them (sections 6.2.5 and 6.3.1–3).

---

[217] This is a recurring problem of the book of J. C. Hawkins, *Horae Synopticae* (Oxford: Clarendon Press, 1968).

[218] The mandate of Matthew 28:20 covers the second part of the apostolic manifesto (1 John 1:3–4) about *writing* materials; the mandate for the *oral* part of the apostolic manifesto (1 John 1:1–2) is Luke 24:46–49.

The Papias theories. These theories from the beginning of the second century say that Matthew possessed a Hebrew source with Gospel stories. He and the other evangelists would have used it to translate information for their books. However, as we have seen, Jesus did not teach in Hebrew or Aramaic but in the Greek language (section 2.3 and 6.4.2). There is also no ground for the theory ascribed to Papias that the Gospel of Mark originated from Peter's preaching while the two were in Rome, and Mark would have functioned as Peter's secretary. This is in conflict with the biblical evidence.

The Q-gospel theory. There was no source Q (section 6.4.3) used by the evangelists Matthew and Luke, as common materials in their books would suggest. They mainly used the source of teaching records and the source of public records for the writing of their Gospels (section 5.6).

Two-source theory. It is widely accepted that Matthew and Luke rearranged and edited the Gospel of Mark, together with a second unknown gospel Q. Not only in the narrative parts but also in the direct speeches, they would have made adaptations, according to their own theologies (sections 4.5.1 and 6.1). However, neither Matthew nor Luke edited the Gospel of Mark according to their own theologies.

The flexible canon theory. The canon of the twenty-seven books of the New Testament was not a flexible entity before the church set the standard of the canon by ecclesiastical decisions. It was the early publication of the four Gospels in the apostolic era that set the standard for all the Christian churches. The four Gospels formed the first canon. The process whereby more apostolic books were added to the Gospels in the course of time was in the nature of things (chapter 10).

It is quite remarkable that a common zeal for the truth in theology has led many to study the Gospels more comprehensively. This has resulted in a lot of books over the last centuries that present the methods above with great scholarship. However, the spoken word of Jesus seems to have become the lost sheep in all these methods. And that should not be so in Christian theology, should it? Jesus's sayings are the only tangible relics he left behind on earth. It is time for the Christians to wake up!

All theories above—and there are more—can be countered

effectively by the documentation theory. Jesus's writers followed him to preserve his deeds and teachings, and that is exactly what the New Testament says in the prologue of Luke, the testimony of Hebrews 2:3–4, and the apostolic manifesto of 1 John 1:1–4. The apostles broadcast during their lifetimes, again and again, "what they had seen and heard" about Jesus, the Living Word. It was part of their apostolic calling from the outset.

The single theory of documentation is not meant as an interesting alternative of all sorts of theological theories about the Gospels. Documentation claims direct truth by observation and representation, which is of a much higher standard than an assumed oral tradition can ever give. Of course, the above theories are not without some benefit for those who want to gain knowledge about the Gospels, but the documentation theory is of a different quality. It is the author's conviction that Christians who recognize the value of the documentation theory will be utterly blessed by it.

Part III

Documentation and Exegesis

7. Reading the Gospels Analytically

The documentation theory, thus far developed, is also important for interpretation and exegesis. Now the moment has come to look more specifically at the contents of the Gospels. Luke, as well as the other Gospel writers, worked as the many and copied only authentic records in their books, as we have learned from Luke's prologue. We have seen that the records originated from the events they describe, and therefore it is possible to look at the contents of the Gospels in a new way.

7.1 Rules Concerning the Interpretation of Discourses

The writers of Jesus worked systematically. We already had a foretaste of their work in section 5.6, how they worked with a concept of distribution. In this section, the purpose is to recognize the rules underlying the reporting work of the direct speech portions by reading analytically. Thereafter, we will do the same for the narrative parts.

There are only a few parallel occasions in the Gospels where the same sayings are repeated verbatim. The few we possess, however, are sufficient to permit us to formulate rules by which we may analytically read the direct speech portions. We will present these rules, followed by examples.

Rule 1. Simple (single) introduction. If direct speech is preceded by an introduction with a single speaking verb, the direct speech has been presented completely. For instance: he said, he answered, he cried, etc. After any of these forms, the complete direct speech follows.

Rule 2. Twofold (double) introduction. If direct speech is preceded by an introduction with two speaking verbs, the direct speech has been presented in part. For instance: he answered and said; he answered them, saying.[219] After this type of introduction,

---

[219] A twofold introduction is not a Greek or Semitic literary figure of speech, as has often been supposed. The fact that in many modern translations, only one speaking verb has been translated, instead of the two, shows adequately that a literary effect is lacking. For the writers, who were not acquainted with all sorts of punctuation marks, the use of the simple or twofold introduction was a means to indicate features of their quotations.

not all of what was said has been rendered but only an important part of it. Unfortunately, in most translations of the New Testament, twofold expressions of speaking have been exchanged for simple ones. If necessary for discussion, the missing forms of the Greek will be presented in square brackets [] in the text of the Revised Standard Version. If a word given in the RSV is lacking in the Greek text, it will be indicated with curly brackets {}, if necessary for discussion.

Rule 3. Plural introduction. If an introduction has the subject in plural, several statements were made, but only one of them has been presented in the direct speech. For instance: they answered him, they cried out, saying.

First example, rules 1 and 2

Peter's Confession		
Matthew 16:15–16	**Mark 8:29**	**Luke 9:20**
¹⁵ He <u>said</u> to them, "But who do you say that I am?" ¹⁶ Simon Peter replied [<u>answered and said</u>], "You are the Christ, the Son of the Living God."	²⁹ And he <u>asked</u> them, "But who do you say that I am?" Peter answered [<u>answered and said</u> to] him, "You are the Christ."	²⁰ And he <u>said</u> to them, "But who do you say that I am?" {And} Peter answered [<u>answering said</u>], "The Christ of God."

This example is taken from the well-known story in which Jesus asks his disciples for their opinion of him. When we read the question, we see that in all three cases, it is exactly the same: "But who do you say that I am?" This is easily explainable because of the simple introduction used in all three cases: said (Matthew), asked (Mark), and said (Luke). The question is presented completely three times (rule 1).

The three Gospels present three different replies of Peter. To understand this, it is necessary to apply rule 2. The introductions are twofold: answered and said (Matthew), answered and said (Mark), answering, said (Luke). In other words, Peter's answers have been presented, in part, three times. The meaning of the expression "answered and said" or "answering, said"' is that while he was answering, the presented direct speech was *among* the things he said. The three answers are part of the same reaction. Peter must

have said something such as, "The Christ of God. You are the Christ.
You are the Christ, the Son of the Living God!" This is a figure
of speech, an enumeration with increasing force. The threefold
repetition of Peter's answer is not strange or unusual. It was not
daily custom among the disciples at that time to talk about Jesus
as the Messiah. When Jesus sent them out to preach the kingdom
(Matthew 10), he instructed them to proclaim the kingdom of
heaven, not to proclaim him as the Messiah. Later on, we read
in John's Gospel that it was dangerous for the people to confess
Jesus as the Messiah, because they could be punished by being put
out of the synagogue.[220] That might be the reason Jesus took his
disciples to the district of Caesarea Philippi, as it was forbidden by
the Pharisees to call him Messiah in the Jewish land. In Caesarea
Philippi, they did not transgress a law by that confession. Anyway,
it is understandable that Peter did not give a short and formal
reaction of one single phrase. On the contrary, he expressed a deep-
rooted conviction with the emotions that go with it, and that is the
cause for the repetitions in his answer.

This example shows also that the rules about direct speech are
related to the way the records that constitute the Gospels came into
being. The expression, "You are the Christ, the Son of the Living
God" is suitable for a teaching record. The aspect of being the Son of
God is mentioned in it explicitly. And Matthew, as discussed earlier,
incorporated teaching records in his Gospel. For a public record, the
expression "The Christ of God" is appropriate (Luke). Without a verb
form, this answer gives a direct and vivid touch, which makes public
reading more interesting. The phrase "You are the Christ" was left
for the remnant record used by Mark.

Second example, rules 1 and 2

(See table.) What the man cried out in the synagogue is, in
both cases, recorded verbatim, with one exception. Luke has the
exclamation "Ah," which is lacking in Mark. Luke gives the spoken
word completely and thus uses a simple introduction (rule 1): "He
cried out with a loud voice." As Mark does not give a complete direct
speech, he uses a twofold introduction (rule 2): "He *cried out [saying]*."
It is possible to consider *rebuked* as a speaking verb, as Jesus rebuked

---

[220] John 9:22; 12:42.

135

Healing of a Demoniac	
Mark 1:23–26	**Luke 4:33–35**
[23] And immediately there was in their synagogue a man with an unclean spirit; [24]: and he <u>cried out</u> [saying], "What have you to do with us, Jesus of Nazareth? Have you come to destroy us? I know who you are, the Holy One of God." [25] But Jesus <u>rebuked</u> him, <u>saying</u>, "Be silent, and come out of him!" [26] And the unclean spirit, convulsing him and crying with a loud voice, came out of him.	[33] And in the synagogue there was a man who had the spirit of an unclean demon; and he <u>cried out</u> with a loud voice, [34] "Ah! What have you to do with us, Jesus of Nazareth? Have you come to destroy us? I know who you are, the Holy One of God." [35] But Jesus <u>rebuked</u> him, <u>saying</u>, "Be silent, and come out of him!" And when the demon had thrown him down in the midst, he came out of him, ...

the spirit with his words (i.e., by speaking). In that case, it seems that Jesus actually said a little bit more than "Be silent, and come out of him!"[221]

The third rule has to do with plural introductions. It is not difficult to see that if an introduction has the subject in plural, several statements occurred, but *only one* of them has been presented. The example below shows how Jesus asked his disciples what the public opinion was about him. He asked it several times and in each case several answers came: they said, they told, they answered. Three reactions and all of these reactions are similar in meaning, but there are differences in rendering.

Third example, rules 2 and 3

(See next table.) It is quite natural in life that reactions differ, and it would be strange if they were exactly the same. In matters of biblical exegesis, however, people have often difficulties with these differences, and they get the feeling that the Gospels are not in agreement (in some way contradicting each other).

---

[221] Luke has an important variant, which is most likely original: "Be silent, and come *away from* him!" The twofold introduction gives room for this variant. In this case, Jesus had rebuked the spirit two times.

Who Is the Son of Man?		
Matthew 16:13–14	**Mark 8:27–28**	**Luke 9:18–19**
[13] Now when Jesus came into the district of Caesare'a Philippi, he asked [examined] his disciples [saying], "Who do men say that the Son of man is?" [14] And they said, "Some say John the Baptist, others say Elijah, and others Jeremiah or one of the prophets."	[27] And Jesus went on with his disciples, to the villages of Caesare'a Philippi; and on the way he asked his disciples [saying], "Who do men say that I am?" [28] And they told him [spoke to him saying], "John the Baptist; and others say, Elijah; and others one of the prophets."	[18] Now it happened that as he was praying alone the disciples were with him; and he asked them [saying], "Who do the people say that I am?" [19] And they answered [answering said], "John the Baptist; but others say, Elijah; and others, that one of the old prophets has arisen."

The explanation is often given that the oral tradition caused these differences to creep in to the text. From the documentation point of view, we see—on the contrary—a completely normal situation; many reactions to a topic under debate. That was the way of higher education at that time. A teacher, by putting forth a question, opened a discussion.[222] The purpose was to consider a matter from all angles, and the disciples were supposed to come back with remarks and new questions, as starting points for the master to reveal his knowledge (diatribè style). Mark 8:28 has an important variant with a twofold introduction (spoke to him saying). Luke also has a twofold introduction. This means that in these cases, the answer has been presented in part (rule 2).

Rule 3 also is applicable when someone speaks in the name of a group or reads a message from a document representing all. In Matthew 22:16–17, we read, "And they sent their disciples to him, along with the Herodians, saying, 'Teacher, we know that you are

---

[222] In Mark and Luke is used for asking: eperoota-oo, i. e. asking a specific question with emphasis on the speaking aspect. In Matthew is used eroota-oo: asking, examine, inquire. The context shows whether the emphasis is on asking or on examine, inquire. In the last case it refers to a series of questions. A second speaking verb *only* refers then to one saying of the investigation (single introduction). Compare Luke 23:3. See also Appendix. Highlights of the Passion and Resurrection Story, 2, Table 3, 4.

true, and teach the way of God truthfully, and care for no man; ... Is it lawful to pay taxes to Caesar, or not?'" Certainly this message was spoken by one person as part of a group that was listening. The speaker probably read the message from paper or a wax tablet, as the vernacular suggests (they sent ... saying; that is, they sent ... to say, etc.). In Luke 7:6, we read, "the centurion sent friends to him, saying to him, 'Lord, do not trouble yourself, for I am not worthy to have you come under my roof.'" It is clear from the first person (I am not worthy) that the friends possessed a letter containing the words of the centurion. Of course, only one of the centurion's friends read the message.

So far, we may say that the rules for interpretation of discourses show a refined system for reporting the spoken word. This system, in turn, provides the tools for exegesis to understand the many nuances concerning the spoken word in the Gospels and Acts, nuances that are no changes, due to a so-called oral tradition.

7.2 Rules Concerning the Interpretation of Narratives

A second set of rules deals with the course of events: succession and interruption of events or actions. To discover the rules about the course of events, there is much more material for comparison than for the rules of the spoken language in the discourses. The synoptic Gospels have many narratives, and the use of specific conjunctions at the beginning of a sentence tells a lot about the course of an event.

Rule 4. Succession. In the first place—without any conjunction at the beginning of the sentence (asyndetic connection). In the second place—when a sentence starts with *Immediately* (or *And immediately*). In the Gospel of Mark, this construction is often used. In the third place—a principal sentence starting with *Then*. The Gospel of Matthew very often uses this construction instead of *Immediately*.[223]

---

[223] Matthew has an extreme predilection for *Then* (Greek: *Tote*), while Mark very often uses *Immediately* (Greek: *Euthus*) instead of *Then*. The Septuagint, the Greek translation of the Old Testament (ca. 200 BC), is much more acquainted with *Tote* and seldom has *Euthus*. That may be a possible explanation for Matthew's predilection.

Rule 5. Interruption. There is one significant way to refer to an interruption in the course of events, that is when a sentence or a clause starts with *And/and* (Greek: Kai).[224] The Gospel of John has often the word 'then' in the second or third position in the sentence to create interruption (Greek: 'oun' in the second or third position).[225] Let's give an example to show these rules (4 and 5).

(See table page 140.) The conjunctions and asyndetic connections are underlined, and they tell us a lot about the course of the events. The conjunctions *immediately* and *but* are used by the writers to stress an uninterrupted course of events.

Directly following Jesus's encouragement, Peter asks permission to also come onto the water. Matthew 14:28 begins with *And*, but it is not in the Greek original, as the curly brackets show. So verses 28–31 show an uninterrupted discourse.

Mark uses an interruption before Jesus enters the boat. He makes clear with the word *And* (51) that Peter's walk on the sea is lacking. But Matthew also has *And* here (32), and that is because he does not give a description of the return of Jesus and Peter into the boat.

John uses a typical way of reporting. He starts with Jesus's reassurance to not be afraid. Then interruption follows, as John uses *then* in the second position (21). He creates a contrast between the fear in the beginning and gladness at the end of the event; and in his company they arrived at the precise spot for which they were making.

At last Matthew and Mark say something about the reactions of the disciples. Matthew—that they worshipped. Mark—that they were astounded. Last but not least, John uses the expression *and immediately* (21) to express that the ship set course for the coast as soon as Jesus and Peter were on board.

---

[224] Sometimes the Greek particle *de* in the second position of the sentence has been translated as *and*. In this case, only a sort of contrast with something in the previous sentence is expressed and not interruption; however, although the context more often means succession, interruption cannot always be excluded.

[225] Unfortunately the translation of *then* in second position for *oun* is often lacking.

Walking on Water		
Matthew 14:26–33	**Mark 6:49–51**	**John 6:19–21**
²⁶ <u>But</u> when the disciples saw him walking on the sea, they were terrified, saying, "It is a ghost!" And they cried out for fear. ²⁷ But <u>immediately</u> he spoke to them, saying, "Take heart, it is I; have no fear." ²⁸ {And} <u>Peter</u> answered him, "Lord, if it is you, bid me come to you on the water." ²⁹ <u>He</u> said, "Come." <u>So</u> Peter got out of the boat and walked on the water and came to Jesus; ³⁰ <u>but</u> when he saw the wind, he was afraid, and beginning to sink he cried out, "Lord, save me." ³¹ Jesus <u>immediately</u> reached out his hand and caught him, saying to him, "O man of little faith, why did you doubt?" ³² <u>And</u> when they got into the boat, the wind ceased. ³³ {And} <u>those</u> in the boat worshiped him, saying, "Truly you are the Son of God."	⁴⁹ <u>but</u> when they saw him walking on the sea they thought it was a ghost, and cried out; ⁵⁰ for they all saw him, and were terrified. But immediately he spoke to them and said, "Take heart, it is I; have no fear." ⁵¹ <u>And</u> he got into the boat with them and the wind ceased. <u>And</u> they were utterly astounded,	¹⁹ <u>When</u> they had rowed about three or four miles, they saw Jesus walking on the sea and drawing near to the boat. [<u>And</u>] They were frightened, ²⁰ <u>but he</u> said to them, "It is I; do not be afraid." ²¹ {Then} they <u>then</u> were glad to take him into the boat, <u>and</u> immediately the boat was [came] at the land to which they were going.

7.3 The And-Style of Mark

Mark has many more And-sentences than the other Gospel writers. Mark used remnant records, and it is understandable that the writers of Jesus—after preparing a teaching record and a public record—finished their work with rather uncomplicated records. With And-sentences together with and-clauses, they could sum up a lot of observations, without taking pains to produce eloquent editorial expressions. That is indeed what we see in the remnant records. To give an example of it, we will sum up the twenty-nine *Ands/ands* in the first twenty verses of Mark 11 (KJV—Jesus enters Jerusalem; barren fig tree; expulsion of the dealers from the temple).

[1] And when they came nigh to Jerusalem, [2] and saith unto them, [4] And they went, and found, and they loose him. [5] And certain of them, [6] and they let him, [7] And they brought, and cast, and he sat upon him. [8] And many spread, {and} others cut, and strawed, [9] And they, and they that followed. [11] And Jesus entered, and when he had looked, {and} now the eventide, [12] And on the morrow, [13] And seeing a fig tree, and when he, [14] And Jesus answered, And his disciples heard it. [15] And they came, and Jesus, {and} began, and overthrew, [16] And would not, [17] And he taught [and said], [18] And the scribes, and sought, [19] And when even, [20] And in the morning.

Mark uses the word *And/and* twenty-nine times; Matthew and Luke use it twenty and twelve times, respectively, in the parallel passages.

In the Gospels this and-style is a permanent part of the narratives, especially in Mark. It is not wrong; it only looks a little bit loose. The Gospel writers did not change the records they copied; unmistakably, their respect for them was too great to do that. They refused to change them, as these records were written during Jesus's activity, under his responsibility, and through the inspiration of the Holy Spirit.

Reading the Gospels analytically has important benefits. In matters of exegesis, it always gives relevant answers, where otherwise only a somewhat vague reference can be given to "changes within the oral tradition." There also is a set of tools available for explanation, which makes exegesis less arbitrary. The explanation becomes transparent and verifiable for the common reader. And last but not least, we get the feeling that we are coming nearer to the source, nearer to the events, and nearer to the central person of the Gospels, Jesus Christ. Let's have a look to some well-known examples.

7.4 Cure of the Centurion's Servant

The story of the centurion who wanted his servant to be healed through Jesus has been preserved in two records: a teaching record in the Gospel of Matthew and a public record in the Gospel of Luke. (See table page 143.)

When the writers of Jesus had collected their notes and had to decide how to compose their reports, they made it quite easy for themselves. They divided the information on their wax tablets into roughly two parts.

The first part (number I in the columns) was particularly applicable to a public record. It contains many interesting details necessary for such a report—Jewish leaders with good connections with a Roman officer. They are willing to do something for him and his critically ill servant. Formerly the officer had helped to build their synagogue. The second group sent out by the officer has the message for Jesus to stay outside his house. Obviously the officer is acquainted with Jewish feelings about the house of a Roman as a heathen place, with all sorts of symbols and idols, which is forbidden for a Jew to enter. Also very interesting is the letter that was written by the officer and which was read by the friends, as is clear from the I-style in their words: "I am not worthy," etc. How could a proud Roman centurion speak in that way to a Jew? And we see how astonished Jesus is after hearing the letter. It seems superfluous to make mention of Jesus's healing command (between verses 9 and 10 of Luke 7, such a command is lacking); the public understood instantly that the healing did not fail to occur.

In Luke's report, the Revised Standard Version gives three and-sentences (verses 4, 6, and 10). However, only verse 10 is a real one, as the word *and* (kai) does not occur in verses 4 and 6 of the Greek text. So just before verse 10, there is an interruption in the course of the event. That is the place, then, where we may insert the other

The Centurion of Capernaum	
Matthew 8:5–13	**Luke 7:2–10**
II ⁵ As he entered Caper'na–um, a centurion came forward to him, beseeching him ⁶ and saying, "Lord, my servant is lying paralyzed at home, in terrible distress." ⁷ And he said to him, "I will come and heal him." ⁸ But the centurion answered him [answering him said], "Lord, I am not worthy to have you come under my roof; but only say the word, and my servant will be healed. ⁹ For I am a man under authority, with soldiers under me; and I say to one, 'Go', and he goes, and to another, 'Come,' and he comes, and to my slave, 'Do this,' and he does it." ¹⁰ When Jesus heard him, he marvelled, and said to those who followed him, "Truly, I say to you, not even in Israel have I found such faith. ¹¹ I tell you, many will come from east and west and sit at table with Abraham, Isaac, and Jacob in the kingdom of heaven, ¹² while the sons of the kingdom will be thrown into the outer darkness; there men will weep and gnash their teeth." ¹³ And to the centurion Jesus said, "Go; be it done for you as you have believed." And the servant was healed at that very moment.	I ² Now a centurion had a slave who was dear to him, who was sick and at the point of death. ³ When he heard of Jesus, he sent to him elders of the Jews, asking him to come and heal his slave. ⁴ {And} when they came to Jesus, they besought him earnestly, saying, "He is worthy to have you do this for him, ⁵ for he loves our nation, and he built us our synagogue." ⁶ {And} Jesus went with them. When he was not far from the house, the centurion sent friends to him, saying to him, "Lord, do not trouble yourself, for I am not worthy to have you come under my roof; ⁷ therefore I did not presume to come to you. But say the word, and let my servant be healed. ⁸ For I am a man set under authority, with soldiers under me: and I say to one, 'Go,' and he goes; and to another, 'Come,' and he comes; and to my slave, 'Do this,' and he does it." ⁹ When Jesus heard this he marvelled at him, and turned and said to the multitude that followed him, "I tell you, not even in Israel have I found such faith." III ¹⁰ And when those who had been sent returned to the house, they found the slave well.

143

column, the report of Matthew.

The second part of the entire event lent itself admirably to use in a teaching report. It contained the meeting of Jesus and the officer. Obviously, the centurion had followed the second group with the letter for Jesus to see the outcome. When Jesus praised the faith of the centurion after hearing the letter, he could certainly not remain hidden. Maybe bystanders, recognizing him, shouted that the centurion was present.

Not only was the presence of the centurion important for the teaching record, but some other things also were.

1. Jesus's words about Gentiles who would enter the kingdom from east and west. This was a rather strange idea for Judaism in Jesus's days. The first Christians, who were all Jews, also had problems when Peter baptized the first Romans (Acts 11:1–18).[226]
2. His painful words about people who would weep in the darkness outside the kingdom. It's most important that Jesus spoke about this issue to the inner circle of his disciples and not to the crowd who followed him (Luke 7:10). His clear objective was to motivate the multitude, not by fear but by encouragement. To his close disciples, however, who were supposed to live in the kingdom, he showed the boundaries of the kingdom.
3. The healing command. Again and again we are confronted in the teaching records with Jesus's ultimate power. And the teaching aspect of it is that Jesus is more; he is the Messiah.

Thus far, the exegesis is in complete order—only one and-sentence in the public record (Luke 7:10), and that is exactly the place for the teaching record (Matthew 8:5–13) to be incorporated when we combine the occurrences in Luke and Matthew. The words of the centurion to Jesus (Matthew) are nearly the same as those of the friends (Luke), which were part of a letter written by the centurion a few moments earlier. He just repeated, with slight differences, what he had dictated earlier. So far, so good.

But what would the defender of the oral tradition preceding the

---

[226] May we learn from Acts 11:1–18 that no Gentiles were baptized within Jesus's ministry? This seems to agree with the fact that Jesus's calling was to bring his message only to the lost sheep of Israel.

Gospels say about these two messages? He must try to score in quite a different manner. He would surely put forth the supposition that we don't know whether the centurion actually came to Jesus because the Gospels are not clear about that. He would say that one Gospel says that the centurion met Jesus, but the other says that only elders and friends came up to Jesus, so it remains uncertain whether the officer was there or not. Moreover (the advocate of the oral-tradition would argue), since the differences between the words of the centurion in Matthew and the words of the friends in Luke are small, we must conclude that they are dependent (i.e., within the oral tradition, they had been changed). Otherwise, the two—Matthew and Luke—used the written source Q and made changes according to their own theology. And, the defender of the oral tradition would continue, we don't know who really met Jesus, what was said to Jesus, or what he said. And if we cannot be sure about that, we also cannot be sure whether or not the servant was healed ... or if he was actually ill.

This line of reasoning sounds like a joke, but this sort of argument is not infrequent, and we see that the idea of the oral tradition essentially destroys the power of the Gospels and of Jesus. One then continues as follows: According to the oral tradition, we must take this story as a pious confession of Jesus's power but not as reliable historical writing. The Christians only wanted to express their faith as to how powerful they believed Jesus was but not that he actually did this healing miracle. This jargon is not infrequent among modern exegetes, who base their suppositions on the theory of the oral tradition. Of course, not every advocate of the oral tradition will go this far in explaining the Bible, but on the other hand, we should not close our eyes to the faculty of the oral tradition to totally disintegrate the biblical records. As water flows into every hole, the theory of the oral tradition is able to fill any ignorance in Christian thinking—and that is a lot! For that reason, we have the right to ask of modern theology that it present conclusive evidence in favor of the so-called oral tradition preceding the Gospels. But there is no hard evidence. The oral transmission preceding the Gospels is a collective misunderstanding, and thus each theological result based on it is powerless.[227]

---

[227] There exists a mass of exegetical notions in favor of the so-called oral transmission preceding the Gospels, but conclusive argumentation is

7.5 The Gerasene Demoniacs

A storm on the Sea of Galilee brought Jesus and his disciples to a place they had not planned to arrive. Once ashore, they were confronted with frightful screaming.

Healing of Demoniacs		
Matthew 8:28–30	Mark 5:6–11	Luke 8:28–32
I a 28 <u>And</u> when he came to the other side, to the country of the Gadarenes, two demoniacs met him, coming out of the tombs, so fierce that no one could pass that way. 29 And behold, they cried out [saying], "What have you to do with us, O Son of God? Have you come here to torment us before the time?" 30 Now a herd of many swine was feeding at some distance from them.	I b 6 <u>And</u> when he saw Jesus from afar, he ran and worshiped him; 7 and crying out with a loud voice, he said, "What have you to do with me, Jesus, Son of the Most High God? I adjure you by God, do not torment me." 8 For he had said to him, "Come out of the man, you unclean spirit!" II b 9 <u>And</u> Jesus asked him, "What is your name?" He replied, "My name is Legion; for we are many."	I c 28 <u>When</u> he saw Jesus, he cried out and fell down before him, and said with a loud voice, "What have you to do with me, Jesus, Son of the Most High God? I beseech you, do not torment me." 29 For he had commanded the unclean spirit to come out of the man. (For many a time it had seized him; he was kept under guard, and bound with chains and fetters, but he broke the bonds and was driven by the demon into the desert.) II a 30 <u>Jesus</u> then asked him, "What is your name?" And he said, "Legion"; for many demons had entered him.

something else and is lacking. Libraries have been filled during the last centuries with studies about or based on it. Form criticism and redaction criticism are still respected fields of scientific research into the oral transmission. However, nobody can deny anymore that a wrong translation of Luke 1:1–2 is the only foundation of the theory of the oral tradition.

The unclean spirits want to reign over people, and they don't like intruders in their area of influence who want to thwart their plans. God, however, wants people to be free, to be masters of their own lives, and he likes to help them to be. These ill people were torn apart when Jesus entered their region. There were the strange powers, who wanted them to stand their ground. By a struggle, the liberation came; these men could win only as Jesus interfered and became their helper.

It is an old question as to whether one or two demoniacs were healed. Matthew's description mentions two, while Mark and Luke have only one. It is not difficult to guess what the explanation of the oral tradition is. People started to honor Jesus's power more and more, and the result of it in the oral transmission was, of course, exaggeration. After a period of time, the one demoniac had grown to two demoniacs, which doubled Jesus's power. However, from our point of view, we have to deal with *speaker reduction*. That means that the only person mentioned is one whose words are reported and who clearly speaks for himself, which is to be seen in the singular form (instead of the plural). How many people may accompany him does not matter; only he is in the picture (e.g., Mark 5:7—"What have you to do with me?"). One of the demoniacs ran to Jesus and reached him before the other one. From that moment on, he is speaking for himself, while at the beginning of the story, two demoniacs came out of the tombs while they were screaming together, "What have you to do with us?" (Matthew 8:29). There are many more examples of this phenomenon in the Gospels, and it is clear that exaggeration can be ruled out in all these cases, according to the documentation theory.

It is striking that the teaching reports of Matthew often show the same structure. They start with a short description of the beginning of the event, followed rather quickly by Jesus's word of power that changes the whole situation. What happened in between seems to be less relevant. It was certainly the primary teaching aspect of Matthew's records to show Jesus's Messiahship and his majesty by relating his power above all other powers. We recognize the same method of reporting in the story of the cure of the centurion's servant, as we have discussed, and in the resurrection of Jairus's daughter (see further).

One of them ran in front the other one and arrived at Jesus

first. He fell on the ground, and we have two of his sayings. The introductions are twofold in Mark (crying out, he said), as well as in Luke (cried out, and said). Which of them was first is not clear, but it does not seem to be important to answer this question.

Then Jesus asked the name of the man. He asked it twice; the first time as reported in Luke, the second one as in Mark (and-sentence of Mark—And Jesus asked him). After Jesus's first question (Luke: What is your name?) an and-sentence followed. The man did not immediately want to answer "Legion." Jesus was probably surprised, as he asked him a second time (Mark), "What is your name?" The Greek, in the second question, has a different word order, which may show surprise: "What is the name of you?" or "What name do you have?" Now the man also gave an explanation of the name "for we are many."

Matthew 8:31–32	Mark 5:12–13	Luke 8:32–33
IV b [31] {And} the demons begged him [saying], "If you cast us out, send us away into the herd of swine." [32] And he said to them, "Go." So they came out and went into the swine; and behold, the whole herd rushed down the steep bank into the sea, and perished in the waters.	III b [10] And he begged him eagerly not to send them out of the country. [11] Now a great herd of swine was feeding there on the hillside; IV a [12] and they begged him, "Send us to the swine, let us enter them." [13] [And] So he gave them leave. And the unclean spirits came out, and entered the swine; and the herd, numbering about two thousand, rushed down the steep bank into the sea, and were drowned in the sea.	III a [31] And they begged him not to command them to depart into the abyss. [32] Now a large herd of swine was feeding there on the hillside; IV [32] ... and they begged him to let them enter these. So he gave them leave. [33] Then the demons came out of the man and entered the swine, and the herd rushed down the steep bank into the lake and were drowned.

After the question of the name, the evil spirits began to negotiate with Jesus. At first they proposed not to be sent into the abyss (III a). In the place of evil spirits, it is not pleasant for spirits at all, it seems. Then via the possessed man, they asked to send them out in the country (III b). They forgot that Jesus did not come to hurt people, as they do. As soon as they understood how wrong their question was, they asked him to send them into the swine (IV a, b). The demons were anxious and forced the man to speak for them. Then the Lord permitted them to enter into the swine. Strangely enough, it looks very much like Jesus communicated with the evil spirits and that he accepted their request to enter into the swine. Jesus communicated with the man and consequently ordered the evil spirits who spoke through the man, who was their messenger (rule 3).

After the healing of the two demoniacs and the dying of the swine, the drama became complete. The evil spirits submitted to Jesus, but the people did not. The local population forbade Jesus to enter the region. Jesus drove off the spirits; the people drove off Jesus, and he obeyed them. And that was it? No, Mark and Luke go on to tell that the man who had spoken for the spirits started to speak for God all over the country and tell what God had done for him in his grace. The apostle Paul sayd, "But the word of God is not fettered."[228] Fortunately, this is still the case.

7.6 Jairus's Daughter Raised to Life

The well-known story of Jairus, who came to Jesus for the healing of his daughter, is told in the three synoptic Gospels. Jairus was the ruler of the synagogue of Capernaum. He had probably seen how Jesus had healed a possessed man in his synagogue on a Sabbath much earlier.[229] Jesus had forced the screaming man to be silent, and the evil spirit had left the man. Even if Jairus had not attended that synagogical service, he certainly would have been informed in full about this occurrence. Never had anything like that happened in his synagogue. And of course he must have heard that Jesus healed many people on that same Sabbath after sunset. It seems reasonable that he

---

[228] 2 Timothy 2:9.
[229] Mark 1:23–25; Luke 4:33–35.

also was acquainted with the cure of the centurion's slave, who had helped to build his synagogue.

However, Jairus also knew about the mixed reactions to Jesus's deeds. Division of opinion had resulted from Jesus's appearance in Capernaum. Before he cured a lame man, Jesus had forgiven his sins, to the great scandal of the party of the Pharisees.[230] And of course, as a ruler of the synagogue, Jairus surely had noticed that a delegation from Jerusalem had come to the city to inquire as to Jesus's teachings, and it had resulted in a negative judgment.[231] Jairus knew the ins and outs of all these things. But none of that could change Jairus's positive first experience with Jesus, which was put into words by the people in the synagogue: "What is this? A new teaching! With authority he commands even the unclean spirits, and they obey him!"

Maybe because of the bad publicity around Jesus, Jairus did not have the courage to go to Jesus for healing earlier. But when he saw the death mask[232] on the face of his child, he understood that her illness was serious. His child was about to die. At that moment he knew that there was no time to lose. His feelings for his child were stronger than his fear of the disapproval of his fellow citizens. He arose and went to Jesus.

Most translations say that according to Matthew, the girl already had died when Jairus met Jesus. The same versions in Mark and Luke say that the girl was not already dead at that point. That is quite strange. It's easy, however, when we realize that we are reading the report of that very moment.

Jairus's first words are found in Matthew because he knelt at that moment (9:18). The Greek here has a so-called aorist form, which only gives the action of the verb (to die) without saying anything about the result of it. And so this implies that only the beginning of the action is meant, and that should be the translation here. When we translate *she died*, we can think only of the result: She is dead. But in Greek, it is also a reasonable possibility to translate it as "she is dying" (ingressivus).

---

[230] Mark 2:1–12.

[231] Mark 3:22.

[232] The death mask is a deathly expression on the face of someone who is terminally ill. The message of it is that the end is about to come.

The Request of Jairus		
Matthew 9:18–19	**Mark 5:22–24**	**Luke 8:41–42**
[18] While he was thus speaking to them, behold, a ruler came in and knelt before him, saying, "My daughter has just died; but come and lay your hand on her, and she will live." [19] And Jesus rose and followed him, with his disciples.	[22] [And] Then came one of the rulers of the synagogue, Jairus by name; and seeing him, he fell at his feet, [23] and besought him, saying, "My little daughter is at the point of death. Come and lay your hands on her, so that she may be made well, and live." [24] And he went with him. And a great crowd followed him and thronged about him.	[41] And there came a man named Jairus, who was a ruler of the synagogue; and falling at Jesus' feet he besought him to come to his house, [42] for he had an only daughter, about twelve years of age, and she was dying. As he went, the people pressed round him.

Jairus speaks about the last picture he saw, the death mask on his daughter's face. After Jairus's request, Matthew has an and-sentence, which means that something more happened before Jesus rose and followed Jairus. Indeed, more was said, and some of it has been preserved in Mark, but not all (5:23, twofold introduction: "and besought him, saying"). Luke makes the picture complete, mentioning that Jairus also told Jesus that the girl was about twelve years old (8:42).

After Jairus's request, as described in Matthew, Mark, and Luke, Jesus followed Jairus to his house. However, a fateful message reached them.

At least two messengers came up to Jairus to tell him that his daughter had died, as we may learn from Mark 5:35 (some who said). Luke uses speaker reduction, as he has "a man … came and said." Maybe both spoke to Jairus, as we have two differing sayings: (Mark) "Why trouble the Teacher any further?" and "Do not trouble the Teacher anymore." Jesus's answers also differ a little. The explanation is that Jesus reacted to each saying of the messengers, one after the other. Jesus encouraged Jairus to keep faith, and, as in a dream, he went to his house.

Do Not Fear, Only Believe	
Mark 5:35–36	**Luke 8:49–50**
[35] <u>While</u> he was still speaking, there came from the ruler's house some who said, "Your daughter is dead. Why trouble the Teacher any further?" [36] But ignoring what they said, Jesus said to the ruler of the synagogue, "Do not fear, only believe."	[49] <u>While</u> he was still speaking, a man from the ruler's house came and said, "Your daughter is dead; do not trouble the Teacher anymore." [50] But Jesus on hearing this answered him, "Do not fear; only believe, and she shall be well."

When Jairus and Jesus arrived at the house, the weepers had to be driven away. Their reaction of laughing and unbelief was not completely wrong, as they had not had the experiences of Jairus,

Resurrection of Jairus's Daughter		
Matthew 9:25–26	**Mark 5:39–42**	**Luke 8:52–55**
[25] <u>But</u> when the crowd had been put outside, he went in and took her by the hand, and the girl arose. [26] And the report of this went through all that district.	[39] And when he had entered, he said to them, "Why do you make a tumult and weep? The child is not dead but sleeping." [40] And they laughed at him. But he put them all outside, and took the child's father and mother and those who were with him, and went in where the child was. [41] [And] Taking her by the hand he said to her, "Talitha cumi"; which means, "Little girl, I say to you, arise." [42] And immediately the girl got up and walked (she was twelve years of age), ...	[52] {And} all were weeping and bewailing her; but he said, "Do not weep; for she is not dead but sleeping." [53] And they laughed at him, knowing that she was dead. [54] But taking her by the hand he called, saying, "Child, arise." [55] And her spirit returned, and she got up at once; ...

who had been brought into his position of faith, step by step, by Jesus's words: "Do not fear, only believe!" At any rate, the disparaging reaction of the weepers made clear later on that there could not be any mistake that the girl had passed away.

Their reaction may also serve as an illustration for Jesus's instruction to the elders after the resurrection of the child to not speak to others about the event. They certainly would have met unbelief, and it seems that Jesus wanted to protect the elders from it. When Jesus, who had performed so many miracles, was treated with total lack of comprehension by the weepers, how much more lack of understanding would they have met as ordinary people? Jesus gave his resurrection command two times: in Mark, by speaking with authority (in Hebrew) the words "Talitha cum(i)," and in Luke, by calling, "Child arise" (in Greek). In the latter case, something more was said (rule 2). The sequence of these sayings is not clear.

The only purpose of Matthew's record was to teach of Jesus as the Messiah: "He went in and took her by the hand, and the girl arose." Can it be any more concise? The use of an and-sentence leaves enough room for the spoken words of Jesus, as in Mark and Luke.

Mark has a more extensive record than Luke, and it has the typical Marcan style. Mark and Luke give the same information, but Mark has eleven and-sentences versus Luke's five. Mark has repetitions throughout the entire story (in contrast with Luke): ruler of the synagogue, tumult, James. Mark has expressions with added emphasis: besought him (Greek, urgently), great crowd, wailing loudly, strictly charged. These features suggest that we are confronted in Mark with the first impressions of the writers. The public record of Luke is shorter, but it doesn't leave out relevant information in accordance with Mark. The public record was not permitted to bring out, because of Jesus's word "that no one should know this." Of course, everyone spoke about the occurrence, as Matthew remarked (v. 26), but nobody came to know exactly what had happened inside the house (Mark 5:43, Luke 8:56).

7.7 James's and John's Request

While Jesus prepared himself for his Passion in Jerusalem, he was confronted with the career ambitions of his disciples. And career is also important for the family. So when James and John came to speak with Jesus about their personal future desires, their mother was there to take care that everything went as desired. The question was, who would sit at the immediate right and the immediate left of Jesus in his kingdom?

In Mark's record, the attendance of the mother is not mentioned, as she has no speaking role (speaker reduction), while in Matthew, the mother is dominantly attendant. The brothers start posing the question, and later on, their mother repeats it. We can conclude this from the prudent opening by the two brothers: "Teacher, we want you to do for us whatever we ask of you" (Mark 10:35). This is very much in contrast with the opening of the mother: "Command that ..." (Matthew 20:21).

The Best Places	
Matthew 20:20–22	**Mark 10:35–38**
I	II
[20] Then the mother of the sons of Zeb'edee came up to him, with her sons, ...	[35] And James and John, the sons of Zeb'edee, came forward to him, and said to him, "Teacher, we want you to do for us whatever we ask of you."
III	[36] {And} he said to them, "What do you want me to do for you?"
... and kneeling before him she asked him for something. [21] {And} he said to her, "What do you want?" She said to him, "Command that these two sons of mine may sit, one at your right hand and one at your left, in your kingdom." [22] But Jesus answered [answering said], "You do not know what you are asking. Are you able to drink the cup that I am to drink?" They said to him, "We are able."	[37] {And} they said to him, "Grant us to sit, one at your right hand and one at your left, in your glory." [38] But Jesus said to them, "You do not know what you are asking. Are you able to drink the cup that I drink, or to be baptized with the baptism with which I am baptized?"

Mark has several sentences starting with *and* in the Revised Standard Version, but in the Greek, there is only one real and-sentence (v. 35), "And when the ten heard it, they began to be indignant at James and John." In the interval of "And" their mother intervened (Matthew's report), "And kneeling before him she asked him for something." Her behavior is remarkable. She had already heard the reply to her sons, and now she was trying to force Jesus in her own direction. She had seen regularly how people in great despair came to the Lord and knelt before him. Kneeling was an expression of faith and obedience, not a tool for pressure. God is not interested in knees but in hearts. And he is certainly willing to react mercifully and abundantly but in his sovereignty.

Later the other disciples blamed James and John for their selfishness, and implicitly they also blamed their mother. The attitude of the other disciples shows enough that they also had aspirations to the high places in the kingdom. Strangely enough, Jesus was without reproach; he did not blame the two, the mother, or the others. Obviously, he is not against people who think about their future. On the other hand, he took the opportunity to teach them a principle of the kingdom: He who wants to climb has to descend.[233]

The writers of Jesus who had to distribute the materials to various reports, followed nearly the same method as in the reporting of the cure of the centurion's servant. After collecting their material, they made a sober division into two parts. First they prepared a teaching record, and for that they chose Jesus's final answer to the mother for the outcome. It is not without reason that no public record is available in Luke's Gospel. The subject was certainly not an issue for the public but for the inner circle of the twelve. Therefore, only a teaching record (Matthew) and a remnant record (Mark) have been delivered.

7.8 Eschatological Discourses

During Jesus's last visit to Jerusalem, he taught his disciples about the future to come. He had in mind his own departure from this world, of which they were unaware. In fact, we possess three discourses of

---

[233] Matthew 20:27; Mark 10:44.

Jesus about eschatological matters. The supposition (oral tradition) that we are dealing with three versions of one single discourse does not contribute to our knowledge of the subject. Also, the suggestion that the three discourses would be compilations of scattered sayings of Jesus on the subject only obscures their clear messages. We will see that much clarity can be brought to eschatological doctrines by reading these discourses analytically, and in the following, an impetus for it is given.

Announced Fall of the Temple		
Matthew 24:1–3	Mark 13:1–4	Luke 21:5–7
III ¹ [And] Jesus left the temple and was going away, when his disciples came to point out to him the buildings of the temple. ² But he answered [answering said to] them, "You see all these, do you not? Truly, I say to you, there will not be left here one stone upon another, that will not be thrown down." ³ As he sat on the Mount of Olives, the disciples came to him privately, saying, "Tell us, when will this be, and what will be the sign of your coming and of the close of the age?"	II ¹ And as he came out of the temple, one of his disciples said to him, "Look, Teacher, what wonderful stones and what wonderful buildings!" ² And Jesus said to him, "Do you see these great buildings? There will not be left here one stone upon another, that will not be thrown down." ³ And as he sat on the Mount of Olives opposite the temple, Peter and James and John and Andrew asked him privately, ⁴ "Tell us, when will this be, and what will be the sign when these things are all to be accomplished?"	I ⁵ And as some spoke of the temple, how it was adorned with noble stones and offerings, he said, ⁶ "As for these things which you see, the days will come when there shall not be left here one stone upon another that will not be thrown down." ⁷ {And} they asked [asking said to] him, "Teacher, when will this be, and what will be the sign when this is about to take place?"

Luke reported the first of the three discourses. Jesus and his disciples were in the temple, and previous to this teaching, they had discussed the value of the gifts that people put into the treasury, in particular the high value, according to Jesus, of two copper coins of a poor widow (21:1–4). It is quite logical that the disciples looked at the rich ornaments of the temple in a different way from that moment on, and Jesus himself started a new discussion when he heard them speaking about it. "As for these things which you see, the days will come when there shall not be left here one stone upon another." At the end of Luke's discourse, he remarks that Jesus was teaching in the temple every day and that the people came to him in the temple to hear him (21:37–38). So we certainly have a public report in the Gospel of Luke about the issue of the end of the world.

Many supposed that the temple would stand for ages, until the end of the world.[234] From this concept of history, his disciples asked him about the end of the world (Luke 21:6). "Teacher, when will this be, and what will be the sign?" So Jesus started his oration, as given by Luke, with an overview of history up until the end of the world (vv. 8–19); then he turned back to the issue of the destruction of the temple, which would come much earlier than the end of the world. With this tragic occurrence, he connects an overview of the history of the Jewish people from that moment on until the end (vv. 20–24). "And Jerusalem will be trodden down by the Gentiles, until the times of the Gentiles are fulfilled" (Luke 21:24). With this point of view, he thwarted all the expectations of his listeners about the future. Certainly, many hearers were flabbergasted, and no doubt his disciples would ask him more about this when they were alone with him without the crowd (see Matthew and Mark). Finally, he combines the two lines of history (end of the temple; end of the world) with a description of the circumstances connected with his great return (vv. 25–28), and the discourse is closed with a few parables and warnings (vv. 29–36). "But watch at all times, praying that you may have strength to escape all these things that will take place, and to stand before the Son of man" (Luke 21:36).

---

[234] As many Jews believed that the temple would stand until the end of the world, Jesus could say without protest among his hearers, "For truly, I say to you, till heaven and earth pass away, not an iota, not a dot, will pass from the law until all is accomplished" (Matthew 5:18). Everyone believed that the holy scrolls of Israel would remain safe in the temple until the very end of human history. However, Jesus meant something else (see also section 10.7.2).

After Luke's eschatological discourse of Jesus, he left the temple. On the way to the Mount of Olives, his disciples wanted to return to the subject, and one of them said (see Mark), "Look, Teacher, what wonderful stones and what wonderful buildings!" He did not refer to the ornaments, as one of them had in the temple, with the result being a shocking oration. No, as a pious Jew, nobody might blame his drawing Jesus's attention to the imposing building of the temple, the house of the Lord (Mark 13:1). Jesus's answer to him, however, was like the previous one in the temple: "There will not be left here one stone upon another." In Matthew we see that others also started pointing to the temple, and Jesus had to repeat his answer to them (Matthew 24:2). Matthew has a twofold introduction, which means that Jesus's reply has been presented in part. Again, the disciples don't understand or don't dare to ask further.

Having crossed the River Kedron, the four close disciples, Peter, James, John, and Andrew, dared to ask again (Mark 13:3–4): "When will this be, and what will be the sign when these things are all to be accomplished?" At this point, Jesus gives them his teaching in private. This oration of Mark has the same structure as that of Luke, and it is of the same length—first, an overview of the future of those who follow Jesus, the Christians (vv. 5–13); then he goes again to the future destruction of Jerusalem and the temple by the Romans, followed by the history of tribulation of the Jewish people. Now Jesus warns his four intimate disciples, and he gives them strict guidelines on how to conduct themselves at that time of destruction (vv. 14–23). He even speaks through the writers, James and John, to his future followers, who will read this oration with these words: *let the reader understand.* "But when you see the desolating sacrilege set up where it ought not to be—*let the reader understand*—then let those who are in Judea flee to the mountains" (Mark 13:14). And finally, the third part of this oration deals with the return of Jesus (13:24–27), connected with parables and warnings, just like those found in Luke.

By the time Jesus had ended this discourse to his closest disciples, the others had arrived, and they also decided to ask the question of the when and what the sign would be. For the third time, Jesus taught the same things but to the twelve, as they were all present now. Also, in Matthew, Jesus spoke directly to his future readers: "Let the reader understand!"[235] This oration is much longer than those of Mark and Luke, as many parables and examples are connected at the end in chapter 25—the wise and the foolish virgins, the parable of the talents, and the last judgment.

It is obvious that the writers took the longest discourse for the teaching record that was used by Matthew in his Gospel. We have already seen that the writers used the discourse to the crowd in the temple for the public record (Luke). So the remnant record that was left was the oration to the intimate disciples, Peter, James, John, and Andrew.

7.9 Conclusions

When we look back to the method of analytical reading (a. r.), we may conclude that the benefits of this method are relevant enough:

1. With the use of the saying-introductions, it is possible to study carefully the course of the spoken word, as presented in the Gospels.
2. Conjunctions at the beginning of a sentence often give signals that help define the course of events.
3. Comparison of identical Gospel stories makes it possible to give all sayings a proper place in their context.
4. Details in the narrative parts, as well as in the spoken word portions, are never accidents of the oral tradition but specific observations of the original writers.
5. Analytical reading (a. r.) certainly does increase the transparency (understanding) of the texts and the dynamics of the contents and, by that, the impact of the Gospels.

---

[235] In our concept of accurate reporting of somebody's words, it is not acceptable to suppose that at a later stage a Gospel writer incorporated his own ideas and words into the spoken word he presented. For example, Matthew 24:15—"Let the reader understand!"—is part of Jesus's own words. (See also Mark 13:14.) Only in the narrative parts do we sometimes find a remark from the Gospel writer that he makes clear is his work; for example, "who became a traitor" (Luke 6:16). Of course, this remark was not part of the record Luke copied. Other reader indications are Mark 7:2 (that is unwashed); Mark 7:3–4 (For the Pharisees ... of bronze); Matthew 27:46 (that is "My God, my God, why hast thou forsaken me?"), etc.

8. Documentation Exegesis

In this chapter, we will present a new way of explaining the Gospels, based on the documentation theory and the analytical principles, as presented in chapter 7. We have seen that it is often necessary in analytical reading to compare Gospel texts. In the given examples, it was always clear that the compared passages related to the same event. The two messages of the healing of the centurion's servant certainly described the same event. This is also true of the three stories of the resurrection of Jairus's daughter. However, in some cases, it is not so easy to establish the fact that similar stories relate to the same event.

8.1 Orderly! But What Order?

Many stories in the Gospels are similar with regard to contents, style, and language but may be shown as related to different events for several reasons, especially the aspect of time.

Early in the beginning of Jesus's ministry, we read about his cleansing of the temple.[236] Much later, shortly before his Passion, he again cleansed the market of the temple.[237] Many commentators take it as a starting point for their explanation that the same event is at issue and that the evangelists just put their descriptions of it at different places in their books. According to them, John put it in the beginning of his book to instantly show Jesus's attitude toward the temple and the priesthood. The other evangelists, putting this episode before the Passion of Jesus, would underline the growing conflict between Jesus and the priests, according to these exegetes. Nevertheless, many scholars hold that not one but several similar events were described in these cases. That would mean that Jesus cleansed the temple market more than once. The position of these stories in the Gospels and the meaning of this placement will be discussed in this chapter. Moving forward, we will see the relevance of this subject to our goal: documentation exegesis.

Four times we are confronted in the Gospels with the accusation that Jesus was able to cast out demons through Be'elzebul, the prince of

---

[236] John 2:14–22.
[237] Matthew 21:12–13, Luke 19:45–46, and Mark 11:15–17.

demons. Three times Jesus parried the accusation with the remark that a kingdom or house divided against itself cannot stand. Matthew puts it shortly after the Mission of the Twelve, while Mark has it much earlier, before the mission. Luke has it much later than Matthew, where Jesus is then on his last journey to Jerusalem.[238] Again, many suppose that only one event lies at the root of the descriptions and that the oral tradition caused the different placements in the Gospels. However, the differences in the spoken word drive us to the conclusion that Jesus had to defend himself against this accusation many times. The same discussion is possible regarding the parable of the sower. We possess three versions of this parable with Jesus's explanation. In Matthew, it is after the storm on the sea, and in Luke and Mark it is before the storm. Did the oral tradition cause these different positions in the Gospels, or did Jesus tell this parable several times? Indeed, with regard to the analysis rules, we have to decide that Jesus told this parable at least three times.[239]

In Bible exegesis that has oral tradition as a starting point, it is standard procedure to take a single event as the basis for similar stories and assume that the evangelists gave the stories a placement that they liked (or that would be in accordance with their theology). This working method seems to be generally accepted in theology, but there are two weighty objections against it. First, there are often details in similar stories that are not in accord with one another. That would mean that these details contradict each other frequently, and therefore many theologians take that as an argument that the Gospels are liable to have errors. Second, the gospels create the impression of presenting a continuous story of what happened; that is, that the temporal sequence of the events was the same as the order in which they are described. It is rather brutish to brush aside this general impression unblushingly with the remark that the evangelists arranged their materials according subject or theme. This argument has such a scholarly sound that it appears it must be true, without any verification. However, the lack of any sound basis defines this opinion as no more than a pretentious supposition.

Employing the rules of analytical reading (a. r.), it is possible, in most cases, to establish whether stories are derived from one and the same event or from different events. With the rules for

---

[238] Matthew 12:22–30, Mark 3:22–27, and Luke 11:14–23.

[239] Matthew 13:1–9, Mark 4:1–9, and Luke 8:4–8.

analytical reading, it is always possible to examine accurately the direct speeches and the course of an event. Details in a description are, in fact, the observations of the speedy writers and stenographers, which are decisive for the uniqueness of an occurrence. It is realistic to accept a lot of similar events in Jesus's ministry. According to the documentation theory, there are many sound and practical explanations for this phenomenon.

According to the Revised Standard Version of the Bible, Luke says in his prologue that he wrote "an orderly account" (Luke 1:3). The Greek word for orderly is *kat'hexès*, with the standard meaning being "in sequence, in order."[240] Older versions, such as the King James Version and the American Standard Version, translate it as "to write unto thee in order." Most modern translations have "to write an orderly account for you" (RSV, AMP, ESV, NIV). Neither in the older versions nor in the modern ones is it clear what is meant by *order* or *orderly*. Does it mean an arrangement according sequence or an arrangement according to theme or subject? The vague translation of *kat'hexès* (sequence) as "orderly" is the result of the general theological feeling that a real sequence of occurrences is demonstrably missing in the Gospels. Yet Luke uses the term, which means "to write unto you in sequence." The term *kat'hexès* is certainly not capable of misinterpretation.

Luke says in his prologue that he followed the many in writing his Gospel. That means again that he followed the sequence of the occurrences, as the many worked in that manner. They added new stories to former ones, and in that way they compiled their narratives. Of course sometimes they may have missed a story, but with an and– sentence they were able to continue their narratives. Luke wrote his Gospel in the same way, and so did the other evangelists. In the Gospels, we are dealing with the temporal sequence of events, unless, of course, a different approach is mentioned explicitly.

---

[240] Already in the oldest Greek texts of Homeros, *hexès* means: in a row. In the time of the New Testament, this meaning still remained. *Kat'hexès* is: der Reihe nach, eins nach dem anderen, nacheinander, in richtiger Reihenfolge (Walter Bauer, *Wörterbuch zum Neuen Testament*). Or: one after another, successively, in order (Thayer, *A Greek-English Lexicon of the New Testament*). In modern Greek, the terms *kai houtoo kat'hexès* means: et cetera, and so on. Also in modern Greek, the expression *hoos hexès* means: as follows.

8.2 The Blind Men of Jericho

All three of the synoptic Gospels have a narrative telling us that Jesus cured a blind man—or two blind men—in the neighborhood of Jericho when he passed through the city on his journey to Jerusalem. It is an interesting example of the question of how many events were involved. Was it one, or were there two or even three occurrences? And did it happen before Jesus entered Jericho or when he left the city?

What Do You Want Me to Do?		
Matthew 20:29–34	**Mark 10:46–52**	**Luke 18:35–43**
[29] And as they went out of Jericho, a great crowd followed him. [30] And behold, two blind men sitting by the roadside, when they heard that Jesus was passing by, cried out [saying], "Have mercy on us, Son of David!" [31] The crowd rebuked them, telling them to be silent; but they cried out the more [saying], "Lord, have mercy on us, Son of David!" [32] And Jesus stopped and called them, saying, "What do you want me to do for you?" [33] They said to him, "Lord, let our eyes be opened." [34] {And} Jesus in pity touched their eyes, and immediately they received their sight and followed him.	[46] And they came to Jericho; and as he was leaving Jericho with his disciples and a great multitude, Bartimaeus, a blind beggar, the son of Timaeus, was sitting by the roadside. [47] And when he heard that it was Jesus of Nazareth, he began to cry out and say, "Jesus, Son of David, have mercy on me!" [48] And many rebuked him, telling him to be silent; but he cried out all the more, "Son of David, have mercy on me!" [49] And Jesus stopped and said, "Call him." And they called the blind man, saying to him, "Take heart; rise, he is calling you." [50] {And} throwing off his mantle he sprang up and came to Jesus.	[35] As he drew near to Jericho, a blind man was sitting by the roadside begging; [36] {and} hearing a multitude going by, he inquired what this meant. [37] They told him, "Jesus of Nazareth is passing by." [38] And he cried [saying], "Jesus, Son of David, have mercy on me!" [39] And those who were in front rebuked him, telling him to be silent; but he cried out all the more, "Son of David, have mercy on me!" [40] [And] Jesus stopped, and commanded him to be brought to him; {and} when he came near, he asked him,

	[51] And Jesus [answering] said to him, "What do you want me to do for you?" {And} the blind man said to him, "Master, let me receive my sight." [52] And Jesus said to him, "Go your way; your faith has made you well." And immediately he received his sight and followed him on the way.	[41] "What do you want me to do for you?" He said, "Lord, let me receive my sight." [42] And Jesus said to him, "Receive your sight; your faith has made you well." [43] And immediately he received his sight and followed him, glorifying God; and all the people, when they saw it, gave praise to God.

The similarities are so numerous that most exegetes suppose that it was one event. In all three records, the following words are used:

- Jericho
- blind
- sitting by the roadside
- crowd/multitude
- heard/hearing
- cried
- have mercy
- Son of David
- rebuked him/them
- to be silent
- cried out (all) the more
- Son of David (repeated)
- have mercy (repeated)
- Jesus stopped
- What do you want me to do for you?
- Immediately
- received (their) his sight

There are also similarities in wording between two records in Mark and Luke (e.g., "Your faith has made you well").

There are so many similarities and in the same sequence that coincidence must be excluded. Exegetes generally conclude that we have three descriptions of one event. There are a few dissimilarities—Matthew has two blind men, and the place of action is after Jesus's visit in Jericho. Mark and Luke have one blind man; in Mark it's after Jericho, and in Luke before the city. In spite of the dissimilarities in these stories, orthodox theologians have always felt that the overwhelming majority of similarities witness in favor of one and the same event.[241] In their commentaries, none of them explains why just one event is at issue. It either seems evident, or it is a common prejudice that nobody knows the exact origin, nor do they take great pains to show the reasonableness of this point of view. Even among orthodox Bible teachers, this unsupported reductionism in Gospel exegesis always crops up where stories about similar events are under discussion—miracles, healings, teachings, meetings, and so on.

This misconception is so deeply rooted that the superscription above the Luke passage not infrequently is "Cure of Bartimaeus." That, of course, does not fit with the information of Mark—that Bartimaeus was healed after Jericho and certainly was not the same man mentioned in Luke, who received healing one day earlier, when Jesus entered the city.

Not only in orthodox but also in liberal Gospel exegesis, this reductionism of similar stories with details that are not in line with each other is standard procedure. In liberal exegesis, one has a clear-cut answer to the question of why. The answer is the oral tradition. By that process, many changes would have entered into the text, and details that are not harmonious seem to prove this point of view.

In the older orthodox exegesis,[242] exegetes tried to bring

---

[241] Matthew Henry (1710) one event—Mark and Luke are focusing on one of the two blind men. Adam Clarke (1824) idem. Theodor Zahn (1922) one event in front of Jericho. Adolf Schlatter (1947) one event—he says nothing about the place of action. S. Greijdanus (1955) one event. W. H. Gispen (1963) one event. F. Rienecker (1966) two events, each with one blind man. The problem is now that Matthew has two blind men who were together. I. H. Marshall (1978) Mark and Luke one event. G. L. Archer (1982) one healing. R. T. France (1994) one healing.

[242] Reductionism is a real shortcoming in orthodox theology. For example, Abraham Kuyper, *Encyclopedia of sacred Theology its Principles* (New York: Charles Scribner's Sons, 1898), 550 "When in the four Gospels Jesus, on the same occasion, is made to say words that are different in form and

these details into accord with one another. For instance the Dutch theologian S. Greijdanus supposed that there was an old Jericho and a new part of the city, also named Jericho, so that it was possible to speak of a place in between as "before Jericho," which could also be indicated as "after Jericho." And so he could maintain that only one place was involved.[243] G. L. Archer supposed that the blind man started to cry for mercy when Jesus entered Jericho and that Jesus did not listen immediately but that he cured the man when he left the city one day later.[244] Nowadays many orthodox theologians have abandoned these positions, as they seem too artificial to be true, with the result being contradicting details of which nobody speaks openly, as if it's taboo. In their commentaries, they often stress the similarities and remain silent about the dissimilarities. Unfortunately, an attitude of exegetical silence has never solved anything. The more they stress the similarities, the more the irreconcilable details come to the fore. And in doing so, they not infrequently seem to agree with liberal colleagues who hold that many adaptations entered into the Gospels in the course of the oral tradition. As a consequence, liberal and many orthodox theologians hold that the oral tradition and the Gospel writers were responsible for changes in Jesus's sayings and those of his interlocutors in the four Gospels.[245] Liberal theologians

---

expression, it is impossible that He should have used these four forms at once. The Holy Spirit, however, merely intends to make an impression on the Church which wholly corresponds to what Jesus said." (Transl. J. H. De Vries.) Kuyper came to this belief by the idea of "Graphical Inspiration", which he derived from 2 Timothy 3:16. All scripture is theopneust: God inspired. The written part of the Scriptures is inspired, just as the spoken words of the prophets are. In the documentation theory this truth cannot be missed, but there is no place for reductionism. Others held Kuyper's point of view. N. B. Stonehouse, *Origins of the Synoptic Gospels* (London: Tyndale Press, 1964) 110 mentions J. Murray, A. A. Hodge, B. B. Warfield, H. Bavinck and L. Berkhof.

[243] S. Greijdanus, *Het Evangelie naar Lucas II.* (Kampen: Kok, 1955), 132.

[244] G. L. Archer, *Encyclopedia of Bible Difficulties* (Grand Rapids: Zondervan, 1982), 332.

[245] Six of the ten orthodox exegetes (Matthew Henry, Adam Clarke, Theodor Zahn, Adolf Schlatter, S. Greijdanus, W. H. Gispen, F. Rienecker, I. H. Marshall, G. L. Archer, R. T. France) hold that the Sermon on the Mount (Matthew 5:1–7:29) is a redaction of the Sermon in the Field (Luke

like to say that the Gospel writers made these changes "according to their own theologies." Orthodox theologians, instead of solving the questions, like to say that changes does not mean changes in meaning, because the Holy Spirit watched over the work of the Gospel writers.

The question is this: Are orthodox (evangelical) theologians aware of their foundations? How accurate is orthodox Gospel exegesis? Also, an orthodox house that is divided cannot stand. If orthodoxy wants to hold to the infallibility of the scriptures, it has the obligation to explain that. Is the confession of orthodox theology that the Holy Spirit watched over *the meaning* of the words or that he watched over *the words*? It is not difficult to answer this question with Matthew 24:35 in mind, where Jesus says, "Heaven and earth will pass away, but my words will not pass away." Certainly the Holy Spirit watched over the words. And so a lot of work is still to be done. We have to go back to the basics and leave reductionism out of Gospel exegesis. (Of course, speaker reduction, as discussed in section 7.5, is not involved here.)

8.3 The Blind Men of Jericho Analytically Read

What picture do we receive about the blind men of Jericho when we read the texts analytically? It should be mentioned that the author has never seen the next approach in any treatise or book.

One blind man was cured by Jesus before he entered Jericho. That is clear from the use of the singular in Luke: And *he* cried [saying] ... *he* cried out all the more; What do *you* (singular) want me to do for *you*?

The course of direct speeches in Matthew shows that it was indeed two men who wanted to be healed. Have mercy on *us* (two times); *they* cried out; What do *you* (plural) want me to do for *you*?; let *our* eyes be opened.

Finally, there is the blind man in Mark, named Bartimaeus, who was cured after Jesus's visit to Jericho. He did not belong to the group

---

6:20–49). So Matthew enlarged the Sermon in the Field, and he changed it because the wording and expressions of the Sermon of the Mount are in no way copied verbatim from the Sermon in the Field. Two of these exegetes say nothing about the relationship between the two sermons. Two of them (Matthew Henry, G. L. Archer) correctly state that we have to deal with two different sermons of Jesus.

of two in Matthew, which we can deduce from the singular forms within the spoken words: *he* began to cry out; have mercy on *me*! (two times); *he* cried out; Call *him*!; What do *you* (singular) want me to do for *you*?; let *me* receive *my* sight; Go *your* (singular) way; *your* faith has made *you* well.

The conclusion must be that there were four cured men and three events of healing. We don't need to be frightened of the number of healings. Didn't John say at the end of his Gospel that Jesus did many other things and that the world could not contain the books if they all had been written down?[246] Of course, John is using rhetorical exaggeration. He has the intention to say that Jesus did very much more than the Gospels contain about him. Four healings in Jericho were not too much for him, who was a specialist in healing.

Jericho was situated at the caravan route through the valley of the River Jordan in the direction of Jerusalem. Jesus followed that route, as did many others, to be on time for the celebration of the yearly Pasha in Jerusalem. He knew that it was to be his last Pasha. Several times he had spoken to his disciples about his Passion and his crucifixion and resurrection, but they could not grasp the reality of it. To them, it seemed to be talk from a different planet.

Jericho belonged to the southern region of Judea. Many people who were very serious about their religion lived in this area. Many of them expected the Messiah, and many of them were baptized by John the Baptist (Matthew 3:5–6). However, there also existed a rigid religious leadership which, in an early stage of Jesus's ministry, had decided that he could not be the Promised One. According to them, it was an impossibility that the Messiah would come from Galilee. Moreover, with his healings on the Sabbath, he continually transgressed the divine law. Last but not least, by forgiving people he had never seen, he acted as more than man; he acted as God. This was unacceptable for the leadership, which had an excessively strong influence on societal life.

The followers of Jesus in Judea were oppressed. They were not permitted to speak openly of him as the Messiah. Offense of this rule meant that one was put out of the synagogue.[247] In a practical sense, that meant that the person had lost Jewish status, even in public life.

---

[246] John 21:25.
[247] John 9:22; 12:42.

An unreal and impossible situation was the result. Nobody dared to speak up about Jesus, as there was no freedom of speech. And in the meantime, there was an unstoppable stream of people from Galilee who came to the temple to bring their thank offerings for the healings they had received through Jesus.

It is not difficult to guess where the blind man, sitting by the roadside in front of Jericho, had received his information about Jesus and his healing potential. The lively stories he had heard from the people of Galilee who passed him had given him the clear image that Jesus was the Messiah of Israel. He had the time to think and rethink about everything that reached his ears. And when Jesus approached the city, and the blind man heard that it was Jesus, he started to cry for help. "Jesus, Son of David, have mercy on me!" The result was that everybody was shocked. Jesus, Son of David? That was Jesus, Messiah? Immediately the people tried to silence him—for his own good, of course. If he, with his handicap, were to be banned from the synagogue, his life wouldn't be worth living. There would be no possibility of help from the community. With the best of intentions, they fell upon him to impose silence on him. The blind man, however, hated the meddlesomeness of the people. He had learned to look after his own interests, and he also learned to ask for attention from the people on the road. His eyes were blind, but there was nothing wrong with his vocal cords. He cried louder; Jesus heard him, and a miracle happened.

That night while Jesus stayed with Zacchaeus, the healed man walked through the streets of Jericho. He had no problem finding his way; he knew every stone on the road by heart. He could not sleep; he had no time to close his eyes now. Even in the darkness, he enjoyed the use of his eyes. Everything looked splendid, even at night—the dark sky with stars and clouds, the dark shadows of the trees, the shining lights in the houses. No, he did not want to sleep now. And so he arrived at his friends—his blind friends—and he started to tell them circumstantially what had happened a few hours ago. And then they made a plan. The next day when Jesus left the city, they would sit by the roadside to do the same thing. Probably none of the men could sleep that night due to excitement.

The blind friends had listened very well. The next day they used almost precisely the same words as their informant had used the day before. And when the people compassionately tried to make them silent, they cried louder and louder, determined to be heard through Jesus. He felt the pressure that the people put on the men. What a comfort it was for them when he prepared them for their healing by posing the same question as the day before: "What do you want me to do for you?" It is too easy to say that he played the game. The situation was too threatening. Jesus revealed himself to these men first as their comforter and then as their healer.

In this approach to the blind men of Jericho story, all the details have their proper places. There exists a natural explanation for the more than seventeen similarities in the three Gospel records. When the stories are taken as reports of one event, then many interesting details are underexposed because they are contradictory to this view; the result is an intellectual but unconvincing exposition that ultimately does not explain anything. But when we accept the details as true observations and the stories as reports of different events, then the dynamic of the occurrences spring forth. We might speak of *documentation dynamic* because of the consequent view that gospel exegesis relies on copied documents (copied by the gospel writers). Again and again, when the rules for analytical reading are taken seriously, we will discover different, multiple events instead of one single event. Often, details of the events are interrelated, as in the case of the blind men of Jericho. The details belong to a living pattern, the living context. It is the task of the exegete to give a proper explanation for these details, to expose that living context. The rules for analytical reading make this task doable.

8.4 Look-alike Stories in the Gospels

There is an inconceivable number of parallel stories in the Gospels, due to many similar events. In only a few cases, they are similar descriptions of one event. And what about the many nearly identical sayings of Jesus scattered all over the Gospels? It is a pillar of the scholarly theory of the oral tradition to take look-alikes of stories and sayings as if they emerged from one single event or moment of the public life of Jesus Christ. Is there a way to falsify this deep-rooted evil in scholarly exegesis? Yes, documentation exegesis is applicable in all cases, as the rules for analytical reading are always necessary. In the following overview, the most important cases of look-alikes in the Gospels will be presented; from Jesus's baptism onward, until the conspiracy to put Jesus to death.

The overview of look-alikes is based on anchor points (bold, numbered a. p. 1–a. p. 30). When the features of similar descriptions have only points of contact, and we can be reasonably sure that a single event is meant, we have to deal with an *anchor point*. This working method makes it possible to define many events or sayings as dissimilar when they stand before or after an anchor point, which functions as an arbiter. Of course, the rules for analytical reading are extremely helpful to indicate anchors. Through the accurate observations of the speedy writers and steno writers, it is possible to evaluate almost all occurrences and spoken words (sayings and speeches) in the Gospels as either look-alikes or anchor points.

The overview shows that the Gospels contain many similar stories about different occurrences. How is it possible that there are so many of them? Or better yet, how is it possible that there were so many similar events in Jesus's ministry? What are the causes for all of these look-alikes?

First, many who were ill spontaneously followed an *example of healing*. Striking examples are given of this phenomenon. Lepers in a certain area approached Jesus in the same way (see points 4 and 9 in the overview). The second one must have heard of the cure of the first, as he used nearly the same words.

Overview Look-alikes in the Gospels						
Numberings, Titles	*a. p.*	*Parallels*	*Matthew*	*Mark*	*Luke*	*John*
Baptism of Jesus	1		3:13–17	1:9–11	3:21–22	
Temptations*	2		4:1–11	1:12–13	4:1–13	
1. Cleansing of the temple I		72, 74				2:14–22
Calling first disciples	3		4:18–22	1:16–20		
Demoniac in synagogue	4			1:21–28	4:33–37	
2. Simon's mother-in-law I		21		1:29–31	4:38–39	
3. Cures in the evening I		22		1:32–34	4:40–41	

Numberings, Titles	a. p.	Parallels	Matthew	Mark	Luke	John
4. Cure of a leper I*		9		1:40–45	5:12–16	
5. Cure of a paralytic I		6, 24		2:1–12		
6. Cure of a paralytic II		5, 24			5:17–26	
Call of Levi I	**5**	25		**2:13–17**	**5:27–32**	
7. Picking corn on Sabbath I		30		2:23–28	6:1–5	
8. Cure of a withered hand I*		31		3:1–6	6:6–11	
9. Cure of a leper II		4	8:1–4			
The centurion's servant	**6**		**8:5–13**		**7:1–10**	
10. The Baptist's question I		27			7:18–23	
11. About John the Baptist I		28			7:24–35	
12. Jesus and Beelzebul I		26, 32, 57		3:22–27		
13. Blasph. against the Spirit I		33, 62		3:28–38		
14. Parable of the sower I		17, 36			8:4–8	
15. Why parables? I		18, 37			8:9–10	
16. Explanation, parable sower I		19, 38			8:11–15	
Mother and brothers I*	**7**	35		**3:31–35**	**8:19–21**	
17. Parable of the sower II		14, 36		4:1–9		
18. Why parables? II		15, 37		4:10–12		
19. Explanation parable sower II		16, 38		4:13–20		
20. Parable mustard seed I		39, 61		4:30–32		
21. Simon's mother-in-law II		2	8:14–15			
22. Cures in the evening II		3	8:16–17			

Numberings, Titles	a. p.	Parallels	Matthew	Mark	Luke	John
23. Foxes have holes I		55	8:18–22			
Calming a storm	8		**8:23–27**	**4:35–41**	**8:22–25**	
24. Cure of a paralytic III		5, 6	9:1–8			
25. Call of Levi II		after 6	9:9–13			
Jairus's daughter	9		**9:18–26**	**5:21–43**	**8:40–56**	
26. Jesus and Beelzebul II		12, 32, 57	9:32–34			
Mission of the Twelve	10		**10:1–42**	**6:7–13**	**9:1–6**	
27. The Baptist's question II		10	11:2–6			
28. About John the Baptist II		11	11:7–19			
29. Lamenting the lake-towns I		56	11:20–24			
30. Picking corn on Sabbath II		7	12:1–8			
31. Cure of a withered hand II		8	12:9–14			
32. Jesus and Beelzebul III		12, 26, 57	12:22–30			
33. Blasph. against the Spirit II		13, 60	12:31–37			
34. Sign of Jonah I		43, 58	12:38–42			
35. Mother and brothers II		after 16	12:46–50			
36. Parable the sower III		14, 17	13:1–9			
37. Why parables? III		15, 18	13:10–17			
38. Explanation parable sower III		16, 19	13:18–23			
39. Parable mustard seed II		20, 61	13:31–32			
40. Parable of the yeast I		62	13:33			
Death of John the Baptist	11		**14:3–12**	**6:17–29**		
Return apostles	12			**6:30–31**	**9:10**	

Numberings, Titles	a. p.	Parallels	Matthew	Mark	Luke	John
Loaves for 5,000	13		14:13–21	6:32–44	9:10–17	6:1–15
Walking on water	14		14:22–33	6:45–52		6:16–21
41. Mother and child (Syroph.) I		42		7:24–30		
42. Mother and child (Canaan.) II		41	15:21–28			
Loaves for 4,000	15		15:32–39	8:1–10		
43. Sign of Jonah II		34, 58	16:1–4	8:11–12		
44. Yeast of Pharisees I		59	16:5–12	8:13–21		
Peter's confession	16		16:13–20	8:27–30	9:18–21	
45. Passion prophecy I*		51, 68	16:21	8:31–32	9:22	
46. Following Christ I		47, 48			9:23–27	
Peter rebuked	17		16:22–23	8:32–33		
47. Following Christ II		46, 48	16:24–28			
48. Following Christ III		46, 47		8:34–9:1		
Transfiguration	18		17:1–4	9:2–10	9:28–36	
49. Return of Elijah I		50		9:11–13		
50. Return of Elijah II		49	17:10–13			
Lunatic cured	19		17:14–21	9:14–29	9:37–43	
51. Passion prophecy II*		45, 68	17:22–23	9:30–32	9:43–45	
The first place*	20		18:1–5	9:33–37	9:46–48	
The name of Jesus	21			9:38–41	9:49–50	
52. Warning to tempt I		53		9:42–50		
53. Warning to tempt II		52	18:6–9			
54. The lost sheep I		64	18:10–14			
Journey to Judea	22		19:1–2	10:1	9:51	
55. Foxes have holes II		23			9:57–62	

Numberings, Titles	a. p.	Parallels	Matthew	Mark	Luke	John
56. Lamenting the lake-towns II		29			10:13–16	
57. Jesus and Beelzebul IV		12, 26, 32			11:14–23	
58. Sign of Jonah III		34, 43			11:29–32	
59. Yeast of Pharisees II		44			12:1	
60. Blasph. against the Spirit III		13, 33			12:10	
61. Parable mustard seed III		20, 39			13:18–19	
62. Parable of the yeast II		40			13:20–21	
63. Jerusalem admonished I		87			13:34–35	
64. The lost sheep II		54			15:1–7	
Blessing the children*	**23**		**19:13–15**	**10:13–16**	**18:15–17**	
65. The rich man I*		66, 67	19:16–30			
66. The rich man II*		65, 67		10:17–31		
67. The rich man III*		65, 66			18:18–30	
68. Passion prophecy III*		45, 51	20:17–19	10:32–34	18:31–34	
John and James	**24**		**20:20–24**	**10:35–41**		
69. The blind man of Jericho I		70, 71			18:35–43	
70. The blind man of Jericho II*		69, 71		10:46–52		
71. The blind men of Jericho III*		69, 70	20:29–43			
Entrance into Jerusalem	**25**		**21:1–11**	**11:1–11**	**19:28–44**	**12:12–19**
72. Cleansing of the temple II		1, 74	21:12–13		19:45–46	
Barren fig tree	**26**		**21:18–19**	**11:12–14**		
73. About barren fig tree I		77	21:20–22			

Numberings, Titles	a. p.	Parallels	Matthew	Mark	Luke	John
74. Cleansing of the temple III		1, 72		11:15–17		
75. Jesus's authority questioned I		78	21:23–27			
76. The wicked tenants I		79, 80	21:33–46			
77. About barren fig tree II		73		11:20–26		
78. Jesus's authority questioned II		75		11:27–33	20:1–8	
79. The wicked tenants II		76, 80			20:9–19	
80. The wicked tenants III		76, 79		12:1–12		
Tribute to Caesar*	**27**		**22:15–22**	**12:13–17**	**20:20–26**	
81. About resurrection I		83, 88			20:27–40	
82. Son of David I		85, 90			20:41–44	
83. About resurrection II		81, 88	22:23–33			
84. Greatest commandment I		89	22:34–40			
85. Son of David II		82, 90	22:41–46			
86. Against scribes (and Phar.) I		91	23:1–36			
87. Jerusalem admonished II		63	23:37–39			
88. About resurrection III*		81, 83		12:18–27		
89. Greatest commandment II*		84		12:28–34		
90. Son of David III		82, 85		12:35–37		
91. Against scribes II*		86		12:37–40	20:45–47	
The widow's mite	**28**			**12:41–44**	**21:1–4**	
92. Destruction of the temple I		After 93			21:5–6	
93. Eschatological discourse I		94, 95			21:7–36	

Numberings, Titles	a. p.	Parallels	Matthew	Mark	Luke	John
Destruction of the temple II	29	92	24:1–2	13:1–2		
94. Eschatological discourse II		93, 95		13:3–37		
95. Eschatological discourse III		93, 94	24:3– 25:13			
Plans to arrest Jesus	30		26:1–5	14:1–2	22:1–2	

* Mutual location (or sequence of the spoken word) uncertain.

When Luke tells us that much later, ten lepers came for healing (Luke 17:12), only one conclusion is possible. Such a great a group meant that they had heard, (and/or seen) real convincing testimonies about Jesus's power, which motivated them to take action together. In other words, examples of healing were the strongest motivation for people to act in the same way. We have already seen the blind men of Jericho. The first one who became healed motivated the others to do the same, whether unintentionally or purposefully. Many other examples of this are found in the Gospels.

Second, Jesus followed the method of *teaching by repetition* for several reasons. It has been shown historically that pupils need to hear information again and again—the same ideas, rules or principles. It has nothing to do with indoctrination, but education and training are based on repetition. It was certainly also the rabbinic way of teaching disciples and, in that respect, Jesus acted like the rabbis. He regularly made use of the same parables and metaphors. When he sent the twelve out on their mission, he started to teach new disciples, and of course he used the same teachings he had taught to the twelve earlier—the parable of the sower (14, 17, 36), with explanation (16, 19, 38), and the parable of the mustard seed (20, 39, 61). And of course, when the question was repeated, "Why parables?" (15, 18, 37), Jesus replied with the same answers as earlier. There is every reason to suppose that it was a rule in rabbinic teaching to standardize lessons and answers.

Third, as a teacher, Jesus was regularly confronted by his hearers with identical questions. It was the classical practice of higher education that the teacher and his pupils follow the so-called *diatribè* style of learning. In a relaxed way, teacher and disciples conversed with each other about all sorts of subjects. The teacher would put forth questions and listen to the reactions of his disciples, and they, in their turn, had the same option. The meaning of this for the Gospels is that the same subjects often came up for debate; for example, as they needed more explanation. When John once said to Jesus that they had forbidden a man to cure demoniacs in Jesus's name, as he did not follow the other disciples, Jesus answered, "Do not forbid him; for he that is not against you, is for you" (Luke 9:50). This was a rather confusing answer for John. It was certainly too short to understand, and it needed explanation. So he had to repeat his point. The first time John addressed Jesus with the rather neutral Epistata (overseer)—Sir or Master. The second time he opened with Didaskale; that is, Teacher. By using this title, he made known that he needed more insight in the subject. Now Jesus gave a longer answer about the issue; more than ten verses (Mark 9:39–50). In the overview of look-alikes, the discourse "The name of Jesus" is marked as an anchor point (21, bold). Mark and Luke deliver a part of the discourse. As it was one person (John) who came with it, we can be sure that it was one occasion. It is not realistic to suppose that John had later on again forbidden someone to work in Jesus's name, after an earlier reprimand about it, and again posed his point. Not only disciples but outsiders also could approach Jesus with their questions on moral, spiritual, or practical matters. Identical questions existed among the people, and therefore Jesus was confronted by outsiders with similar questions also, not once but several times.

Fourth, repeatedly Jesus had to deal with the same accusations and countered with the same arguments. More than once he was accused of being a coworker with the devil (12, 26, 32, 57) and that he violated the law of the Sabbath (7, 30). More than once he was challenged to do a miracle as evidence of his prophetical status (34, 43, 58). More than once he had to defend the existence of eternal life against the Sadducees (81, 83, 88). He replied with the same arguments, parables, or metaphors. This is so striking that we can say with a high degree of certainty that it was rabbinic custom to repeat identical answers, which were applicable to standard questions and problems. The benefits were twofold. Nobody could mistake a rabbi's view on a matter, and, particularly in Jesus's case, this was of great importance. "Why do you ask me? Ask those who have heard me, what I said to them; they know what I said."[248] Another advantage was that everybody could return to the subject in future discussions. The rabbi could show further implications of his point of view in all sorts of aspects, theologically and practically.

Fifth, Jesus followed a consequent way of acting with respect to unchanged abuses. For example, several times Jesus cleansed the temple square of merchants. It is a strange position of liberals—who suppose that Jesus did so only one time, and that the four reports in the Gospels about it go back to that single event—that John gave his report at the beginning of his Gospel while Matthew, Mark, and Luke put theirs at the end of their Gospels.[249] If Jesus did not accept the habit of merchandising in the open places around the temple, wouldn't it be strange if he had cleansed the temple only once, even though he was in Jerusalem several times? No, when Jesus went to Jerusalem, his disciples could count on what was possibly to occur again in the temple square.

Finally, in Matthew, two multiplications of loaves are mentioned (five thousand and four thousand fed). This is also the case in Mark. In each of the synoptic Gospels, there are three prophecies about the Passion. When even the Gospels show these repetitions, we should not be surprised that there were many similar events in Jesus's ministry, and it is artificial to dogmatically reduce their reports to one supposed event, due to a so-called oral tradition that never existed. Both orthodox and liberal theology have created and preserved a restricted image of Jesus for centuries by their common preoccupation with the so-called oral tradition. One forgets that the Gospels paint a picture that is overwhelming with respect to the mass of Jesus's teachings and works.

8.5 Documentation Dynamics and Documentation Exegesis

It is obvious that the first result of the documentation theory is that the common Bible reader is enabled to read the Gospels with good conscience. It is possible to read any Gospel story with the knowledge that each direct speech is authentic and that every detail

---

[248] John 18:21.

[249] John 2:13–17; Matthew 21:12–13; Mark 11:15–17; Luke 19:45–46.

is an observation of the writers who followed the Lord. The common reader is given a concept by which he is able to understand what he reads—documentation. It is not necessary for laymen to use the argument, "I know that theologians have problems with these texts, but I am not a theologian. I just need to believe." Now he can say, "I believe, and I understand what I believe."

The second result of the documentation theory is that it preserves a complete facility for professional Gospel interpretation—documentation exegesis. In this section we will summarize the aspects of this method.

Dynamic of the document. It is always necessary to understand that a Gospel text originally was a document that the Gospel writer used for the composition of his Gospel book. Therefore, it is necessary to describe the original document as far as possible by answering questions such as the following: Where does it begin, and where does it end? What type of document is it? What was the purpose of the document? What was the importance of the central message? Answers may be deduced from the contents of the text, the Gospel to which it belongs (teaching record, public record, or remnant record), and sometimes from its position in a Gospel.

Dynamic of the spoken word. We possess the real spoken word in the documents, as if it was said yesterday. We listen, so to speak, together with the writers who were operative in the past. And the questions are as follows: What are the direct speeches? What do the rules for analytical reading teach us about spoken words and their place in the narrative of the description? These questions require serious investigation, according to the rules of discourses.

Dynamic of actions. There are often concise references that show the connections between the actions. By analytical reading, it is possible to define most of the actions within the framework of the occurrence. Signal words and rules for analytical reading reveal the course of actions within an occurrence—connections between them and interruptions. Accurate investigation is needed in this field to establish the proper interrelations between the described actions of a story. By that, the course of events becomes clear.

Dynamic of reinforcing records. When it is possible to establish that reports in the Gospels refer to the same event, the dynamic force of these records becomes much greater by mutual reinforcement.

Questions may be as follows: Are there similar records? What are the similarities, and what the differences? Do they hold similar positions in the Gospels or don't they? Part of this investigation is the question of how the direct speeches relate to one another. Do they exclude or include the possibility of belonging to the same event?

Dynamic of repetitions. Similar reports that do not refer to the same event have a special impact. As repetition is never a result of the oral tradition, there is always a *living pattern*, a living context, underlying the repetition. As this pattern is rooted in everyday life, it is always a dynamic pattern. The question is, what is the living context, that this repetition took place several times?

Dynamic of details. Details nearly always represent specific nuances. Therefore, they need a proper estimation instead of neglect. It always has to do with the first observations of the writers who followed Jesus. Any detail can be of decisive importance. They have a great bearing on the vividness of the described event or subject. Often, only a few details are needed to show that different events are at issue.

We have summed up six central points in relation to documentation exegesis. Often only five are active because numbers four and five are alternatives. When four and five are not relevant because there are not similar reports at issue, only four points remain.

8.6 Genealogies of Jesus in the Gospels

Direct reports of Jesus's writers have been used later for the arrangement of the Gospels, but not only those reports. Earlier, we saw a compilation of events known as the longer Mark-ending (section 6.4.1) incorporated with documentation materials. Matthew and Luke made use of existing genealogies concerning Jesus's descent. In the last cases, only the dynamic of the document remains of interest.

Matthew, in his first chapter (1:1–17), writes that it was fourteen generations from Abraham to David, from David to the exile, and again fourteen generations from the exile to Jesus. It is generally accepted among exegetes that Matthew construed three periods of fourteen generations by omitting a few names (Ahaziah, Joash, Amaziah, v. 8), as Matthew, with his knowledge of the Old Testament, accidentally missed these names.[250] It is generally supposed that Matthew had a theological purpose with these omissions. He would have thought that fourteen was a superb holy number: two times seven. Three series of fourteen (from Abraham to David, from David to the deportation, from the deportation to Jesus) would confirm the divine plan of the time of Jesus's birth, but is it true? Did Matthew construct these genealogies with his knowledge of the Old Testament? Of course not. Matthew knew too much about—and had too much respect for—the Old Testament to manipulate its information in this way. No, he used an existing document that once belonged to Joseph as evidence that he was a descendant of David—his birth certificate. Original genealogies were kept in the archives of the temple.[251] When a new son was born, the father went to the archives, showed his lineage certificate, and the name of the newborn son was added. In Jesus's case, this did not happen, as he was not actually the biological son of Joseph. It is clear from this view that in the past, some kings did not always visit the temple archives to register their sons.

What about the three missing kings, as earlier mentioned? The ungodly King Joram (2 Kings 8:18) started a tradition of neglecting, which was continued by his son Ahaziah (2 Kings 8:27) and later on by his grandson Joas (2 Chronicles 24:17, 18). Joram did not register Ahaziah; Ahaziah did not register Joas; Joas did not register Amaziah. Amaziah (2 Kings 14:3), however, continued the old tradition of registering his sons in the temple archives. Apparently, the priests put a ban on registration of three generations to punish Joram for

---

[250] Names such as Jehoahaz, Jehoiakim (Eliakim), and Zedekiah (2 Chronicles 36:1–11) are missing in Matthew's register. As sons of King Josiah, they all reigned for some time in Jerusalem, but Jechoniah (Matthew 1:11), who was also a son of Josiah, was the real ancestor of Joseph. Jechoniah is to be counted among the fourteen before the deportation, as well as among the fourteen after the deportation, because he belonged to both periods.

[251] Ezra 2:59–63. (1) Israelites who were not able to prove that they belonged to the Jewish people; it seems that they did not have proper birth certificates. (2) Families about which there was doubt whether they belonged to the priestly family. The official archives of the priestly families seemed to be not completely in order after the exile (v. 62).

the killing of all his brothers, an unprecedented criminal act (2 Chronicles 21:2) in the house of David, in former or later times.[252]

The dynamic of this part of the Gospel of Matthew is a look into the family tradition of Joseph, in which these documents existed. When Joseph went to Bethlehem to be enrolled (Luke 2:4), he certainly needed a document as evidence that he was an ancestor of King David. With Matthew's mention of the three series of fourteen generations, he did not refer to a divine plan of the birth of Jesus, but he prevented the insertion of missing names by later copyists. If they did so, the number fourteen would not fit anymore. Of course, the expression "the father of" in Matthew's register has a broad sense also, as the rabbis' hold in relation to genealogical registers: "Sons of sons are sons."[253]

To complete the discussion concerning Jesus's lineage, we will have a look at another document of Jesus's forefathers as presented in the Gospel of Luke (3:23–38). Some take this list as contradicting the list of Matthew because they take the two genealogies as referring to Joseph's lineage, and then there are many dissimilarities between the lists. In Luke, however, we read word by word: "Jesus ... being the son as supposed of Joseph the son of Heli the son of Mattat." Many interpreters have read this as "Jesus ... being—the son as supposed of Joseph—the son of Heli, the son of Mattat." Punctuation marks are missing in the Greek text, so there is no grammatical obstacle to reading the passage in this way. Many theologians reason that it doesn't make sense that Luke would give a long genealogy of Joseph, who has been marked as the supposed father. They feel that this expression automatically excludes Joseph as forming part of Luke's list and that, consequently, Mary's genealogy is meant here.[254] That

---

[252] Comp. Deuteronomy 23:8.

[253] The Greek for "the father of" is *egennèsen* (he brought forth), and this particularly makes a wider sense than the possibility of its meaning only "his own son."

[254] The view that Mary's lineage is presented in Luke 3:23–31 was held by M. Luther, J. A. Bengel, J. B. Lightfoot, C. Wieseler, F. Godet, B. Weiss, A. T. Robertson, N. Geldenhuys, John Wenham, and many others (so Wenham, *Redating*, 216). J. McDowell, *Evidence that demands a Verdict* (San Bernardino: Campus Crusade for Christ International, 1972), 377 takes it that Joseph could be called "son of Heli", being his son-in-law.

would mean that in Luke 3:23–31, we face the documentation of Mary's lineage from King David. Maybe she possessed a copy of it, or Luke had access to an official register or family register with this information concerning Mary's lineage.

8.7 A Greater Picture of Jesus Christ

Reductionism in orthodox and liberal theology has resulted in a reduced image of Jesus. Due to the oral tradition, the dynamic of the many events seems to have disappeared, evaporated, and only a scanty measure of that dynamic remains. However, all the reports are still available in the Gospels, and they still witness about the great Christ events.

Documentation exegesis and the rules for analytical reading are tools that make it possible to reveal the dynamic context of Jesus's public life in a special way. Documentation exegesis and analytical reading reveal the living context in which the reports came into being. This was a dynamic context; the speedy writers and stenographers wrote what they saw and heard—an immense stream of details, even for them, with an overwhelming impact. Is it strange that the Gospels represent this stream of details? Until now, this aspect of Gospel exegesis has remained under the bushel with explanations such as insertions of the oral tradition (liberal) or the same miracle (orthodox). We may wonder whether the future will bring a change in this respect. Will documentation exegesis receive a chance, a forum from which to give light to all in the house?

He who follows the model of stenography and documentation activity as a theory of how the Gospels came into being receives a realistic and greater picture of Jesus. It is clear that the Lord did many more miracles than usually is thought. With our understanding of this, his divine status increases, and the picture of his human character changes because a dynamic Jesus takes the place of a static one. He becomes a man of flesh and blood with the limitations that are connected with that. Nevertheless, he is the one who dynamically fulfilled his God-given commission. The examples of documentation exegesis in the next chapter will unquestionably show the effectiveness of this approach.

9. Living Patterns

In the previous chapters we have seen that documentation exegesis has to do with two types of stories. One type is determined as referring to one single occasion.

There are also stories that certainly do not refer to one single occasion but are look-alikes. Questions are then as follows: How is it possible that these stories have so much in common? How is it possible that these stories also have such peculiar details, which are, however, irreconcilable? To answer these questions there nearly always will be a living pattern, which makes these stories look-alikes.

In the stories of the blind men of Jericho, the pattern was that they contacted each other. This notion cannot be deduced directly from the texts. In terms of exegetes, there is no literary feature as evidence for it. In other words, it is not clearly stated in the texts that these men informed one another. All the features together in the texts, however, compel us to conclude this pattern of contact between the men. In this chapter, we will analyze more look-alike stories to understand what sort of living patterns made them so similar.

9.1 In the Desert

Matthew 4:1–11, Mark 1:12–13, Luke 4:1–13.
The stories of Jesus's temptation in the desert are well known. The Gospels of Matthew and Luke each have a lengthy record of it, while Mark has only a reference to the occasion.[255] The records of Matthew and Luke raise a difficult question: Why don't they have the same sequence of Jesus's temptations?

It is an unsolved exegetical riddle that the sequence of the temptations and the direct speeches in the temptations differ. This seems to give credence to the oral tradition. In documentation exegesis, however, these questions are easily solved in a different fashion.

Temptation works through repetition; that is usually its power. And that is the living pattern underlying these reports. The same temptations

---

[255] Comp. the overview of look-alikes (section 8.4), a. p. 2.

intruded upon Jesus's mind repeatedly.[256] That is the living context of temptations. When a temptation seems to have been overcome, it may come back with renewed force. Jesus, in turn, used the *same* verse from scripture to conquer the repeated temptation, sometimes in different wording.[257] Looking to the course of events, we have to reckon with the following sequence at the end of the desert period:

1. Making bread (Luke 4:3–4)
2. Great power (Luke 4:5–8)
3. Making loaves of bread (Matthew 4:3–4)
4. Leap from the temple (Matthew 4:5–7)
5. Leap from the temple (Luke 4:9–12)
6. World power (Matthew 4:8–10)

First, the temptation to make bread out of stone (Luke). Later on, a repetition came but more intense (Matthew)—to make loaves (plural) of bread out of stones. Through the use of the plural (loaves), the thought is near that Jesus was challenged the second time to make bread not only for himself but also for others. Was he challenged to become a Messiah for bread only? In both cases, Jesus resisted with "Man shall not live by bread alone."[258]

In Luke's report (v. 5), Jesus got a vision of the kingdoms of the inhabited world (Greek: *oikoumenè*; the Roman Empire). The devil

---

[256] We may wonder why the devil tempted Jesus. Maybe he only tried, or he did not believe that Jesus could resist temptations, or maybe he had no other possibility of expression at his disposal than temptation. We may also wonder what temptations meant to Jesus. It is difficult to imagine Jesus as constantly fighting against sin. In my opinion, Jesus, being the Word of God (John 1:1–5,14), lived according to this nature and remained the unblemished lamb by using the Word of God. Probably the devil could not believe or understand this. Hebrew 2:18 says that Jesus suffered being tempted, and therefore "he is able to help those who are tempted." The sufferings of Jesus were not that he failed in temptation but that he was confronted in his feelings—how humankind suffers through temptations.

[257] In Judaism, it was accepted to cite the scriptures with slight differences if one spoke in the spirit of a verse. Moses already did so when he looked back on the Law given on Sinai (Deuteronomy 5:6–22).

[258] Matthew 4:8–11 gives an uninterrupted course of events up to the moment that the devil leaves Jesus.

offered him the power over the kingdoms of the inhabited world, but Jesus, in turn, would have to kneel before and to submit to the devil. Did the devil suggest that Jesus could bring peace in the Roman Empire? Again, a Messiah with a different calling? No war?

Matthew and Luke also tell that Jesus was led to "a pinnacle of the temple", probably a high place on one of the galleries surrounding the buildings of the temple. It seems that Jesus would end his period of fasting in the place of worship in Israel. The devil proposed, "Throw yourself down," with the motivation of a verse from the scriptures: "Angels will take charge of you ... they will bear you up!" A "wonder" Messiah making miracles in the temple and maybe repeatedly at fixed times—wouldn't that be the proof of the existence of God? Jesus, however, did not come to be borne but to bear the lost. Two times he rejected with the same verse from the Torah: "You shall not tempt the Lord your God."

Finally, once more the temptation came to kneel before Satan and to receive, in turn, dominion over all the kingdoms of the world (Matthew 4:8). This last temptation was the heaviest one. The earlier proposition was the offer of power over the kingdoms of the *oikoumenè*, the inhabited world of the Roman Empire. Now the whole world was at issue. The devil did not have any more to offer. However, Jesus ended the temptations by saying, "Go away Satan!"

How is it possible that we possess the story of this struggle of Jesus? The extraordinary nature of this state of affairs is that, in reading the sayings, we face Jesus's annotations, which he made during his spiritual struggle. Jesus could read and write,[259] and so there is no reason to be upset by the fact that we indeed possess writings from him, just as Moses accurately annotated what happened in the desert about one and a half millennia earlier. Jesus taught his disciples with his own experiences as a reference point, they could triumph by quoting the scriptures tenaciously in a world in which curiosity and serious temptation occur side by side.

Matthew has a proper use of then-sentences (1, 5, 11), while Luke has the rather loose structure of and-sentences (2, 5, 9, and 13), which

---

[259] John 8:6.

seems to refer to a second choice. It looks as if Luke used a remnant record, as there was no public record.

9.2 Three Paralytics Cured

Matthew 9:1–8, Mark 2:3–12, Luke 5:17–26
The synoptic Gospels each have a record of a healing of a paralytic.[260] Two of them are nearly identical stories (Mark and Luke), about a man on a bed or pallet who was let down by some others through the roof of the house where Jesus was teaching the people. Matthew also has a record but without the roof story. The question is, are we dealing with descriptions of one, two, or three events of healing.

There are striking similarities. First, in each case Jesus "saw their faith." Second, right after seeing their faith, Jesus said, "Your sins are forgiven." Third, in all cases the scribes started immediately to protest in terms of blasphemy. Fourth, Jesus used the healing as proof that he had the right to forgive. Fifth, the man leaves, bearing his bed/pallet. Finally, the people "feared [Matthew, Luke] and glorified God."

In spite of the many similarities, we have to decide in favor of three separate healings. The direct speeches are so dissimilar in address, in word order, and in their use of expressions that it is not possible to suppose that the descriptions refer to one single occasion—not even to only two occasions.

Many sick people came to Jesus without help of others, but these lame men came with their carriers. Common faith is more visible, and in all these cases, it is said that Jesus "saw their faith." The communion of the saints (living context that brought the living pattern) was what Jesus saw. He, being the bringer of faith, immediately took part in this communion; that meant acceptance. The lame men who came to Jesus's feet saw the joy on his face, and that made them joyful. They knew that he accepted them. And Jesus, seeing their relief about the acceptance, started to verbalize what happened. This relief and refreshing in the presence of the Lord (Acts 2:19) was the experience of forgiveness. Therefore, in all cases, Jesus only explained their experience saying, "Your sins are forgiven."

The scribes had a different idea about forgiveness. It was a

---

[260] See 8.4, the overview of look-alikes: 5, 6, 24.

theological issue for them, and in each case, they raised theological objections. But Jesus did not allow them to frustrate the lame men, who had just experienced forgiveness. In all these cases, the same discourse between them and Jesus developed. In Mark and Luke, the men walked out, straight through the people, as through the Red Sea. Before their healing, they could not pass through to enter, but when they left, there was room enough.

Mark describes the cure of the first paralytic. He tells us that carriers opened the roof by uncovering it before they let down the mat with the man. Luke's record tells that the paralytic was let down "through the tiles." This is a strange formulation, as tiles on a roof are not able to let something pass, particularly not a man on a bed. This is only possible if an opening in the tiles already exists. In other words, the roof had not been repaired yet by the first carriers, and probably they ran downstairs to welcome their healed friend outside the house. The opening in the roof was a minor problem at that moment. That made it possible for the second paralytic (in Luke) to be let down before Jesus.

There are more features in Luke's record that point to a second healing. We read, "And the power of the Lord was with him to heal" (Luke 5:17). When the people saw a paralytic coming through the opening in the roof for the second time, they held their breath because they knew what was going to happen.

"Who is this that speaks blasphemies?" (Luke 5:21). During the first occasion the scribes spoke, "It is blasphemy" (singular), but here in Luke, it is "blasphemies" (plural). Indeed, they heard Jesus for the second time saying, "Your sins are forgiven."

"We have seen strange things today" (Luke 5:26). After the first healing, the reaction of the people was, "We never saw anything like this!" (singular). After the second healing, they spoke in plural that they had seen "strange things today."

The third cure of a paralytic man (the record of Matthew) occurred much later.[261] Also, the situation was different, as there is no mention of a roof act. But yes, there was Jesus's declaration of forgiveness and, of course, the reaction of the scribes in doubting

---

[261] See 8.4, the overview of look-alikes, number 24.

about that, followed by the living pattern of Jesus's defense of the experience of forgiveness, as in Mark and Luke.

Matthew has the shortest record. His main interest is teaching that Jesus is the Messiah. For Matthew, that is Jesus's mighty word against vain human thinking. Luke chose to describe the second healing through the roof. When the public plays a significant and positive role, we see often a public record of it in Luke's Gospel. And that is the case here; the people spoke in plural about Jesus's works (v. 26). The first healing remained as a remnant record and found its place in Mark's gospel.

9.3 Sabbatical Perils

Matthew 8:14–17, Mark 1:29–34, Luke 4:38–41

In three Gospels we read the story of Peter's mother-in-law, who was healed by Jesus from a fever. Connected with it, we read about many healings in front of the house.[262] Certainly the same Peter and the same mother-in-law are involved, so many suppose that we are dealing with three stories of the same single occasion. However, this passage of Matthew occurs much later. There are at least two events.

In two cases (Mark and Luke), the same event is at issue. This can be established as earlier that day, a demoniac was cured in the synagogue. It happened at the beginning of Jesus's ministry. During the day, Peter's mother-in-law was also cured inside the house, as she had a serious fever. Remarkably enough, nobody approached Jesus that day before sunset. Of course, according to the rule of the Sabbath, it was not permitted to work in the daytime. The evening after the Sabbath was counted as part of the next day, and at sunset people with diseases started to move in the direction of Peter's house.

Matthew's record is related to another healing of Peter's mother-in-law, which happened much later and not on a Sabbath. On this day, Jesus had given the Sermon on the Mount, instead of being in the synagogue, as was his custom on the Sabbath day.[263] Also on that day, a leper was healed, and, entering into Capernaum,

---

[262] See 8.4, the overview of look-alikes, numbers 2–3, 21–22.
[263] Luke 4:16.

he cured the centurion's servant. After a long period of absence from Capernaum, they arrived at the house of Peter in the evening. Again, Peter's mother-in-law had a fever and was healed. Because of the late time that they arrived, the people came for healing in the evening.

The living context of the first two circumstances is explained above. It was in the evening after the Sabbath, and the people came after sunset for healing because of the sabbatical rule to rest during the day. The second event was also in the evening, during the week, because of Jesus's late arrival in town.

The repeated cure of Peter's mother-in-law seems remarkable, but is it? Fever is a symptom that accompanies many diseases, and in these cases, it was the dominant symptom. So it looks like a conjunction of circumstances (living context).

Luke gives a public record, in which he tells how Jesus associated with the people. "He laid his hands on every one of them and healed them." That he touched every one shows his compassion and care for each. Luke also tells how he handled a disease in the description of the cure of Peter's mother-in-law: "He rebuked the fever." This shows that Jesus did not acquiesce to illness. These features were part of a vivid story for a large public. Mark used a remnant record (it has no direct speech; Luke has one). Mark shows observations that are very impressive: "who were sick or possessed by demons" (omitted by Luke); "the whole city was gathered together" (Luke doesn't make mention of this); "sick with various diseases" (Luke has the same); and "and cast out many demons" (Luke: demons came also out of many). Mark had the remnant record, and it clearly presents the impact of the first observations of the writers.

Matthew opted for a teaching record of a later period. We don't know why he didn't want to use the teaching record of the earlier event—probably because it lacked the fulfillment quotation of Isaiah 53:4. He found it in the record of the later occasion, and that was certainly the reason why he took the teaching record of that event as a paradigm and explanation of Jesus's healing works. "He took our infirmities and bore our diseases" (Isaiah 53:4). This was a Messianic promise, and with that Matthew referred to Jesus as the Messiah, which is often the main point of his teaching.

9.4 Picking Corn on the Sabbath; Cure of a Man with a Withered Hand

Matthew 12:1–14, Mark 2:23–3:6, Luke 6:1–11

People were not allowed to work on the Sabbath, and many spent their time walking through the fields, enjoying nature. It was certainly common practice to pluck and eat ears of grain when the time of harvest was near. And so did Jesus's disciples, when they walked through the fields on the Sabbath. The Pharisees, however, who were perfectionists in matters of the law, had problems with that. Plucking and eating ears on the Sabbath was harvesting, and so it was forbidden by the law, they thought.

For Jesus's contemporaries, this was a serious matter of debate, and for that reason, Matthew, Mark, and Luke present a discussion about the subject in their Gospels (see 8.4, overview of look-alikes: 2–3, 21–22). This is not so strange. Remarkable is that in each case, a description follows about the cure of a man with a withered hand.

The first important question is this: How many events of healing are involved? The records of Mark and Luke of picking corn on the Sabbath seem to refer to the same occurrence in the beginning of Jesus's ministry. Also, the Mark and the Luke reports of the cure of the withered hand seem to refer to one and the same event. Wording of the two reports is very similar, and the direct speeches of both reports also combine perfectly, according to the rules for analytical reading. All aspects point to the same conclusion—that we are dealing with the same event. However, the features of Matthew's report differ dramatically.

Matthew does not refer to the same event as the records of Mark and Luke; the occurrence after the Mission of the Twelve of Matthew's record makes that impossible. However, one question remains: Isn't the repetition strange that, also in Matthew, after the picking corn on the Sabbath, again the cure of a withered hand occurs in a synagogue and on a Sabbath? It seems coincidental, but it is not, as Luke clearly states that the healing was "On another Sabbath." In Matthew, the two events took place on the same Sabbath: "And he went on from there, and entered their synagogue."

In Luke (also in Mark, different words), we read that they "watched him, to see whether he would heal on the Sabbath, so that they might find an accusation against him." But in Matthew: "And they asked him, 'Is it lawful to heal on the Sabbath?' so that they might accuse him." In Luke and Mark, Jesus's opponents are passive, and Jesus confronts *them* with the question of whether it is permitted to heal on the Sabbath. But in Matthew, the Pharisees take the initiative to confront *Jesus* with the question. That is the difference.

After the healing, according to Mark, the Pharisees went to the Herodians and held counsel with them to destroy him. And of course, this was to occur in a legal way; there was no talk of engaging an assassin. No, they had to collect as many examples of Jesus's transgressions as they could, and then they would be able to take him to court. It was impossible to condemn someone to death if there was no evidence of criminal intent.[264] One had to collect incriminating evidence. That is the living (context) pattern behind Matthew 12:9–14 and the rule that a rabbi was supposed to maintain his standpoint. If Jesus would escape their question—"Is it acceptable to heal on the Sabbath?"—he would disqualify himself as a reliable teacher. If he healed the man, they could increase their incriminating evidence. To be sure of their success, they chose a man with a withered hand, as Jesus had healed someone like him earlier in a synagogue. Jesus couldn't reasonably avoid healing the man. This was the way representatives of the Pharisees created their material to ruin him.

And the healed man? Did he have any notion of the game they played with him? Maybe he was grateful to the Pharisees that they brought him to Jesus. Of course there were many humane individuals (doves) among the Pharisees, but because of that, it was easy for the hawks among them to work without being disturbed. They mingled among the many who followed Jesus and wrote their stories (Luke 1:1). They also did, and they prepared Jesus's fall.[265]

Matthew has the last report of picking corn on the Sabbath, probably because it contains Jesus's longer teaching about the

---

[264] In Jewish jurisprudence, it was a task for the judges to determine the intention of a transgressor. "The man (manslayer) did not deserve to die, since he was not at enmity with his neighbour in time past" (Deuteronomy 19:9). In case of accidental transgression, the accused could get off after bringing an offering (Leviticus 4–5).

[265] Comp. John 15:20. "If they persecuted me, they will persecute you; if they kept my word, they will keep yours also."

subject. And so he chose the cure of a withered hand automatically for the later report. Luke's reports received some editorial improvements in comparison with Mark's. Luke's report lacks the statement about Abiathar, which presumed more knowledge of Israel's history among the readers. As a result, Luke's report was more suitable as a public record.

9.5 From Levi to Matthew

Matthew 9:9–17, Mark 2:13–22, Luke 5:27–39
One of Jesus's first disciples was Levi, the tax collector. It is generally accepted that Levi and Matthew are the same person and also that he was the author of the Gospel in that name.[266] In the synoptic Gospels we read three stories of his calling (see overview look-alikes, section 8.4: a. p. 5; 25). Most interpreters hold that these stories refer to one calling. It is one of the misrepresentations that pursues Christianity— that disciples needed only one calling and, obedient as they were, they immediately followed Jesus. Of course, that is completely beside the truth, and the stories of Levi's callings are conclusive proof of that.

The similarities of the stories are many. Jesus passed the customs house; Levi (Matthew) was sitting there. Jesus noticed him and called, "Follow me!" Levi rose, left everything, and followed. In all cases, we read about a reception in Levi's house with many colleagues, sinners, Jesus, and his disciples. This state of affairs was a horrible thing for the Pharisees, and they posed the question of why Jesus ate with sinners. Thereafter, the question was why they didn't have their fasting, like the Pharisees and the disciples of John the Baptist. In all cases, Jesus answers with the same metaphors.

Looking at the many similarities, it is easy to suppose that the same occurrence is related in three different versions. However, the report in Matthew is much later than in Mark and Luke. The earlier placements in Mark and Luke support an identical occurrence (anchor point). And so, a second call took place later on, of which Matthew's Gospel reports.

How is it possible that we are dealing with two calls? Theologically,

---

[266] Matthew 10:3.

there is no obstacle for that. Peter and John apparently did not give up their boats and their professions after their first call, as we read later on that Jesus regularly made use of their boats.[267] It is a real possibility that Levi followed Jesus after the first call, but he did not immediately leave his profession as tax collector, so that Jesus could repeat his call at a later stage.

In each report, it is said that Levi (Matthew) arose and followed the Lord. However, he did not *immediately* do so, as in all cases an and-sentence followed the call. Before he went with Jesus, he gave orders to his servants to prepare a banquet at his house that night. However, Levi was not so strict in his religious duties—or more accurately, he neglected them.

The days of fasting for the Pharisees and the disciples of John the Baptist were on Monday and Thursday.[268] Usually, one skipped the dinner meal, though it was not a prescribed duty of the Torah. Only in a week with a wedding was one released from the obligation of fasting.

In Mark 2:18, it is said explicitly that it was a day of fasting. It is not clear whether it was a Monday or a Thursday. The banquet was in the courtyard, as houses were for sleeping at night; daily life occurred outside the houses. Of course, the sound of revelry could be heard in the neighborhood of that silent, fasting evening. The whole situation cried out for problems, and the reaction was bound to come: "Why does he eat with tax collectors and sinners?" Who are meant by these sinners? In the opinion of the Pharisees, certainly everyone who was eating at the banquet at that moment was a sinner. They made an exception for Jesus. "Why does he eat ... with sinners?" The fact that they did not reckon Jesus himself among the sinners made it possible for Jesus to answer, "Can you make wedding guests fast while the bridegroom is with them?" Thereafter, Jesus clarified his deviant behavior by comparing it with new garments and new wine. To repair old garments with new and to preserve new wine in old wineskins is not done.

The second call of Levi, who had received the name Matthew in the meanwhile, also took place on a day of fasting. That is clear from

---

[267] Matthew 4:19; Mark 1:17; Luke 5:10.
[268] TDNT IV, 929.

the words, "Why do we and the Pharisees fast?"[269] This second event happened shortly before the Mission of the Twelve. And of course the same tension developed outside the courtyard of Levi's house, where everybody heard the sound of a lively meal. The living pattern of these similar occurrences is, of course, the habit of fasting in the Jewish context, which Jesus put aside.

Matthew preferred the report of the second call. In it, he is named Matthew instead of Levi. A lot happened after the first call; he got a new name, with the meaning "Present of God." Instead of the disdained tax collector, he had become a special gift of God to the people. This name expressed the change that Levi had undergone and why he preferred to use the report with the new name. Probably he wanted his readers to look at him as he had learned to see himself—as a new creation in Christ.

The records of Mark and Luke are nearly parallel. Luke's public record has more stylistic reinforcements: a great feast, a large company of tax collectors and others, the Pharisees murmured, fast often. Mark's remnant report includes aspects like these by repetition: many tax collectors and sinners, for there were many who followed him. Mark has "collectors and sinners" three times (15–16). Not the Pharisees but ordinary people ask him about fasting (without *murmured*, and without *often*).

9.6 Question of John the Baptist

Matthew 11:2–19, Luke 7:18–35
John was imprisoned in Herod's fortress, Macherus, in the desert, east of the Dead Sea.[270] This location was not far from the place where he

---

[269] Matthew 9:14.

[270] About John the Baptist: "Accordingly he was sent a prisoner, out of Herod's suspicious temper, to Macherus, the castle I before mentioned, and was there put to death. Now the Jews had an opinion that the destruction of his army was sent as a punishment upon Herod, and a mark of God's displeasure against him." Flavius Josephus, *Antiquities* 18:5.2, (transl. Whiston, *The Works of Josephus*, 484). The Arab king Aretas was the father of Herod's first wife. When Herod Antipas sent her away to marry Herodias, Aretas mobilized his army against his former son-in-law to humiliate him. He destroyed all Herod's army. And according to Josephus, many Jews saw

had baptized in the River Jordan. During his imprisonment, he had time to think about himself, Jesus, and their relationship. Luke says, "The disciples of John told him of all these things."[271] They certainly read public records about Jesus to him—The Young Man of Nain Restored to Life, Cure of the Centurion's Servant, Sermon in the Field, Choice of the Twelve, and maybe more. In these circumstances, John sent some disciples to Jesus with the question, "Are you he who is to come, or shall we look for another?"

In general, occurrences in the Gospels are presented in chronological order. How is it possible that John's question of Jesus as the Messiah is posed before the storm on the lake (Luke) and in Matthew, much later, after the Mission of the Twelve?[272]

Luke has, as a starting point, the moment of the departure of John's two disciples from the fortress Macherus, and he links their arrival to Jesus in Galilee to that directly. But between departure and arrival, at least one week of traveling (and normally two weeks) must be accounted for. Matthew has the question much later; he chose the moment of the arrival of John's messengers. Matthew writes (a word-for-word translation), "John *having heard* in prison about the deeds of the Christ, *having sent* his disciples, said to him 'Are you he who is to come, or shall we look for *a different one*?'"[273] It was not exceptional to send a second couple of messengers with a changed question or request (comp. Luke 7:6, the centurion's servant).

When comparing the answers of Jesus in Luke and Matthew, we see that the line of reasoning is equal; only the choice of words and the word order differ in some respects. This indicates that John sent at least two groups of messengers with nearly the same question.[274]

---

in this catastrophe as "the hand of God"—a punishment for his actions against John the Baptist.

[271] Luke 7:18.

[272] In 8.4, the overview of look-alikes: see 10, 11 and 27, 28.

[273] Matthew 11:2–3.

[274] "As they went away, Jesus began to speak" (Matthew 11:7). "When the messengers of John had gone, he began to speak" (Luke 7:24). There are slight differences between the speeches of Matthew and Luke that follow. But in both cases, a direct connection between the visit of the messengers and the speech about John is supposed (a. r. 4). That forces one to decide for two speeches and two groups of messengers. In the story of the cure of

The first question (in Luke) is, "Are you he who is to come, or shall we look for another?" In this question, it is not clear why John expects another Messiah. But in the second question (in Matthew)—"Are you he who is to come, or shall we look for *a different one?*"—he reveals his deeper feeling, that he had another type of Messiah in mind. According to the general conception of the Messiah, he probably had a spiritual *and* political leader in mind, but Jesus did not have political aspirations. The adjustment in John's second question shows his agonizing problem. Of course, the second question also was painful for Jesus to hear; maybe for that reason, John did not dare to give the first group this message. But later on, he decided that he had to know, and the second question was really important to him.

Jesus's answers are equal in reasoning; he refers to miracles and to the Gospel preached to the poor. And he gives the command to the messengers to tell John what they see and hear themselves. The similarity of the two answers shows perfectly that Jesus understood John's problem from the beginning, already when he heard the first question. Most important, of course, is that Jesus did not refer to himself (Yes, I am) in his answers but to his deeds. In doing so, he referred to the promise of the Messiah through Isaiah: "The deaf shall hear the words of a book ... the eyes of the blind shall see ... and the poor among men shall exult in the Holy One of Israel."[275] The books of the Old Testament, with the criteria of the Messiah, were Jesus's identification papers. John's problems were by no means solved with Jesus's answer. However, didn't Isaiah also prophesy concerning "liberty for captives" and "opening of the prison" in the era of the Messiah?[276] Of one thing, however, John could be sure: his work was not in vain, and the rest was in the hands of God.

To summarize, the couples of messengers left shortly after one another, and they arrived at Jesus shortly after each other, after the resurrection of Jairus's daughter. For in both answers, Jesus refers to the plural "dead are raised up" (i.e., the young man from Nain and Jairus's daughter). Jesus's expressions to the messengers are also

---

the centurion's servant, we also have seen that a second group of messengers was sent with an adjusted message.

[275] Isaiah 29:18–19 (35:5–6).

[276] Isaiah 61:1.

nearly the same, which indicate that they were spoken shortly after one another. The teaching record in Matthew is based on the adapted question about the *different one*. Obviously, this more searching question was of interest in a teaching record. And so the first question came in the public record that Luke used.

9.7 Two Women Standing Alone

Matthew 15:21–28, Mark 7:24–30
There are two moving stories in the Gospels about mothers who had daughters with mental illness (see look-alikes, section 8.4: 41, 42). When these women arrived at Jesus, seeking healing for their children, their husbands were painfully lacking. To all appearances, they left their wives, who were compelled to care for their disabled children by themselves. Undoubtedly, this was very difficult for them in a culture without any social care.

To add to the misfortune, Jesus refused—in a brutish way, according to our standards of good behavior—to heal their children. It happened outside the Jewish country north of Galilee. Jesus went there to be alone for some time, but he could not remain unnoticed. As Mark remarks, "Yet he could not be hid." Strangely enough, these women did not become discouraged; on the contrary, their faith flamed in their hearts. How could that be?

The chronology—very near in time—makes it easy to decide on two reports of one occasion, as is done traditionally. Both records deal with a girl with mental illness, the cry for help of the mother, her persistence, the seemingly unfeeling refusal of Jesus, and the motivation that it is not right to take the bread of the children and throw it to the dogs. In both stories, the women said that they only wanted to eat the crumbs under the table of the children. And at last, Jesus sent them away with a command for healing.

However, there are differences: (1) Matthew speaks about a Canaanite woman, while Mark about a Greek, a Syrophoenician by birth. The woman in Matthew is of Canaanite ancestors, while the woman in Mark is of Greek ancestors.[277] (2) In Matthew, Jesus honors

---

[277] It is often supposed that Greek here has the meaning of Greek-speaking, instead of Greek descent. However, this is so far from the normal meaning that it doesn't need discussion. It is a good example of how interpreters

the woman for her faith, while in Mark, he honors the woman for her word. Nevertheless, in spite of the dissimilarities, almost all the commentators hold that the same event is presented in these stories. According to our presuppositions, it is impossible to accept that point of view.

The culminating answer of the woman in Matthew (15:27) is introduced with a simple introduction (a. r. 1). "She said, 'Yes, Lord, yet even the dogs eat the crumbs that fall from their masters' table.'" She did not say more at that moment. The answer in Mark 7:29 is definitely not the same, and an insertion of it into Matthew is impossible: "Yes Lord; yet even the dogs under the table eat the children's crumbs." Moreover, it is clearly stated that the woman in Matthew is of Canaanite descent, while in Mark she is of Greek descent. Therefore the evidence is sufficient to show that we are dealing with two separate healings.

The question remains: How could it be that these events occurred precisely according to the same pattern? What is the living pattern of these stories? First, as in so many similar healing stories, a first occasion established the precedent and the model for action. In these cases, one quickly sees that the second woman immediately fell down without crying for help at a distance. That action remained without result in the first case, and therefore, the second woman omitted doing so. She understood perfectly that making personal contact with Jesus, in combination with perseverance, would not fail. Jesus, in turn, did not honor her for her faith but for the word she spoke. It contained the meaning of what her predecessor had said, and Jesus impressed upon her that this word would be the gate of mercy for her in the future. She had to stick with that word.

With the saying that the bread is for the children and not for the dogs, Jesus forced the women to accept that the Jewish people are the chosen people of God to bear his salvation to the world. "The salvation is from the Jews" (John 4:22), and their table of salvation is only for those who wholeheartedly accept that. These women did

---

deal with their embarrassment in their zeal for harmonizing. Greek descent (Mark 7:26) does not harmonize with Canaanite descent (Matthew 15:22); that's the point.

accept that and even contented themselves with a place under the table of salvation. For remaining health, they needed their hearts to be filled with the Word of God (second living pattern). Didn't Jesus teach his disciples, "When the unclean spirit has gone out of a man, he passes through waterless places seeking rest, but he finds none. Then he says, 'I will return to my house from which I came.' And when he comes he finds it empty, swept and put in order. Then he goes and brings with him seven other spirits more evil than himself, and they enter and dwell there; and the last state of that man becomes worse than the first"?[278] Jesus prepared the women and their children for a lasting healing; when they filled their hearts with God's Word, they became immune to spiritual disorder in the future, as evil spirits intensely dislike the Word of God.

Matthew has the teaching report of the first occurrence; he has the remark that Jesus "was sent only to the lost sheep of the house of Israel."[279] In Mark, this is missing. Mark has the typical and-sentences (five times, versus two in Matthew). There is no public record in the Gospel of Luke of one of these healings. This is in accordance with Matthew's remarks that "Jesus withdrew," and Mark said that he "would not have any one know it." This visit outside the borders of the Jewish country was a silent trip without publicity.

9.8 People with Money

Matthew 19:16–30, Mark 10:17–31, Luke 18:18–30
Within nearly the same period, some rich men approached Jesus with substantially the same question: "Teacher, what good deed must I do, to have eternal life?"[280] Strangely enough, the conversations have the same character.

- Jesus refers to God as the one who is good.
- Jesus's answer is, "Do the (ten) commandments and you will live."
- The answer of the man is that he observed the commandments always, from his youth (Mark and Luke).

---

[278] Matthew 12:43–45.
[279] Matthew 15:24.
[280] Matthew 19:16.

- The word of Jesus: "Go, sell what you possess and give to the poor,"[281]
- The man went away sorrowful, as he had great possessions.
- A closing conversation follows between Jesus and his disciples about riches.
- Peter takes the lead in this conversation, with the suggestion that they have left everything to follow Jesus, and what will be their reward?[282]

When we look at the stories of the rich men, we cannot avoid seeing the great similarities: in expressions and in content (line of reasoning), and the enclosures are strikingly identical in the same way.

The classical view is that we are dealing with three reports of one occasion. The famous and devout commentary on the Gospels by John Calvin (Harmony of the Gospels) took this position, and he has been followed until today by an army of commentators. The inescapable consequence of this position is that the sayings of Jesus have been altered when we compare the conversations in Matthew, Mark, and Luke. In the time of the Reformation, nobody saw this as a serious problem, as they had to deal with wars and persecutions. But now, in our time, Christianity is blamed again and again for the inconsistencies in its scriptures. That these inconsistencies are serious will be painfully seen from the next discussion.

The story of the rich young ruler has always been a cornerstone of the theory of the oral tradition preceding the Gospels, for it is undeniable that the parallel conversations are not exactly the same. Furthermore, it is even impossible to explain the dissimilarities by invoking the theory of translation from Aramaic into Greek, somewhere in the process of the oral tradition. When we count the small differences in Greek between the three conversations in Matthew, Mark, and Luke (with regard to the rich young ruler), we find at least thirty small dissimilarities. And in the closing conversations about richness, we find around forty slight differences. Altogether, there are about seventy dissimilarities. But what is the ultimate conclusion of that phenomenon?

---

[281] Matthew 19:21.
[282] Overview of look-alikes: 65, 66, 67.

It's a conclusion that is seldom expressed nowadays by orthodox scholars, but N. B. Stonehouse did so, some decades earlier.

> It is obvious therefore that the evangelists are not concerned, at least not at all times, to report the *ipsissima verba* [Latin: the very own words] of Jesus. … Inasmuch as this point seems constantly to be overlooked or disregarded in the modern situation it may be well to stress again that orthodox expositors and defenders of the infallibility of Scripture have consistently made the point that infallibility is not properly understood if it is supposed that it carries with it the implication that the words of Jesus as reported in the gospels are necessarily the *ipsissima verba*. What is involved rather is that the Holy Spirit guided the human authors in such a way as to insure that their records give an accurate and trustworthy impression of the Lord's teachings.[283]

It is no coincidence that Stonehouse wrote these words in his commentary on the rich young ruler. But what must the conclusion of a student in theology be when he reads this? Or of any nonprofessionally educated Christian? I'm sorry to say that the inevitable conclusion is that we don't possess the actual words of the Lord in the Gospels. And that is simply unacceptable—psychologically, theologically, historically, and grammatically.

Psychologically. In reading Stonehouse's quote, above, don't we get the desperate feeling of Mary Magdalene, who cried out: "They have taken away my Lord, and *I do not know where they have laid Him*"?

Theologically. What can be the significance of the Gospels when what Jesus said is questionable? "Everyone then who hear *these words of mine* and does them, will be like a wise man who built his house upon the rock." Are there words to build upon, then? Maybe Jesus's ideas are left, but we cannot be certain of that either. Maybe it was only the enthusiastic ideas of the apostles who put these ideas into Jesus's mouth, years later. And what about that guidance of the Holy Spirit,

---

[283] Stonehouse, *Origins of the Synoptic Gospels*, 108–110.

about which N. B. Stonehouse spoke? In commentaries, usually the work of the Holy Spirit is not stressed, not even mentioned. Rather, the differences are stressed, and they are explained as products of the oral tradition without any reference to the Holy Spirit, even in orthodox works.

Historically. Isn't the church based on a monomania? If the apostles could lay their own words on Jesus's lips, they could also invent the resurrection as a happy ending. It is impossible to base one's faith on historical facts only, and it is much more impossible to base one's faith on a set of possible ideas. It is only possible to base one's faith on a relationship, and a relationship is based on true sayings, viz. of Jesus. Therefore, the apostles have given us the Gospels, in which more than six hundred times it is clearly stated, "Jesus said" or "Jesus answered and said." The apostles knew perfectly well the value of Jesus's own sayings.

Grammatically. In the first chapter of this book, the proper grammatical evidence was given for the right understanding of the prologues of the Gospel of Luke and of the first letter of John, together with the statement of Hebrews 2:3–4 about Jesus's writers. It has been demonstrated clearly that the traditional grammatical analyses of these texts are *wrong* and that better are needed. These passages underline the riches of the Gospels. We possess, indeed, the very own words of Jesus Christ, the *ipsissima verba.*

It is not the purpose of this book to blame scholars with different views. On the other hand, it is not acceptable to be forced, theologically, to continue with a scholarly and ecclesiastical inheritance that is not in line with grammar, nor with our true Christian inheritance of the Gospels. Therefore, let's return to the stories of the rich men and see how they form together a cornerstone for documentation exegesis.

It is impossible to explain the three stories as descriptions of one occasion. In each instance (Matthew, Mark, and Luke), the discourse between Jesus and the rich man is closed; that is, direct sequence of question and answer (a. r. 4). That makes it impossible to combine the discourses into one great conversation.

The narrative details also refer to three different events. Matthew speaks about a young man, and in Mark and Luke, the man says that he has observed the commandments from his youth onwards (Greek: *neotès*: youth). In these two cases, it is supposed that the speaker is not a young man anymore but an older man. Moreover, the rich man of Luke is "a ruler"; that means a person in authority. In Jewish culture, it was impossible to inherit authority; one could only acquire authority—especially in Jewish society—by experience of life. At the age of about forty, one could become a ruler. Therefore, the ruler in Luke was certainly not the young man of Matthew. The ruler in Luke did not kneel in front of Jesus; he could not do that due to his social position. Therefore, the ruler in Luke is not the rich man of Mark either, who was an older man and knelt before Jesus. Undoubtedly, we are dealing with three rich men. The rich young ruler never existed; he is a composite character of three different individuals.

The imperative form, "sell ... and give (distribute) to the poor," is an aorist form; a principle of acting is meant and not an immediate and complete application. In the course of time, the rich men should sell their property, which they did not use. That was the part of their possessions they were supposed to use for the benefit of the poor. Jesus's word included going home and making a start. This has been interpreted wrong, as if they had to go home and immediately sell all of their belongings. If this were the case, an imperative *present* would have been used. Jesus taught his disciples the same principle: "Sell your possessions and give alms."[284] None of the listeners arose to carry out this command immediately. John the Baptist had followed the same ethic: "He who has two coats, let him share with him who has none; and he who has food, let him do likewise."[285] Phrases such as "Sell all that you have" (Luke) and "Sell what you have" (Mark) mean sell what you *hold* and with which you do nothing.[286] For the rich men of these stories, that was a considerable amount; hearing this command they were very disappointed.

The men did not recognize this word of Jesus as gospel—good news—but as bad news. The life of a rich person at that time was not simple—no insurance, no police with modern criminal investigation departments. The rich had to organize nearly the complete protection of their properties against unreliable slaves,

---

[284] Luke 12:33.
[285] Luke 3:11.
[286] The Greek verb *echoo* has two basic meanings: to have, to hold.

corrupt servants, money-grubbing tax collectors, and plundering gangs. Nobody would lift a finger when a rich man was robbed. They had to organize a small army of "faithful" followers who were reliable, as long as they were paid. The relationships of the rich were nearly all monetary relationships. Jesus offered a personal relationship if they gave up their properties. If they would do so, their monetary relationships would come to an end. Only caring for their daily needs would remain; that was Jesus's liberation for them. They could take as much as they wanted to count for their daily needs, as Peter said to Ananias: "And after it was sold, was it not at your disposal?"[287]

The fact that the rich men came to Jesus at nearly the same time and at nearly the same place indicates that they had had contact with each other (living pattern). Living in the same region and belonging to the same social circle, they had met each other, and they had discussed the rabbi of Nazareth and his message about eternal life. That was an interesting point. Of course they knew that being a Jew did not guarantee eternal life. They knew enough co-nationals who were definitely unreliable. But what would be the condition for receiving eternal life? It couldn't be money; if so, they all possessed the life already. No, there had to be something else, but what? It was not difficult for them to agree on this point, and there they finished; they did not dare to admit that it was a serious question for each of them. If they had done so, they would have come to Jesus *together*. Their contact was not so open that they dared to share their deepest secrets; it was certainly part of their problem that they were unable to handle true personal relationships. However, their discussion revealed their basic need, and each one decided to arrange a meeting with Jesus. By questioning him, it was impossible to become socially incorrect. However, the answers they got were very disappointing to them. Maybe one or some followed Jesus's word later, after mature consideration, and experienced the blessing of it.

After each meeting with a rich man, Jesus started to teach about wealth and faith in God. Peter asked only once, "Lo, we have left everything and followed you. What then *shall we have*?" (Matthew 19:27). Then Jesus started to talk about their rewards (twelve thrones for his disciples). In Mark and Luke, Peter only stated, "We have left

---

[287] Acts 5:4.

everything and followed you." Peter already knew the answer; it was not necessary to ask about that again. He could confine himself to the statement only, to make it possible for Jesus to accomplish his teaching about the rewards of the Gospel. Maybe Peter liked to hear that, or he was concerned that others, who were not present during the other occasions should know that.

Matthew has the largest report. His teaching report with the issue "riches and belief in God" had the specific prophecy about the twelve thrones that the twelve disciples were to inherit. Luke's public record is the smallest one. It doesn't speak about the twelve thrones or about the astonishment of the disciples.[288] These things were not appropriate for the public at the time of the first reports being written. It was probably not only the twelve who were listening in Luke's story as Jesus spoke to "those who heard it" (Luke 18:26) and not specifically to the twelve, as in Matthew (19:23) and in Mark (10:23). Mark's report became the remnant record, as the remark of the twelve thrones for the closest disciples is lacking in it.

9.9 Parable of the Wicked Tenants

Matthew 21:33–41, Mark 12:1–9, Luke 20:9–16
In the last week before his Passion, Jesus remained in the open places around the temple regularly to teach the people. This was the environment and meeting place of the intelligentsia of Israel, and here all the knowledge of the Torah was concentrated. The temple was the religious and political center of Israel and of the Diaspora of the Jews outside Israel. Offerings were the daily rituals of the priests. The books of the Old Testament were preserved, studied, and copied, and the Jerusalem copies found their way to the synagogues all over the Roman Empire and beyond. The rabbis held their conversations with their students in the shady colonnades around the temple squares. Everything was focused on the God-given revelation to Israel in the books and the traditions.

It was risky for Jesus, who had never received rabbinic education, to teach his disciples and the people in this place. His teaching was aimed at the common man who hungered for spiritual and

---

[288] Matthew 19:25; Mark 10:24–25.

practical knowledge to serve the Lord God of Israel. Jesus was not interested in the elite of intelligent students who were busy with acute interpretations of the Law, irrespective of how important these might be in themselves. Jesus's presence in the temple squares was aimed differently, and critical reactions were bound to come.

In this setting, Jesus told the well-known parable of the wicked tenants three times.[289] Some tenants of a vineyard refused to pay tax to the landowner. They assaulted the servants who were sent by the landowner to receive the payment. At last the son of the landowner came to receive the tax, but the tenants killed him. In doing so, they supposed that they could inherit the vineyard, but that was a misconception: What would the landowner do after the murder of his son? The parable ended with this question. In the beginning, the listeners didn't understand the meaning of the story. It seemed to be about a labor dispute getting out of control, but through the repetitions of the narrative, the people came to understand the real significance. This was not simply an interesting story but harsh reality.

In current interpretations, the point of view is that the three variations of this parable are results of the oral tradition in combination with redaction activities of the Gospel writers about thirty to fifty years after the occurrence.[290]

During the oral tradition, step-by-step embellishments would have entered into the parable, which would show the course of history. That would have caused the existence of three variants of the parable. This supposition has brought far-reaching conclusions. First, these parables would not have been uttered by Jesus in the forms in which we possess them. Second, the parables would cover the period in which the Romans conquered the Jews and recaptured Jerusalem. What, then, would the owner of the vineyard do? Third— as an inevitable consequence—the parables got their final form in about AD 65–85, the period of war and oppression by the Romans.

---

[289] Overview of look-alikes: 76, 79, 80.

[290] Marshall, *The Gospel of Luke*, 726–727 assumed that Luke followed Mark by making alterations. "It seems possible, therefore, indeed probable, that we have here an authentic parable of Jesus which had obvious allegorical possibilities; *these were developed in the tradition* [italics pres. author], but in such a way that the genuine latent thrust of the parable was expressed more clearly for a Christian audience."

Finally, the Gospels in which these parables are related must have been written in about this period (AD 65–85).

These conclusions and, of course, their underlying suppositions are dramatically wrong. If these parables had reflected the Roman war of 70 AD and the oppression thereafter by the Romans, the vineyard would have been destroyed in the parable or at least some part of the vineyard, which is not the case. The parables, on the contrary, suggest continuance of the entire vineyard instead of destruction. In the same way, threatening war is not implied in the parables. The conclusion must be that the dating of the Gospels within AD 65–85 is a fabrication.

The parables show a future perspective of a limited group: "When the chief priests and the Pharisees heard his parables they perceived that he was speaking about them."[291] Jesus prophesied punishment of the religious leaders of his own generation. "Therefore I tell you, the Kingdom of God will be taken away from you and given to a nation producing the fruits of it."[292] The parable clearly says that these severe words were addressed to the men with whom Jesus stood face-to-face at that very moment, no more and no less. That "other nation," of course, never meant the Romans. Those pagans were certainly not "the God pleasing nation that brought spiritual fruits for the Lord."

The parables of the wicked tenants fit perfectly into the period of the Jewish Christian Church in Jerusalem, under the guidance of the twelve apostles, after the outpouring of the Holy Spirit. When Jesus spoke about another nation producing the fruits of the kingdom, he certainly followed the Old Testament metaphor of a righteous rest of the people of Israel,[293] not only the visible group of Jews who had recognized Jesus as the Messiah and who were baptized in the Jerusalem church but all those of Israel who longed to do God's will. "And they were all together in Solomon's Portico. None of the rest dared join them, but the people held them in high honor. And more than ever believers were added to the Lord, multitudes of both of men and women."[294] After Pentecost, the temple had become

---

[291] Matthew 21:45.

[292] Matthew 21:43.

[293] Isaiah 10:20–21, Jeremiah 23:1–4.

[294] Acts 5:12, 14.

the central meeting point of the Christians of Jerusalem, and the religious leaders recognized, "you have filled Jerusalem with your teaching."[295] With the parable of the wicked tenants, Jesus had in mind the offspring of the Jewish Church in Jerusalem a short time later, after the Passion and Pentecost. Then remains the question about the relationship between the three parables.

After Jesus's triumphal entry in Jerusalem, he caused a great commotion on the temple square. Jesus expelled the dealers from the open place before the temple, market vendors as well as money-changers (Matthew). And blind and lame people came to him to be healed. [296] That night Jesus left the city to return the next day.

This new day is fully described in the Gospels with all sorts of discussions, parables and riddles. Matthew says about the end of that day: "And no one was able to answer him a word, nor from that day did any one dare to ask him any more questions."[297] Mark and Luke also present discussions of the same day, as there are several short interruptions in Matthew's description.[298]

It all started when Jesus on his way to the city cursed a fig tree that morning, as it had no fruit. It seemed to be a sign of what he would find in the temple. When he arrived there he again found the market vendors and their customers active as the day before. Again he expelled the dealers from the temple square, who had settled there already early in the morning, as Mark tells us.[299] Time for the authorities (chief priests and elders) to establish a provisional inquiry and to approach Jesus with the question of why he acted in this way and from where his power of attorney came. "By what authority are you doing these things, and who gave you this authority?"[300] Standing face-to-face with the authorities, Jesus did not act slavishly at all. "I also will ask you a question; and if you tell me the answer, then I also will tell you by what authority I do these things. The baptism of John, whence was it? From heaven or from men?" Under the eyes of the public, the chief priests

---

[295] Acts 5:28.

[296] Matthew 21:12–14.

[297] Matthew 22:46.

[298] Mark 11:27–12:37 and Luke 20:1–21:4.

[299] Mark 11:15–18.

[300] Matthew 21:23, And-sentence reports interruption: the third cleansing of the temple according to Mark.

and the elders could not avoid answering, and when they said that they did not know the answer, Jesus started to teach them with parables. It looked as if he had forgotten the opening question of the priests and the elders, but certainly he had not. He had turned the situation into his profit and started to influence his listeners.

The priests and the elders were offered the possibility of recovering from their ignorance before the public. He told them two riddle parables, to which they were supposed to reply after a final question. The last parable was that of the wicked tenants (the Matthew variant of the parable), and the question was, "When therefore the owner of the vineyard comes, what will he do with those tenants?" That was easy, the tenants had killed the son of the master of the vineyard, and the priests and the elders answered, "He will put those wretches to a miserable death, and let out the vineyard to other tenants who will give him the fruits in their season." A few moments later they discovered that they had judged themselves, and they became angry. They wanted to arrest Jesus instantly, but the multitude was too large, and therefore they decided to return to Jesus later on that day with a stronger delegation. At the end of the last parable, Jesus had blamed them as bad builders, they who were lawfully chosen as defenders of the temple and the traditions of Israel. Wasn't that blasphemy? And blasphemy meant death penalty. To challenge the owners of the temple and to question their authority might be enough to arrest Jesus. Later on that day, they would return, well prepared with scribes to document everything, and if Jesus would repeat his accusation for the second time, they had a point: they could take action for his arrest.

From the Gospel of Mark, we get the information that Jesus and his disciples "went out of the city when it was late." Mostly, one supposes that *late* means "in the late afternoon," and so it translates as, "When the evening came they went out of the city."[301] But according

---

[301] Matthew 22:46 shows convincingly that all the questions of Mark 11:27–12:37 belong to the day after the triumphal entry. The translations in Mark 11:19 (And when evening came they went out) and 11:20 (passed by in the morning) suggest a night in between. However, in 11:19, the Greek for *evening* is missing, and the translation is, "And late they went out." As the phrase "passed by in the morning" directly follows, it is clear that "late in the morning" is meant. The first meaning of the Greek *opse* is *late* (LSJ, Thayer, Bauer). The second meaning is late in the day.

to the context, the translation "late in the morning" would be better because they passed the fig tree, which was cursed that morning by Jesus on his way to the city. And now, leaving, still in the morning before noon, they saw the tree "withered away to its roots"[302] (Mark 12:20). During the heat of the hours around noon, the people also left the temple for the afternoon rest. Jesus went to the Mount of Olives at the east side of the city for the afternoon rest, where he also remained at night (Luke 21:37).

After the period of rest, Jesus and his disciples returned to the temple to teach the people.[303] The delegation of chief priests and elders also returned but now complete, as they were accompanied by scribes (Mark and Luke). Statements of a rabbi, once made, were binding, in contrast to the words of a disciple. A rabbi could not allow himself to give answers that contradicted former ones. It was quite easy for the weighty delegation to repeat the discussion of that morning. There was no other choice, as the full delegation had to hear what had happened early in the morning (living pattern: repetition in rabbinic teaching). They started immediately questioning Jesus's authority.[304] From there they came to Jesus counter-questioning about John the Baptist. The priests could not find a better answer than "We don't know."[305] And Jesus, therefore, had refused to answer their question. Would Jesus now put their authority up for debate or attack their authority? Yes, he did, but not in the way they had expected.

---

[302] Immediately after the curse, they saw features of desiccation (Matthew 21:20). It would be strange if Peter saw the complete withering of the fig tree—to its roots—the next day and not on the day of the curse. when they came back from Jerusalem. That would mean that he did not see a great change when they passed the tree later, coming from Jerusalem. It is therefore more realistic that Peter would draw Jesus's attention to the tree later that same morning of the curse (Mark 11:20).

[303] Mark 11:27; Luke 20:1.

[304] First Mark 11:28–30, the first challenge in the form of a question. Thereafter Luke 20:2–4 now, impatiently, in the form of a command: "Say us."

[305] The sayings in the conversation within the delegation are introduced with plural introductions (a. r. 3).

Instead of telling them the parable of the wicked tenants, Jesus turned to the people and started to loudly tell *them* the story over the heads of the authorities—the short variation of Luke.[306] And arriving at the quote from scripture, he finished with the harsh statement that this stone will "crush any one" on whom it falls. This was a relentless warning that all authority is from God, and therefore nobody will automatically keep a once-received authority. With this absolute statement, Jesus imposed silence on the delegation; any discussion had become impossible between them.

Because of the silence, Jesus started to tell the parable in Mark's variation (living pattern: repeated teaching) with a lot of additions (Mark 12:1-11). The hedge around the vineyard was the strong wall around Jerusalem. The wine press was certainly the central point in Jerusalem, the altar where the offerings were pledged. The tower to look over the vineyard was the white temple with golden roof on Mount Sion and was visible from every spot in town. All these features were missing in Luke's variation, which Jesus spoke to the people earlier, but when he turned to the delegation of the temple representatives, he added these aspects, and they could not miss the point that the parable meant them and no one else. These details could have brought feelings of acknowledgement and contrition, but that did not happen. Only the confrontation remained.

It is understandable that Jesus's stenographers used the first parable of that morning for a teaching report (the Matthew variation). During the narration, an open opportunity for teaching existed. The conflict between Jesus and the delegates developed openly in the afternoon.[307] The writers used the parable to the people for a public record, which Luke later used in his Gospel. Mark used the remnant record; that means it contained the last version of the parable that was left over and spoken to the opponents.

---

[306] Luke 20:9 succession (a. r. 4). "{And} he began to tell the people this parable."
[307] Matthew 21:45.

9.10.1 Doves and Hawks

In chapter 8, we summed up the most frequent causes for repetition in Jesus's ministry:

1. Healing as a precedent to be followed
2. Rabbinic teaching by repetition
3. Similar questions among the people
4. Repeated accusations
5. Repeated manifestations (positive and negative)

These were living patterns that the Gospel writers did not take great pains to explain, as they belonged most normally to everyday life. A lot of examples are already given in this chapter to show the relevance of this state of affairs. Only the manipulating activities of Jesus's opponents—some of which we have seen—are still to be demonstrated.

From the beginning of Jesus's ministry, he stood under control of the religious power that worked from Jerusalem all over the country.[308] Many times the hawks among the Pharisees had tried to collect evidence against him or even create that evidence. However, much material was arbitrary. What about healings on the Sabbath? For them, it was working on the day of rest, a trespass. But Jesus defended himself with this objection: When your donkey is thirsty on the Sabbath, you unbind it to lead it to the well, and you blame me as I unbind this man or woman from his or her illness on the Sabbath?

Then there were his claims of his divine origin, although he himself did not use that in his teaching. He always spoke about himself as the Son of Man. It was usually others who called him the Messiah. Even his nearest disciples did not use that title for him. It would be difficult, therefore, to accuse him of teaching the people wrongly, against Jewish theology. Nevertheless, Jesus did not fit into Jewish life. His forgiving of all sorts of people he had never met was completely out of order. Wasn't it up to God to forgive people? And Jesus's attacks on the Jewish religious traditions hit hard. In Jerusalem, he did not submit to the highest religious authorities of the temple. No, there could be but one conclusion for those who

---

[308] Mark 3:22. After the death of John the Baptist: Mark 7:1, Matthew 15:1.

were in power. Jesus was strange and dangerous; something had to be done. But what?

In a conflict, opposing parties try to find the weak spots in the defense of the other side. Manipulation and conflict are then the lines of action. The large religious parties that worked in and around the temple were priests, Pharisees and Sadducees. Dominant personalities as well as moderate-minded persons belonged to each group—hawks and doves. Jesus did not blame every Pharisee. Sometimes he would accept invitations to eat with them. It is therefore historically unjust to speak curtly about the bad Pharisees and Sadducees. It was the Pharisees who saved Judaism after the destruction of the temple in AD 70. Because of their peaceable mentality, they received permission from the Romans to study the law in Jamnia and to give guidance to the Jewish people. They were the preservers of the temple text of the Old Testament.[309] Yet Jesus had to blame them as a group repeatedly because of severely wrong presuppositions they cherished in matters of tradition, which were man-made instead of God-given and which formed real obstacles to serving God wholeheartedly. It was the hawks that gave direction to each party. We would call them fundamentalists, as they were ready to impose their traditions and opinions unconditionally on everyone else, and they did not shrink from harsh measures.

---

[309] The term "temple text" is used for the text of the Old Testament books that were preserved in the temple from Ezra onward. In theology, it is accepted custom to constitute a history of the text of the Old Testament, based on an evolutionary process, with the final result as the Masoretic text. However, all the supposed constituting texts represent vulgar text forms outside the second temple. It is historically undeniable that in the second temple, a temple text existed. The Pharisees had that text form at their disposal in the form of three copies used to correct texts with copy errors. The majority (two) of the three was seen as the correct reading. This text form at last has been preserved in the Masoretic text form (St. Petersburg Codex and Aleppo Codex, with minuscule differences) on which all current translations of the Old Testament rely.

9.10.2 The Sign of Jonah

Matthew 12:38–42, Matthew 16:1–4, Mark 8:11–12, Luke 11:29–30
Jesus repeatedly compared himself with the prophet Jonah.[310] We
have to deal with four descriptions, and the occasions of Matthew 16
and Mark 8 may be identical.

What might be the importance of the repeated question to Jesus
to show a sign from heaven, a miracle? And what was the importance
of Jesus's referring constantly to the prophet Jonah? The Pharisees
argued as follows: Moses had shown himself as a prophet before
Pharaoh by two signs. His stick could change into a snake, and his
hand could get the illness of leprosy. And as they argued, Jesus also
had to show signs to convince them, as evidence that he was a real
prophet. No signs, no prophet! A religious court in a rigid, religious
environment could use this as an argument to punish Jesus, maybe
with the death penalty, as this was the punishment for false prophecy.
But there was more—if Jesus would do a sign in response to their
challenge, he would affirm himself to be a prophet. And wasn't that
blasphemy to put yourself on the level of an Old Testament prophet?
In other words, there were several dangerous traps for Jesus within
this single question.

Jesus's answer demonstrated that they used a false superficial
trick. Indeed, Moses had given the two signs before the people.[311]
But in the later tradition of prophecy in Israel, the word of a prophet
could be enough without a sign. As the word was spoken from God, it
possessed spiritual and moral power, and it had to be in accordance
with God's revelation in the past. In his answer, Jesus referred to the
prophet Jonah, as in spite of the great signs ascribed to this prophet,
the people of Nineveh did repent due to his message, *without seeing
any miracle.* That was Jesus's evidence that the word of a prophet
should be enough without a sign. Jesus simply proved that their
question was wrong, and so he bypassed the underlying threats. The
Pharisees tried to collect incriminating material against Jesus again
and again (living pattern), while Jesus, with the same frequency,
disproved their arguments as unscriptural and manipulating.

---

[310] Overview look-alikes 34, 43, 58 (section 8.4).
[311] Exodus 4:30.

Matthew has two longer reports about Jonah—one a teaching report with references to several signs of Jonah and with a prophecy that Jesus will be three days in a sepulcher, as Jonah was three days in a sea monster (12:38–42). The other report was with the teaching of signs in the sky that make the prediction of a change of weather possible (16:1–4), but why then couldn't they recognize the time in which they lived? It is clear that Matthew, with his Gospel for teaching, focused on Jesus as the Messiah, the era of the Messiah, and the resurrection of the Messiah. Luke has a shorter report about Jonah, but his material also shows that the public was informed by Jesus about his conflict with the Pharisees concerning signs. Remarkably, Jesus finished it with a reference to himself: "And behold, something greater than Jonah is here." Mark's variation shows that the example of Jonah could be used briefly in a one-liner.

9.10.3 Paying Taxes

Matthew 22:15–22, Mark 12:13–17, Luke 20:20–26
Why was Jesus approached three times with the question of whether it was lawful to pay taxes to Caesar? Wasn't it enough to hear his answer only once?

There were two parties in Israel who had many convictions in common, but differed in one point of view—paying taxes to Caesar. The Pharisees and the Zealots were at "daggers drawn" over the tax question. In the year AD 6, Judas the Galilean mobilized many people who refused to pay tax to the Romans.[312] These zealots argued on religious grounds that it was forbidden to pay taxes to the Romans, for in that case they were not free Jews anymore but slaves. Many zealots had been crucified, but the movement was still alive in Jesus's time, especially in Galilee.

The Pharisees of Jerusalem, who were confronted with a multitude of Galileans in Jerusalem because Easter was near, probably felt unhappy with so many suspicious persons from Galilee around, and they supposed that Jesus, being a Galilean, would teach the people to refuse to pay taxes. Maybe they had heard that there were zealots among his disciples (Simon the Zealot—Matthew 10:4).[313] They decided

---

[312] Acts 5:37.

[313] In older translations, Simon the Cananaean.

to trap Jesus using this issue "as to deliver him up to the authority and jurisdiction of the governor."[314] If he had the zealot point of view, they had the possibility of arresting him as a rebel. If he rejected this standpoint, they had discredited him with the people from Galilee.

According to Matthew, the Pharisees sent their disciples to Jesus to question him.[315] In Mark they are simply called Pharisees, and in Luke, spies. They looked very much like innocent young people who wanted to debate about an issue they were discussing together. These students were doves, but behind them were the hawks, waiting for their booty. In the synoptic Gospels, we have three different conversations on the subject. The rules for analytical reading demonstrate that the conversations are without interruptions, and it is not possible to combine the sayings into one greater discourse. In other words, the Pharisees had chosen to take the offensive and sent several different groups of disciples to Jesus with the same question. If Jesus gave a negative answer three times, legally there couldn't be a misunderstanding about his teaching.[316] If he taught that it was permitted to not pay taxes, he was certainly subject to arrest as a revolutionist. With the three groups of disciples, the hawks among the Pharisees were creating incriminating evidence (living pattern).

Jesus understood that it was arranged; it was theater. However, the Gospels do not inform us how he knew. Jesus's well-known answer was a counter-question: "Show me a coin. Whose likeness and inscription has it?" When they answered that it was Caesar's, Jesus said, "Then render to Caesar the things that are Caesar's, and to God the things that are God's." The Pharisees' intention with this attack was to receive evidence to bring Jesus before a Roman court, but it failed. The most simple-minded person could understand that he underlined the law to pay taxes. He did not lose but won the goodwill of the people, as simplicity is the hallmark of truth. Of course, many have understood the deeper message of Jesus, which is still applicable—his encouragement to his hearers to give themselves to God because they bear the image of God, as the coin bears the image of Caesar.

---

[314] Luke 20:20.

[315] Matthew 22:16.

[316] "Only on the evidence of two witnesses, or of three witnesses, shall a charge be sustained" (Deuteronomy 19:15). Also for death penalty, Deuteronomy 17:6.

9.10.4 Resurrection

Matthew 22:23–33, Mark 12:18–27, Luke 20:27–40

There are three reports in which the Sadducees put a question to Jesus about the issue of resurrection. According to the rules for analytical reading, it is impossible to combine these conversations into one long discourse; we have to consider three different conversations between Jesus and the Sadducees. The theology of the Sadducees differed greatly from that of the Pharisees, as they did not accept the existence of eternal life—life after death.

At the very start of Jesus's ministry, the Pharisees and Sadducees already had worked together to undermine Jesus's work.[317] Their unanimity was striking, as the differences between them were many and important. The Sadducees belonged to the upper class, while the Pharisees were held in great respect in the middle class of society. The Sadducees rejected eternal life in contrast to the Pharisees, who believed in it strongly. Paul once cleverly made use of their disagreement on this point. In a meeting with the Pharisees and Sadducees, he arose and declared loudly that he was being accused because of his belief in eternal life.[318] The result was a violent brawl between the two parties, and the Pharisees even started to defend him. In their rejection of Jesus, however, the two groups were surprisingly unanimous.

After the offense of the Pharisees about taxes for Caesar, the Sadducees also tried to trap Jesus. They came with a theological question, and indeed they could not use it as a threat for a death penalty, but they considered it to be an efficient means to discredit Jesus as a religious leader. Central in Jesus's teaching was eternal life. They must have supposed that if they could weaken his teaching in this respect, Jesus's popularity certainly would come to an end. In their case, they also needed several answers from Jesus to establish his view, and so several delegations approached him with the same riddle parable (living pattern). The Sadducees had a standard example by which it was proven beyond doubt— according to them—that resurrection did not exist. There were seven brothers. The oldest had married but he died. According

---

[317] Matthew 16:1, 6.
[318] Acts 23:6–9.

to the law of Moses, the second brother married the widow, but he also died. And so all the brothers had her as their wife, each after the death of an older brother. None of them had a child with her. And the question the Sadducees posed was this: "In the resurrection, whose wife will she be?" It seemed an insoluble problem, and therefore the Sadducees claimed resurrection was impossible. What would Jesus say?

He made short work of it. In the first place, there are no weddings in heaven, no marriages. People do not marry there; they are as angels in heaven. Second, according to the scriptures, the Israelites believe in the God of Abraham, Isaac, and Jacob. As God is not a God of the dead but of the living, Abraham, Isaac, and Jacob are living in God's presence. So there is resurrection. Jesus's refutation was short and powerful. Three times this riddle came up to him, and three times he replied in the same way. The Sadducees felt certain that they were disproved, as the Pharisees earlier had experienced.

Matthew, Mark, and Luke remark that shortly thereafter, nobody dared to pose questions to Jesus. He had demonstrated painfully that he mastered both the Pharisees and the Sadducees.[319] For Matthew, who preserved the teaching records, this was also an important moment. "And when the crowd heard it, they were astonished at his teaching."[320] In Matthew's concept, Jesus's teaching was not intended only for the closest disciples but also for the crowd. Matthew has the same sentence in the beginning of his Gospel after the Sermon on the Mount (Matthew 7:28). Matthew's teaching records contain lessons not only for the closest disciples but also for the crowds, universally. In these cases, we see hardly any difference between the reports of Matthew and Luke.

---

[319] Matthew 22:46; Mark 12:34; Luke 20:40.
[320] Matthew 23:33.

9.11 Documentation Exegesis

The many passages of the synoptic Gospels here discussed show that documentation exegesis is a viable means of Gospel interpretation. We have presented the tools that are to be used in this field of work and how useful they are:

1. Rules for analytical reading
2. Discrimination of descriptions that refer to one or several events
3. Living patterns as explanations for repeated events

Enough material has been brought forward to show that there is an alternative to form-critical exegesis, dominated by the theory of the oral tradition. Details and dissimilarities are much better explained as real observations of speedy writers and stenographers, than as embellishments or transformations due to a so–called oral tradition or form history. Documentation exegesis directly reflects the work of Jesus's writers. There is no need for the so-called search for the authentic sayings of Jesus. We possess them already.

Part IV

Documentation and Canon

10. The Gospels and the New Testament Canon

After a thorough study of the origins of the Gospels in the previous chapters, we will now focus on the relationship between the Gospels and the canon of the New Testament. The twenty-seven books of the New Testament together form the canon, and from the outset, the four Gospels have always been the first of these books. At the end of the second century AD, the Gospels were unquestioned as scripture and were accepted as the undeniable gift of the apostles. A presentation of the history of the canon usually incorporates the question of how the canon came into being.

Generally, Paul's letters are considered to be the first writings of the New Testament. Subsequently, all the other books were added, as one supposes, until the list of twenty-seven books was completed. According to the documentation theory, however, the four Gospels— not the letters of Paul—are the first writings of the Christians. This is meaningful with regard to a discussion about the canon of the New Testament.

10.1 Ellipse or Straight Line?

Discovering the origin of the canon often begins with the question, "How can we be sure that the twenty-seven books of the New Testament were really written by those who usually are named as the authors?" Or "Are the names mentioned above the books really those of the authors?" These are serious canon questions. The issue of the canon is a penetrating one, as may be illustrated in a quote by Bible scholar John Wenham: "There is, then, no absolute proof that our canon is precisely the true canon, and no absolute proof that any one word of the text is precisely as God gave it."[321] This is not a statement from a cynical theologian but a concerned evangelical theologian who draws his serious conclusion according to present orthodox theological knowledge. Therefore, this statement is not

---

[321] John Wenham, *Christ and The Bible* (Guildford: Eagle Inter Publishing Service, 1993), 192. In matters of faith, we don't need to speak in terms of absolute proof but rather in terms of unshakable trust and of an unshakable canon.

negative; rather, it's significant about the nature and magnitude of the problem with which we are faced.

The canon problem, as it is posed nowadays, looks like an ellipse. This geometric figure of a regular oval has two centers (foci) on the diameter, and these foci determine the form of the ellipse.[322] The resemblance is that the canon problem is focused on and moving around two main questions, which are insoluble. As the ellipse never reaches its centers, the canon problem, in its current form, turns around two main questions, without ever reaching the answers.

The first main question is this: How did these books come into being? In current liberal theology, we may suppose that the gospels were written when the apostles came to the end of their lives, and the people started to write down the apostolic remembrances in the Gospels. In the churches, they put names of apostles or other authoritative persons, such as Luke and Mark, above the books and started to use the books in the churches. According to this view, some letters of the New Testament also would have been written in the same way, rather than by the persons by whose names they are known. Of course, this model of origins is based on the theory of the oral tradition. In orthodox theology, one says that the apostles John and Matthew, as well as their helpers Mark and Luke, wrote their books after some decades or a lifetime of preaching. The idea is that in the preaching activity of the apostles words and expressions changed before they wrote the Gospels with all these changes. Also in this view, the oral tradition determined a final text, which would not represent the spoken word as contained in the Gospels.

The second main question is this: How did the Gospels receive authority in the church when they were published late, after the apostles had died or even after the disappearance of the apostles? The usual answer is that after a long canon history, which started with Marcion in about 150, the authority of the New Testament books was established in the fourth century, after a series of decisions in the church. In the third and the fourth centuries, the church would have come to the final decision after a long search. Liberal as well as orthodox theology follows the same path of reasoning, and the

---

[322] The definition is that the sum of the distances of each point on the oval to the centers (foci) is a constant.

problem is that nobody knows how the churches could establish the right decisions after so many years. Is the canon man-made or God-made? According to the liberal view, it is man-made.[323] That means it's possible—or better, probable—that wrong decisions were made. If so, it is not correct anymore to present the canon as the Word of God. According to the orthodox view, the canon is God-made. The books that were brought together had been accepted in the church already. However, this does not answer the included question of how anyone *knew* what the accepted books were. And so from both sides, the subject seems undecided, and we arrive again at John Wenham's quote: "There is, then, no absolute proof that our canon is precisely the true canon, and no absolute proof that any one word of the text is precisely as God gave it."

The two main questions with their answers are totally inadequate for the constitution of an authoritative canon. It is completely unsatisfactory that the first Christians would be so naïve that they (or the apostles themselves) began to write after decades or when the apostles were dying out. In the same way, it is not conceivable that they mentioned repeatedly in the Gospels "and he said," instead of "approximately he said." Adepts of the oral tradition theory regularly suppose that the faith of the first Christians was so great that they thought Jesus could have said so, and their great belief in Jesus would be the justification to write in the Gospels, "and he said." Or one refers to the phenomenon of pseudepigraphic books in classical times, and therefore it would not be a great disadvantage that the gospels were written quite late and that the names of apostles were used to give these books apostolic authority. All this reasoning does not take into account that faith in God is of a different kind. Faith requires that things are as it says. The books of the New Testament are necessarily of a totally different quality, as they are books of faith.

---

[323] Roman Catholic theology solves this problem with the idea that the Holy Spirit has always led the church and so the Church of Rome cannot be misled in accepting the right canon. We can agree with the first statement that the Holy Spirit has always led the church, but that doesn't necessarily mean that the Church of Rome did not make mistakes in the past. The guidance of the Holy Spirit is of such clarity that we are certainly able to understand how that guidance worked in relation to the canon for the whole church.

In the same way, the supposition that the Gospels and some other books of the New Testament didn't have authority right from the beginning, but received that authority after a long canon history is completely unsatisfactory. Can these books have any value for us if we are forced to believe that great value and authority were attached to them only after many centuries? If we are convinced in advance that the authority of these books is not authentic, then it is only interesting for historians to study these books. In that case, they can't serve a divine purpose anymore. We have to conclude that the two current scholarly starting points in matters of canonicity must lead to devastating results. The ellipse of the standard canon discussion will never reach its own centers, and the debate will circle around the questions forever without reaching the final answer as to how the canon of the New Testament is God's gift to humankind.

Fortunately, there are better presuppositions for the study of the canon. First, the books had their value and authority right at their appearance. Speedy writers and shorthand writers who followed Jesus were responsible for the reports in the Gospels. The apostles John and Matthew were the writers of their Gospels, while Luke and Mark worked under their supervision. The letters of the New Testament bear the names of the persons by whom they were written. Second, the churches never produced books but received the books from the apostles and their coworkers. With these two New Testament propositions, the geometric figure has been left in favor of the figure of a straight line. A clear-cut consideration on the canonicity of the New Testament is possible, as a straight line is defined by two fixed points.

10.2 The Canon Formula of the New Testament

Shortly after the outpouring of the Holy Spirit, Peter led the first church in Jerusalem. And already at this very beginning, the apostles started to teach the people as Jesus had taught them (Acts 2:42). They immediately used the reports provided by the speedy writers and shorthand writers in Jesus's ministry. Moreover, they decided to compile Gospel books out of these reports. An explosion of Gospel writing was the result, as the books were copied again and again for the growing church. As John states in the apostolic manifesto, "And we are writing this that our/your joy may be complete." As showed earlier, the complete joy that John mentions includes the joy of the hearers who became new creations in Christ ("your joy") by receiving written documents about the life of Jesus (Gospels). John speaks about the rule of their apostolic preaching. The apostolic preaching was always accompanied by reports out of Jesus's ministry. "We are writing"; the distribution of correct texts was a constant part of their apostolic task. The Gospels contain the best possible description of Jesus and his message.

Writing the Gospels was not the only part of their responsibility; conservation of the correct teaching in the churches also was the task of the apostles. The churches they and their coworkers founded used to read their books apart from the scriptures of the Old Testament. And so a process of conservation came into being. Each time when Christians came together, they read the books of the apostles. Books from other sources were excluded; non-apostolic books, no matter how spiritual they might be, were set aside. There was a strong conviction among the first Christians that they had to rely on God and his revelation. They needed the books in which God himself spoke—through Jesus (the books of the Gospels) or through the Holy Spirit (the apostolic letters).[324] The process of conservation that came into being may be put in a formula as follows:

$$S \rightarrow C$$

Selection gives conservation. The apostles gave the new churches their Gospel texts to read in the church. By doing so, the people conserved these texts, which were the authentic and normative books. In apostolic time, pseudonymous books already were appearing with the name of an apostle but not written by him. Paul said, "We beg you,

---

[324] A question is, why didn't the apostles in their letters quote from the Gospels, if these books existed already? And why did they quote so much from the Old Testament? The answer may be that the apostles didn't use Gospel material to support their own teachings, as they didn't want to subordinate Jesus's sayings to their words. They spoke through the Holy Spirit in their own words and used the Old Testament as teaching material in their letters because the prophets of old had spoken in the same way. Moreover, in the Jewish culture in which they operated, they underlined with their references how important the Jewish Bible (Old Testament) remained to them.

brethren, not to be quickly shaken in mind or excited, either by spirit or by word, or by *letter purporting to be from us.*"[325] The formula shows that these pseudonymous books and letters were rejected as long as the apostles lived to supervise the churches. The apostles formed the limiting condition in relation to the formula. Pseudo-apostolic books did not obtain a foothold in the churches as long as they lived. When an apostle or a coworker left the newly founded church, the formula also received the form:

$$C \rightarrow S$$

When the Christians came together, they read the books they had received from the apostles and their coworkers. And so the two forms of the formula can be represented as:

$$S \leftrightarrow C$$

The formula shows that the reading of the books in the churches formed a closed circuit. No book could enter into the system, and no book could disappear from it. A vast stock of apostolic books remained in each church. Reading books and letters from apostles meant that the letters of the apostles to other churches also were important to read.[326] That gave the final formula:

$$S \text{ (total)} \leftrightarrow C \text{ (total)}$$

At an early stage, churches started to accept books from each other, S (total). In all the churches that were founded by apostles,

---

[325] 2 Thessalonians 2:2.

[326] "Paul wrote to you according to the wisdom given him, speaking of this as he does in all his letters. There are some things in them hard to understand, which the ignorant and unstable twist to their own destruction, as they do the other scriptures" (2 Peter 3:15–16). It is generally accepted that Paul's letters existed in almost complete collections when Peter wrote this. In our concept that the Gospels were the first written books of the canon, we have to reckon in this passage of 2 Peter that a canon of four Gospels and collections of Paul's letters were generally known among the Christians.

books and letters were ready to be added. At least a hidden canon of the New Testament existed in the apostolic church, C (total).

Were the apostles blind to the final formula? These men, who were so concerned with the preaching of the Gospel, who were so adequate in their transmission of Jesus's teaching in script—were they blind to the final form of the formula? Of course not. They understood perfectly the value and importance of it. Who were the twelve appointed by the Lord to be his witnesses? Who were the men who were designated to supervise? All the answers to these questions point to the apostles as those who established the canon of the New Testament during their lifetimes. They could not allow the churches to change the stock of books after their departure.

10.3.1 Completion of the Apostolic Canon I

It has been brought forward frequently in this study that there was a great writing activity in the Roman Empire and especially among the Jewish people in the first century. Therefore the question is, how is it possible that the number of apostolic letters in the New Testament is so small?

It is easily conceivable that the twelve apostles wrote ordinary letters without bringing their apostolic authority into account and without reference to their apostolic calling. Undoubtedly, they were overwhelmed by the authority of Jesus Christ and did not have the desire to put forward their authority instead of his. If someone didn't want to submit to the words of Jesus, how could they suppose that he would submit to their words? Just around the fifties and sixties of the first century, they saw the need to determine some matters for the future. They followed the example of Paul, who had sent already several apostolic letters to the churches or to individuals with his directives for the future.

Also, for Paul, the written documents with the words of Jesus (Gospels) formed the standard for the Christian churches he founded. He called them "the sound words of our Lord Jesus Christ" that were available for the Christians, as he was their Messiah.[327] It can best be presented that Paul, at some critical moment, felt it necessary to

---

[327] 1 Timothy 6:3

write something to a church from this idea: you must know this and bring it into practice; otherwise, the Gospel I preached to you has lost its meaning. In such a case he brought his apostolic authority explicitly forward, either in the opening of his letter[328] or by stressing the importance of his words and the necessity of bringing them into practice.[329] His letters were written approximately in the fifties of the first century until about the year 63. Because of the importance of his letters, he required that the addressees should read them to all the saints and that they had to stick to the traditions as he had delivered them.[330] These directives presupposed the regular reading of his letters. And by that, the canon grew slowly.[331]

In his two letters, Peter clearly followed Paul's example. In the opening of the first letter, he says, "Peter, an apostle of Jesus Christ." And in the opening of the second letter he says, "Simon Peter, a servant and apostle of Jesus Christ." We know that these two letters from Peter are connected and that the second was written shortly after the first, because in the second, Peter says, "This is now the second letter that I have written to you, beloved, and in both of them I have aroused your sincere mind by way of reminder; that you should remember the predictions of the holy prophets and the commandments of the Lord and Savior through your apostles."[332] The canon that Peter is teaching is roughly the Old Testament (the holy prophets) and the Gospels (the commandments of the Lord and Savior). He also included the letters of Paul that were known at

---

[328] Ephesians 1:1; Romans 1:1.

[329] 1 Thessalonians 5:27; 2 Thessalonians 3:14.

[330] 1 Corinthians 11:2; 2 Thessalonians 2:15; 3:6.

[331] Paul did not invent the great theological issues in his letters; he merely found them in the Gospels and developed them e.g., Christ in creation: Col. 1:16 and John 1:3; dwelling of Christ in the believer: 2 Cor. 13:5 and John 17:11, 22, 26; necessity to accept Christ: Col. 2:6 and John 1:12; living in Christ: Rom. 6:11 and John 15:4, 7; law and grace: Rom. 6:14 and John 1:17; remaining significance of Israel: Rom. 3:1–2, 11:1, and Matthew 23:3, John 4:22; prophecies about the Messiah: Rom. 1:2–4 and John 5:39, Luke 24:27; divine nature of Christ: Phil. 2:9, Rom. 9:5 and John 1:1, 20:28; human nature of Christ: 1 Tim. 2:5 and John 1:14, and many others.

[332] 2 Peter 3:1–2. For the authenticity of 2 Peter, see Guthrie, *New Testament Introduction*, 847–848.

the time of writing his second letter, as he equated them with "the scriptures" a little bit further in his letter: "There are some things in them hard to understand, which the ignorant and unstable twist to their own destruction, as they do the other scriptures" (2 Peter 3:16).

In the second letter, Peter seriously took into account the probability of a quick death: "Since I know that the putting off of my body will be soon, as our Lord Jesus Christ showed me."[333] That means that these letters of Peter must be dated between the years 60 and 64, because Peter's death is placed commonly during the prosecution by Emperor Nero in 64.[334] The first letter was written during Peter's tour to the Christian churches in the northeast of Syria, on the east side of the River Euphrates; he speaks concerning these churches as "She who is at Babylon, who is likewise chosen, send you greetings."[335] Babylon is to be taken in a broad sense as the region of Mesopotamia.

Peter didn't aim to enumerate an exact list of books in 2 Peter 3:1–2 and 16, but he referred in general terms to the books that were already being read, and he reminded his readers to continue in that way. It is of great importance that Peter sent the two letters to the west coast of Asia Minor—Paul's old working field. Also churches in other areas of Turkey are mentioned: Pontus, Galatia, Cappadocia, and Bithynia. These churches must have been started by missionaries and

---

[333] 2 Peter 1:14.

[334] This happened as a result of the disastrous fire of Rome in 64, for which Nero accused the Christians. Two-thirds of the city was destroyed in the flames. The letter of Clemens Romanus (V) communicates that Peter and Paul perished through the persecution. "Through envy and jealousy the greatest and most righteous pillars [of the church] have been persecuted and put to death." The death of Peter and Paul must have been at the beginning of this persecution, as Clemens says that many were tortured after them (VI).

[335] 1 Peter 5:13. One frequently supposes that the city of Rome is mentioned with "Babylon." However, this is not obvious. The letters of Peter excel in clarity of thought and language. Metaphors, as in the Revelation of John, are practically absent. Therefore, there is no need to see Babylon as a metaphor for Rome. Babylon was the area where a large Jewish community lived since the Babylonian exile. It is not strange that early Christian churches already existed there at the time of the writing of 1 Peter (Acts 2:9).

coworkers of Paul, because Peter calls Silvanus, who was an employee of Paul, as a name that was well known among them.[336]

It seems that Peter, who didn't previously write apostolic letters to churches, temporarily took over Paul's work. Why didn't Peter send general letters to all Christian churches instead of only to those in Paul's missionary region? Paul was a prisoner for at least four years—at least two years in the Jewish country, followed by two years in Rome. During these years, the churches he had founded were without apostolic supervision. It seems that Peter filled that gap. The second letter appears especially dominated by the warning against false teachers. Apparently, they started to become manifest in that particular period.[337]

10.3.2 Completion of the Apostolic Canon II

The apostle John, in his first general letter, also warned against false teachers and pseudo-prophets,[338] just as Peter had done in his second letter. John, however, didn't write only to Paul's old working area; he wrote to all existing churches. That was new. In the opening words of his first letter, John refers immediately to the Gospels, which all the churches had received. "That which we have seen and heard, we proclaim to you from the source ... and we are writing this that our joy may be complete." Afterward, he turns quickly to the antichrists and pseudo-prophets who went out among the Christians. This letter may have been written in the fifties or the sixties of the first century.

The apostle John, however, also wrote to Paul's old working area. He wrote the Revelation to seven churches in the center of this region: Ephesus, Smyrna, Pergamum, Thyatira, Sardis, Philadelphia, and Laodicea.[339] The Revelation must also have been brought out within the sixties of the first century, in the period of the completion of the canon.[340] The temple still existed when John wrote Revelation.

---

[336] 1 Peter 5:12.

[337] 2 Peter 1:2.

[338] 1 John 2:18–24; 4:1–6.

[339] Revelation 1:4, 11.

[340] Revelation is traditionally dated ca. AD 95, but that is not necessarily right. Robinson, *Redating the New Testament*, 252 dated the book in the period AD 68–70 (albeit on different grounds than in our approach).

He got the task: "Rise and measure the temple of God and the altar and those who worship there, but do not measure the court outside the temple; leave that out, for it is given to the nations, and they will trample over the holy city for forty-two months."[341] It is clear that the temple in Jerusalem was still there. But John had to measure the temple; that means that the period of the second temple came to an end (comp. 2 Kings 21:13; Isaiah 34:11). This metaphor wouldn't be useful after the devastation of the temple. It speaks of a threat that is to be executed; as a matter of fact, the Revelation breathes the spirit of a turbulent time to come: "for the time is near" (1:3); "Now write what you see, what is and what is to take place hereafter" (1:19); "and I will show you what must take place after this"(4:1). The fall of Jerusalem indeed brought an enormous change for Jewry as well as for Christians. From that time onward, the Christians were persecuted, and the Jews were abused in the Roman Empire.

The canon received its form under the apostleship of John. Different from his Gospel and letters, in the opening of Revelation, John calls his name, and he defines his apostolic calling with appeal to his position as a reliable eyewitness of Jesus Christ (1:2). "His servant John, who bore witness to the word of God and to the testimony of Jesus Christ, even to all that he saw." This is striking, because in his other writings, he didn't make known his name within the text. His name is only mentioned in the authorizations above his Gospel and his letters. It seems that a change took place; in the Revelation, John gives his name explicitly in the text (1:1, 4, 9; 22:8). He claims apostolic authority as a witness of the Word of God and as an eyewitness of what he had seen of Jesus. In another way, we may also learn that John exercised apostolic authority. In the second and third letter he calls himself 'the Elder'. The anonymous and absolute use of this term[342] in these letters makes it clear that he exercised

---

[341] Revelation 11:1–2. Those who date Revelation in 95, after the fall of Jerusalem in 70, take these verses as referring to the church as the new temple of God: 3:12, 7:15. However, the context (mentioning the altar) is plain enough that the church can't be meant here but rather the temple of Jerusalem. That means that Revelation must be dated before AD 70.

[342] This terminology is from John Stott, *The Letters of John*, 44. "The use of the title tends to confirm the unique position of the person who held it." He concludes that this term indeed refers to John the apostle.

apostolic authority. That is perhaps the most important significance of these small letters.

Historically, the last book of the New Testament, which was also written by the year 70, is the letter of Jude. He introduces himself as the brother of James. It is generally accepted that the two brothers of Jesus are meant here: Jude and James.[343] In his letter, Jude speaks of "the faith which was once for all delivered to the saints" (3), and "remember beloved, the predictions of the apostles of our Lord Jesus Christ; they said to you" (17).[344] These expressions make clear that the apostolic era had come to an end at the time of its writing. Jude, the brother of the Lord, wrote a catholic letter, which he addressed to all Christians: "To those who are called, beloved in God the Father and kept for Jesus Christ" (1). He warned in the letter of false teachers who troubled the churches. If apostles had been alive, it would have been the duty of an apostle to write such a letter. Yet in a very special way, Jude submitted himself to apostolic authority, as nearly all the ideas in his letter are borrowed from the second letter of Peter. The false teachers of whom Peter had warned were everywhere in the churches when Jude wrote. The difference with Peter is that Jude wrote not specifically for the old working area of the apostle Paul but to all the churches.

It is reasonable to take Jude's letter as having been written still before the year 70. Jude uses two quotations from the authoritative sources that must have been lost with the devastation of the temple. The quotations are ascribed to Enoch and Michael, the archangel.[345] From the early church history onward, one has supposed that Jude cited the apocryphal book of Enoch and an unknown Jewish tradition about Michael, the archangel. From Origen (ca. 250) to Augustine (ca. 400), this is the unchallenged explanation. But is it correct?

---

[343] "Is not this the carpenter, the son of Mary and brother of James and Joses and Judas and Simon, and are not his sisters here with us?" (Mark 6:3).
[344] The letter of Jude has many similarities with 2 Peter. It has always been a problem as to whether Peter used Jude's letter, or vice versa. We follow that Jude used Peter's letter. Because of the many similarities, it is correct to take the same meaning in the expressions "remember, beloved, the predictions of the apostles" (Jude 17) and "remember the predictions of the holy prophets" (2 Peter 3:2). In other words, just as the prophets did not live anymore (2 Peter), the apostles also were not alive anymore (Jude).
[345] Jude 9, 14–15.

Did Jude really quote an apocryphal book? Wouldn't he be setting a very bad example if he summoned all the saints worldwide to stick to the words of the apostles (3, 17)? And was he the first to not do so? The apostles had repeatedly warned the faithful to keep the words of the prophets, the words of Jesus Christ, and the words of themselves. Undoubtedly, Jude was also fully aware of that, and it cannot be seriously thought that he quoted apocryphal traditions to teach the churches. Of course the question remains: What exactly did Jude quote?

Apart from the Law of Moses and the prophets, many songs were preserved in the temple from antiquity onward. Many of these songs did not belong to the book of Psalms. This tradition of hymns in the temple ran parallel with the holy books from times of old. David ordered the writing of a hymn in the "book of Jashar" (2 Samuel 1:18) to teach the people. This hymnbook descended from the time of Joshua (Joshua 10:13). The famous prayer of Moses (Psalms 90), which entered later in the book of Psalms, may have also belonged to the book of Jashar. The lament of Jeremiah for King Josia was very popular among the people of Israel, and it was written in another book of songs, named the *Book of Laments* (2 Chronicles 35:25). In spite of the fact that the singers in the temple made it a tradition to sing this song, it is missing in the biblical book Lamentations. After the exile, the singers resumed their work as from the time of David onward (Nehemiah 12:45, 46). That means an uninterrupted tradition of songs was kept alive in the second temple from the time of Moses. What is more logical than that Jude took quotations out of these prophetical songs, which were well known among the people and which were appropriate for his subject? Maybe Jesus himself also quoted from this tradition of songs with reference to the "Wisdom of God" (Luke 11:49).[346] Apparently that stream of classical songs was also used by the author of the apocryphal book Enoch. That doesn't mean, of course, that Jude cited that apocryphal book. The old song tradition, which was centered in the second temple, must have been lost with

---

[346] In Luke 24:44, Jesus uses the triplet "Law of Moses and the Prophets and the Psalms." The fact that he makes reference especially to the psalms is remarkable as the book of Psalms already belonged to the "prophets." It seems that Jesus referred to a much wider meaning of the psalms: the tradition of hymns together with the biblical book of Psalms.

the devastation of the temple. That means that soon after the fall of Jerusalem this prophetical tradition of hymns lost its authority. The Pharisees, who were responsible for the safeguarding of the Jewish traditions and institutions after 70, concentrated mainly on the pure text of the Torah and the prophets and on the education of the teachers (Mishnah), as they used to do before the devastation of the temple. They certainly are not to blame that they didn't consider the tradition of hymns as part of their responsibility, and so the tradition of hymns was compelled to disappear in the end. Concluding, then, we may say that Jude quoted hymns with prophetical authority before the year 70, and so he wrote his letter before that year.

The conclusion of the canon of the New Testament took place before the year 70. After a quick start with the compilation of the Gospels, a period followed in which mainly Paul wrote letters with apostolic authority. Generally speaking, we may say that the other apostles followed this example when they felt that directives were necessary during the time that they couldn't lead the churches anymore. John marked the end of this period with the writing of the Revelation. Finally, the canon was brought to completion with the letter of Jude. Within forty years, the New Testament received a fixed form under apostolic supervision. Jesus said, "And you shall be my witness in Jerusalem and in al Judea and Samaria and to the end of the earth."[347] With the canon of the New Testament, the apostles modeled a structure that made the fulfillment of this prophecy possible. And the fulfilling is still ongoing.

10.4 From Apostolic to Ecclesiastical Canon

The apostles were considered the authorities of the church as long as they lived. They were the reliable witnesses of Jesus's resurrection, of what he had done and said. Their letters were held in the same authority. After their departure, the question occurred as to what exactly the right books were for the church. Strangely enough, it was a long time before anyone found the answer. It is generally accepted that the end of a long canon history came with a letter from Bishop Athanasius of Alexandria (Egypt). Each year at Easter, he sent a letter

---

[347] Acts 1:8.

to his coworkers in his diocese to encourage them in their faith and service. In the letter of the year 367, he gave the list of the twenty-seven books of the New Testament and finished with these words: "These are the springs of salvation, so that someone who thirsts may be satisfied by the words they contain. In these books alone the teaching of piety is proclaimed. Let no one add or subtract anything from them."

It is remarkable that Athanasius, about three hundred years after the apostles, worked exactly according the canon formula:

> But inasmuch as we have mentioned that the heretics are dead but we have the Divine Scriptures for salvation, and I am afraid that, as Paul wrote to the Corinthians, a few of the simple folk might be led astray from sincerity and purity through human deceit and might then begin to read other books, the so-called apocrypha, deceived by their having the same names as the genuine books, I exhort you to bear with me if, to remind you, I write about things that you already know, on account of the church's need and advantage.[348]

It is clear that Athanasius distinguished between the true books, the divine scriptures and apocryphal books (i.e., of spurious, not apostolic, origin). These qualifications are particularly remarkable in combination with the accurate list of twenty-seven books. How did he know? That's the question. From where did Athanasius obtain his list? His bishop's town Alexandria was as important as Rome, according to an ecclesiastical decision.[349] He could not permit himself to make a stupid move. The eyes of the world were turned toward him.

For hundreds of years, discussions had blazed in the church concerning the question of the right books of the church. Of course, Athanasius knew of those discussions. He knew that in the second century, Marcion had established a canon of the Gospel of Luke and some letters of Paul and that it was rejected. He knew about Irenaeus

---

[348] Translation: E. L. Gallagher and J. D. Meade, *The Biblical Canon Lists from Early Christianity* (Oxford, University Press, 2017), 120–21.
[349] Canon 6 of the Council of Nicea.

and Tertullian, who used nearly all the books of the New Testament in the second century. And of course he knew the views of Christian scholars, such as Novatianus, Cyprianus, Origenes, and Eusebius, who worked in the third and fourth centuries. He knew the classifications used by these teachers to determine the books that should be read in the church. It had been a point of discussion in the Council of Nicea of 325, but no decision had been taken. Athanasius had experienced that council as a young servant of Alexander, who was at that time bishop of Alexandria. Again, from where did Athanasius obtain the list of twenty-seven books?

The answer to this question is not so difficult, if we look in the right direction. Scholars are usually focused on the history of the canon, and generally, the letter of Athanasius in the year 367 is seen as the end of that history. And so one supposes that the motive for his canon decision is found some time earlier, before the year 367. That is hard to deny. However, the key to understanding Athanasius's decision doesn't lie before but *after* the year 367.

Athanasius's decision had a great impact on the history of the church thereafter. In the year 382, Pope Damasus (Italy, France, and Spain) presented a list with the same books as canonical for the church (the books, however, were not in the same order as Athanasius's list). In 397, Bishop Augustine accepted the canon in Carthago (North Africa). And around the year 500, the canon of twenty-seven was also accepted in Syria, together with the Jewish country that was, at that time, a province of Syria.[350]

After Athanasius's decision for the canon, substantially the same canon was accepted in the other regions around the Mediterranean Sea, with one exception: Paul's old apostolic region, Turkey–Greece. In that area, no ecclesiastical decision is known concerning the canon in the history of the church. According to the canon formula, this

---

[350] In Syria, a slow process of acceptance of the canon started. It took years before the four Gospels were accepted, as the *Diatessaron of Tatian* (an anthology of Gospel stories) was very popular in the churches. The Peshitta, the Syriac version from about AD 400, contained only 22 books; without 2 and 3 John, 2 Peter, Jude, and Revelation (Wikenhauser, *Einleitung in das Neue Testament*, 86–87). The completion of this process for the Western Syrian Church came when Philoxenus translated the general epistles and Revelation in the year 508 (T. Zahn 1901, 62).

is completely reasonable. Under the guidance and authority of the apostles, a canon already had been established there in apostolic time, as it is impossible to hold the view that a canon could have been accepted in this area at a later time without an ecclesiastical discussion. And that is the answer to the question of where Athanasius obtained his canon. He had seen for many years how those twenty-seven books existed and functioned within the church in Greece and Turkey, across the Mediterranean Sea.[351]

As there is a lack of any ecclesiastical decision in Turkey–Greece for the canon of twenty-seven before and after Athanasius's decision in 367, no other conclusion is possible. Athanasius, bishop of Alexandria, simply presented the canon that was already in use for centuries on the other side of the Mediterranean Sea. The twenty-seven books were known in Egypt for a long time. Athanasius had only to draw the line where it should be. With his decision, he challenged the bishop of Rome to take a stand, because it had been determined at the Council of Nicea that the bishop of Alexandria controlled a diocese as important as the bishop of Rome. Fifteen years later (382), Pope Damasus confirmed Athanasius's decision with the acceptance of the canon of twenty-seven books, though not in the order of Athanasius.

Augustine had great influence on the decision for the canon in the northwest part of Africa. An ecclesiastical canon decision took place in Carthago in 397. In his book *De Doctrina Christiana*, he answered the question of how to find out which books were to be considered as canonical in the church. From that, it is clear that Augustine also worked accurately, according to the canon formula of the New Testament. He wrote,

> In the matter of canonical Scriptures he should follow the authority of the great majority of catholic churches worthy to have apostolic seats and receive apostolic letters. He will apply this principle to the canonical

---

[351] The importance of the region of Paul's missionary activity is also visible in the five ecumenical councils held in Asia Minor: Nicea (325), Constantinople (381), Ephesus (431), Chalcedon (451), and Constantinople (553).

> Scriptures: to prefer those accepted by all catholic churches to those which some do not accept.[352]

In Augustine's time, it was still possible to visit the cities mentioned in the Acts of the Apostles, which had been seats of an apostle—that means cities in which apostles had founded a church or to which they wrote their letters. In the Jewish land, the apostolic churches had disappeared after the wars in the years 66–70 and 132–135, or they had a severely interrupted history. So generally, the cities where Paul founded churches remained, according to Augustine's rule for finding the right canon. Those cities are mentioned in chapters 13–28 of the book of Acts. Augustine's rule refers, in fact, to the region where Paul had preached the Gospel: the region of Turkey–Greece. And so Augustine's testimony confirms the thesis that Athanasius accepted the canon of twenty-seven from the other side of the Mediterranean Sea. The canon question existed particularly outside of Paul's original work area. From the regions around the Mediterranean Sea, where for a long time obscurity existed concerning the canon (Syria, Egypt, North Africa, Spain, and Italy), pressure rose to reach a solid solution.

Before and after Athanasius's decision of 367, there were and have been church teachers who rejected some books of the New Testament canon. As long as a rule did not exist, or where the rule did not meet general acceptance already, they followed their own insights. Thus, the Revelation of John remained suspicious in the eyes of some scholars and was rejected by them—(practically) by Eusebius; Gregorius of Nazianze (ca. 380); Amphilocius of Iconium (ca. 390); Chrysostomus (ca. 400); and Theodor of Mopsuestia (ca. 415). The last two flourished in Constantinople. Teachers with derogatory opinions concerning the canon of twenty-seven usually received their theological training in cities where Paul had not founded a church: Antioch (Syria), Caesarea, and in Alexandria. These cities outside Paul's missionary activities had theological schools that were unfamiliar with the canon of twenty-seven and remained often loyal to their Antiochan, Caesarean, or Alexandrian school.

---

[352] *De Doctrina Christiana* II, 12. Translation: E. L. Gallagher and J. D. Meade, *The Biblical Canon Lists from Early Christianity* (Oxford, University Press, 2017), 226-27.

The canon formula is still important to come to solid evaluation of the past. Authors claim triumphantly that there never existed a canon in the apostolic period or that the decision of Athanasius had the simple aim of protecting the authority of a church establishment. Some prefer to quote old pseudepigraphic books with so-called "secret words of Jesus."[353] These books would have been found in the Gnostic library of Nag Hammadi (Egypt) in the twentieth century. And so it all has an appearance of academic authority. The canon of the New Testament, however, is the apostolic gift to the church, according to the apostolic manifesto, and therefore, it could not be erased from history.

10.5 Acts, James, the Pastoral Letters, and the Canon

The New Testament is a collection of books from the period of the thirties until the year 70 of the first century. The foundation of the canon was formed by the Gospels; the other apostolic writings were added slowly. The term *apostolic* is to be taken in a broad sense, not only written by apostles (the twelve) but also under their approval.[354] In addition to the books that were discussed in the previous section, some other books also have a particular place in the canon. It's about the Acts of the Apostles, the letter of James, and some controversial letters of Paul: 1 and 2 Timothy, Titus, and Hebrews.[355]

The importance of the Acts of the Apostles with regard to the canon is that the book functions as the link between the Gospels and the letters of Paul. With the knowledge of Acts, we are able to understand the historical setting of Paul's life, and we can understand his letters in that historical context. Peter's letters, which he wrote to Asia Minor during the long period of Paul's captivity, also get a logical place in that historical context through Acts. The book of Acts

---

[353] Books from a later date with the name of an apostle or coworker in the title (e.g., Gospel of Thomas).

[354] The term *apostle* in New Testament times was not limited to the circle of twelve. There were more apostles, but the twelve had the special task to be the reliable witnesses of Jesus's life, as they had seen it.

[355] The so-called letter of Paul to Laodicea (Colossians 4:16) will remain outside of consideration. The letter of Philemon may be meant by it. If so, *yourselves* (Colossians 4:9) is to be taken in a broad sense.

connects two periods, two missionary fields, two important apostles, and two types of Christians.

The beginning of Acts describes the first period of the church in Jerusalem and the Jewish country, where the inspiring character of Peter steps forward. The second part of Acts describes the period of Christianity in Turkey and Greece and even in Rome, with the thirteenth apostle, Paul, in the center of interest. In Acts, Christianity starts as a Jewish movement, which develops further in the book into a movement that is also for Gentiles. Approximately halfway through the book, the directives are formulated for the lifestyle of the non-Jewish Christians.[356] The book was written around the year 62, at the end of Paul's captivity in Rome, because this is the last that we read in the book about Paul.[357]

The book of Acts is an indispensable supplement to the Gospels, and it was never a disputed book in early church history. The author was Luke, although he doesn't mention his name in Acts. In the introduction, he shows clearly that he dovetails the Acts with the Gospel he had written earlier. Luke dedicated the Gospel (1:3) as well as the Acts (1:1) to Theophilus. The working method of collecting documents and copying them in sequence, as Luke did in his Gospel, was certainly the method he followed in Acts. The Acts of the Apostles describes the occurrences of the church in the same way as Luke had done in his gospel with the deeds and teachings of Jesus.

In the letter of James, the name of Jesus Christ occurs only two times. The letter deals mainly with a Christian lifestyle. The letter of James got sharp criticism from Martin Luther; he called it "a letter of straw," a letter of inferior quality and without evangelical character. In this letter, Luther missed the doctrine of justification through faith. D. J. Moo has rightly stated that "his criticism should not be overdrawn." And "He did not exclude James from the canon and, it has been estimated, cites over half the verses of James as authoritative in his writings."[358] However, Luther's opinion has given grounds to

---

[356] Acts 15:19–20; 21:25.

[357] Acts 28:30–31. If Paul had already died when Acts was written, certainly the author would have made it known at the end of the book.

[358] D. J. Moo, *The Letter of James, an Introduction and Commentary*. Tyndale New Testament Commentaries (Leicester, Grand Rapids: Inter-Varsity Press, W. B. Eerdmans, 1986), 18. For the quotations of James by Luther, Moo refers

reject the authenticity of the letter and many theologians doubt it's canonicity. But is there a serious reason for that decision.[359] Because this letter belongs to the canon, the name of the author belongs to the man who was known in the apostolic circle as James, without any further addition. In Paul's letter to the Galatians, we meet him as "the brother of the Lord" and simply as James.[360]

Little account is usually given to what it means that this letter was written by the brother of the Lord. A man is speaking who experienced Jesus as a brother over many years. Initially, Jesus's brothers did not believe in him.[361] But later a change took place, and they also believed in him as the Messiah.[362] So James was a person who could describe as no one else the perfect example of Jesus's way of acting in daily life. When James wrote his letter, he undoubtedly had this delicious example in mind. And reading this letter transparently, we see Jesus himself and how he acted in all sorts of everyday situations. It is moving how simplicity, humility, and releasing covetousness go together with a true knowledge of God. If anyone was equipped to present what it meant to follow in Jesus's footsteps, it was James.

The date of James's letter is not certain but probably is between AD 50 and 62.[363] In that period, Paul wrote his letters. As James wrote to "the twelve tribes of the Dispersion," he certainly wrote for the ears of Jewish Christians, which also is seen in 4:11, where he challenges his hearers to act as "doers of the law." That was the ideal of a pious Jewish lifestyle. Earlier, James uses the expression "doer of the word" (1:22). Which word does he mean? The word of truth

---

to D. Stoutenberg, *Martin Luther's Exegetical Use of the Epistle of St. James* (MA thesis, Trinity Evangelical Divinity School, Deerfield, Illinois, 1982), 51.

[359] There are about five possibilities for James: (1) apostle and brother of John (Mark 1:19); (2) apostle and son of Alphaeus (Mark 3:18); (3) the brother of Jesus (Mark 6:3); (4) James the younger (Mark 15:40); or (5) father of Judas, the apostle Thaddaeus (Luke 6:16, Mark 3:18). James, the brother of John, was martyred in the year 44 (Acts 12:2), and the letter of James seems to have been written much later. James, the brother of the Lord, was martyred in the year 62 (Flavius Josephus, *Antiquities* 20:9.1).

[360] Galatians 1:19 and 2:9.

[361] John 7:5.

[362] Acts 1:14.

[363] See Guthrie, *New Testament Introduction*, 764.

as the word of the Gospel that brought new life (1:18, 21). A doer of the word is someone who surrenders himself to that word of the Gospel to act according to it. In fact, just as Paul could apply *word* to the Old Testament as a personal Word of God, so did James. *Law* has an impersonal connotation and therefore can't bring faith or trust. James's point is that only by doing the word is it possible to be called a doer of the law. And so he is in line with Paul's use of these terms.[364]

As we learn from the life of Paul, the law kept its value, especially for Jewish Christians (Colossians 4:10–11). James met the Jewish ideal of being a doer of the law by giving the example of Jesus's humble and practical acting in everyday life; that was how Jesus fulfilled the law in relationship with his heavenly Father. That was the answer the Jewish Christians needed—to understand the importance of the law, as seen through the life of Jesus.

The pastoral letters, 1 and 2 Timothy and Titus, are in Paul's name. Moreover, in each of them the author starts with his name: Paul. Nevertheless, it is an often-heard assumption in theology that he was not the author of the letters. That would imply a serious canon problem. If these letters were not written by the apostle as they are said to be, then they do not deserve a place in the canon. Of course, many will reject that also, saying that in pseudepigraphic letters, God can speak to us, but that is not the point. The question is, will God do so? The answer must be negative, as God is the wellspring of truth and not of equivocations. And so with the pastoral letters, a canon question is at stake. Especially during the last two centuries, serious arguments have been brought forward against the Pauline authorship of the pastoral letters. The use of words and style differ from the other letters of Paul, the historical context does not seem to be correct, the theology seems rather moralistic, and the tight church organization would not be appropriate in the apostolic time.[365] But how appropriate are these judgments? How was it possible that pseudepigraphic letters could penetrate into the canon under the supervision of the apostles, when they already warned the churches against that phenomenon?[366]

---

[364] Comp. Paul's use of the terms law and word in Romans 13:8–9.

[365] For a complete discussion about the subject, see Guthrie, *New Testament Introduction*, 584–620.

[366] 2 Thessalonians 2:2.

How could it happen that while under the apostolic authority of Peter, John, and Jude, the canon was concluded in the sixties of the first century? In the following paragraph, a number of considerations will be presented that confirm the authenticity of these letters.

J. van Bruggen has convincingly shown that the pastoral letters fit perfectly into the life of Paul.[367] The first letter to Timothy and the letter to Titus are written at the end of Paul's third missionary journey. The second letter to Timothy was written in Rome, during Paul's imprisonment. This is meaningful for the contents of the letters, as Paul had worked daily as a teacher for two years in Ephesus in the hall of Tyrannus.[368] Moreover, he had been faced with all kinds of church problems—in Corinth, for example. During this time, Paul had developed into a teacher and church builder, as his use of words and style show. And of course, his style in the pastoral letters is much more personal as compared with that of his churchly letters. Therefore, the earlier mentioned issues (use of words, style, historical context, church organization) are not serious problems, as they fit into the developments of the church at the time of writing. In antiquity, nobody had problems with the differences in speech and style between the pastoral and the other letters of Paul. They always have been accepted as true Pauline letters. Today, this also is completely acceptable. Only through a complete misunderstanding of a flexible canon concept of the New Testament could this strange opinion about the pastoral letters arise in theology (for hundreds of years).

10.6 The Letter to the Hebrews and the Canon

Finally, we have to discuss the letter to the Hebrews. Its position in the canon and significance for the documentation theory are very important. In section 1.4, the key passage Hebrews 2:3–4 has been discussed.

Whereas questions about the authorship of the pastoral letters arose just in the last two centuries, the questions of authorship and canonicity of the letter to the Hebrews has a long history. In the early western church (Rome and the western part of the Mediterranean),

---

[367] J. van Bruggen, *Die Geschichtliche Einordnung der Pastoralbriefe* (Wuppertal: Brockhaus Verlag, 1981), 31–40, 48–58.

[368] Acts 19:9.

the letter was quite unknown in the first centuries. In the eastern part of the early church, the book had canonical status, as far as we know. There, the book was counted among the letters of Paul, but some doubted the Pauline authorship. The main reason probably was that the author did not put his name on the work, nor did he mention his name in it. Consequently, many possible authors have been proposed, from the past until now: Paul, Barnabas, Luke, Apollos, Silvanus, Philip, Priscilla, and Clement. Still famous about this subject is Origin's statement: "But who wrote the Epistle God only knows."

In the time of the Reformation, a new argument against the Pauline authorship arose. Hebrews 2:3 traditionally reads, "So great a salvation; which at the first began to be spoken by the Lord, *and* was confirmed unto us by them that heard him; God also bearing them witness, both with signs and wonders, and with divers miracles, and gifts of the Holy Ghost" (KJV). Luther supposed that this passage clearly showed that Paul could not have written this. He reasoned as follows: Paul did not receive salvation through those who heard the Lord ("by them that heard him"); on the contrary, Paul got salvation through the revelation of Jesus on his way to Damascus. The Gospel was not proclaimed to Paul by Jesus's hearers but revealed directly by divine mediation. And so, according to Luther, Hebrews 2:3–4 could not have been written by Paul. Men such as Erasmus and Calvin followed his rejection of Pauline authorship. Luther decided that Apollos was the best to designate as the possible writer of the letter to the Hebrews.

Nowadays, Luther's argument has met general agreement in the Protestant interpretation of the New Testament. As the name of a writer is lacking in the letter, no serious dogmatic objection seems to exist against this point of view. However, there is a serious exegetical objection against it, as the traditional translation of Hebrews 2:3–4 is not appropriate, as we have seen (section 1.4). The correct translation of this passage differs fundamentally, and by that the whole scene is changed: documentation. The author is saying that we need the words of the Lord just as they were written, just as he spoke them. That is the "great salvation." And of course Paul also needed these words, even after the revelation of the Lord to him. And so this passage is in no way an obstacle to taking Paul as the author of the letter to the Hebrews.

This letter has no opening in which the writer expresses who he is or in which he is greeting his addressees. This is significantly strange with regard to the other letters of the New Testament. Given the inclusion of this letter in the canon, it seems that it was an appendix or an accompanying letter with another apostolic letter, in which the writer had already made himself known. What letter could that be?

In the New Testament, we have letters of Peter, John, James, Jude, and Paul. Peter and John must be excluded as possible authors of Hebrews, especially because of the passage in Hebrews 2:3–4. If one of them was the author, this verse would be "a salvation; which at the first began to be spoken by the Lord, being established *by us* who heard (Him); God also bearing witness." And *by us* is lacking.

James and Jude are also to be excluded as possible authors of Hebrews. James had already written his letter to the twelve tribes in the dispersal (1:1, Christians of Jewish origin), and it seems strange that he would have provided a separate one (Hebrews) attached to it. Jude must also be ruled out, as he referred in his letter only to the words of the prophets and apostles; he didn't want to present new teachings (1:3). There is only one possible author of the letter to the Hebrews: Paul. And Hebrews could only be received by the churches if connected to a different letter of Paul. Hebrews indeed has many Pauline features.

1. It ends with Paul's standard greeting: "Grace be with you all. Amen." In nearly all his letters, he refers at the end to the need of grace, except in Romans, where he says, "The God of Peace be with you all. Amen" (15:33) and a doxology in 16:27. No other letter of the New Testament has this greeting. Only at the end of the Revelation does John pronounce the blessing of grace. Maybe he did so as he wrote to the region where Paul had worked and where this greeting was so familiar.

2. Another Pauline feature of the letter to the Hebrews is the impressive authority of the author. It is almost inconceivable that someone outside the apostolic circle of thirteen could exercise such authority.

3. The addressees had a warm relationship with the author and with Timothy, and this relates to the cooperation of Paul and Timothy.

4. Although there are differences in approach and new theological developments in Hebrews, there are also many specific, well-known Pauline themes: Christ's previous glory

and part in creation, his self-humbling, his obedience, his self-offering, the new covenant, Abraham's faith as example, gifts of the Spirit, use of similar Old Testament passages, and the athletic metaphor of the Christian life.[369]

Having established the apostle Paul as the author of the letter to the Hebrews, the question remains: With which letter (of Paul) was Hebrews connected? There is only one possibility: the letter to the Galatians.[370] And for the place where Paul wrote Galatians and Hebrews, the best possibility is Ephesus, where Paul remained for a long time during his third missionary journey.[371] He was still in contact with the churches of Galatia,[372] which he founded on his first missionary journey in the southern region of Turkey.[373] There were churches with Christians of Jewish and non-Jewish background, and Timothy originated from this region.[374]

It is clear that the letter to the Galatians and the letter to the Hebrews strongly differ in style, speech, and content. A lot of Pauline

---

[369] (a) Hebr. 1:2–6/1 Cor. 8:6, 2 Cor. 4:4, Col. 1:15–17. (b) Hebr. 2:14–17/ Rom. 8:3, Gal. 4:4, Phil. 2:7. (c) Hebr. 5:8/Rom. 5:19, Phil. 2:8. (d) Hebr. 8:6/2 Cor. 3:9 etc. (e) Hebr. 11:11–12, 17–19/Rom. 4:17–20. (f) Hebr. 2:4/1 Cor. 12:11. (g) Psalms 8 in Hebr.2:6–9/1 Cor. 15:27; Deut. 32:35 in Hebr. 10:30/Rom. 12:19; Hab. 2:4 in Hebr. 10:38/Rom. 1:17, Gal. 3:11. (h) Hebr. 12:1/1 Cor. 9:24. In Guthrie, *New Testament Introduction*, 722.

[370] In Hebrews, Paul and Timothy are not together (13:23). In many of Paul's letters, they are together: Romans (16:21), 2 Corinthians (1:1), Philippians (1:1), Colossians (1:1), 1 and 2 Thessalonians (1:1), Philemon (1). First Corinthians is no option, as Timothy is free and on his way to Corinth (14:7, 16:10), which is in conflict with Hebrews 13:23. Ephesians is not an option, as Paul is imprisoned (6:20), which is not the case in Hebrews (13:23). The pastoral letters are no options, as they are personal letters. Only Galatians remains as a letter of which Hebrews could be an attachment.

[371] An objection against Ephesus might be Hebrews 13:24. "Those who come from Italy send you greetings." Isn't Italy the place/area from which the letter to the Hebrews was written? No, Paul is speaking about the Jews who were pressed to leave Rome (and Italy) under Emperor Claudius and who settled around the Aegean Sea, also in Ephesus (Acts 18:2).

[372] 1 Corinthians 16:1.

[373] Acts 13:14–28.

[374] Acts 16:1–3.

expressions occur in Hebrews, of which only a few occur in Galatians. How is that possible? Isn't it expected that two letters written at nearly the same time would contain the same subjects and expressions? Galatians was written to the churches of Galatia, and the dominating subject is the warning to the Christians of non-Jewish background to not be circumcised and to not let themselves be brought under the law.[375] It is Paul's only letter to a group of churches in a large area instead of a city letter. Jewish non-Christian teachings penetrated with power into the Christian churches of Galatia. It wouldn't be satisfying if Paul didn't also send a message to the Christians of Jewish origin. Not only could they easily be ignored by the non-Jewish Christians as a consequence of the strong doctrines of Paul in the letter to the Galatians, but also a letter to the Hebrews of the region of Galatia was a necessity for the church. In it, he explained the Christological meaning of the law and the prophets.[376] He challenged the Hebrews to teach their fellow Christians, saying that they ought to be teachers already.[377] It seems that he urged them to teach their non-Jewish fellow Christians in order to make them strong against the seduction of legalism.

Many non-Jewish Christians in Galatia were sensitive to the argument that circumcision was a commandment of God to Abraham and his posterity. Weren't they also descendants of Abraham through the faith? Commandments were given by God to fulfill, and if they didn't obey, what then? They could come into serious inward conflict. They needed a new meaning of the Old Testament, a Christological meaning of the law and the prophets. And indeed, that is exactly what the letter to the Hebrews gives. In this letter, Paul showed that he was a Jew to the Jews—though not under the law. And in the letter to

---

[375] Galatians 5:3–10; 6:12–16.

[376] Chapters 1. Christ, son of God, superior to angles. 2. Necessity of the Word of God. 3. Christ superior to Moses. 4. Christ superior to Joshua. 5. Christ the high priest. 6. God's promise to Abraham and his descendants. 7. Priesthood of Christ (according to Melchizedek) and higher than Aaron. 8. Christ high priest of the New Covenant. 9. Christ high priest of a heavenly tabernacle. 10. Christ and his superior offering. 11. The ancestors lived by Faith. 12. The new Zion in Christ. 13. Encouragements to be united in Christ.

[377] Hebrews 5:12;:9–12; 12:12–15; 13:15.

the Galatians, he showed that he was as one outside the law, though not without the law.[378] There is no other combination of two Pauline letters that complete each other in such a remarkable way.

The discussion has shown that a right understanding of the canon has a great impact on a thorough understanding of the individual books of the New Testament. The history of exegesis of the New Testament shows that when the canon has lost its meaning, the separate books lose their meaning also. And where the books lose their meaning, they lose their Gospel power. On the other hand, history also has learned that where the Gospel comes, interest in the canon and its structure grows. A secret of the canon is the Gospel, and a secret of the Gospel is the canon.

10.7.1 Ambiguity of the Byzantine Text Form

It is generally accepted from antiquity onward that those who deal with the Greek text of the New Testament have to face the phenomenon of the variant readings. The canon formula S (total)↔C (total) shows how it is possible that the twenty-seven books of the New Testament are all authentic, but the formula is not related to the purity of the deliverance of the text of the canon. Copyists of the New Testament books made copy errors.

Copy errors were replicated by later generations, and as a result, text families came into being. There are four text families with a rather vast stock of variant readings (copy errors).[379] Not only unintentional errors are found in the texts but also intentional changes.[380] J. H.

---

[378] 1 Cor. 9:19 etc.

[379] The families are signed with capitals: A. Byzantine text form, Koine in Codex Alexandrinus for the Gospels (fifth century); B. Egyptian text form, Alexandrian or neutral text in Codex Sinaïticus (fourth century) and in Codex Vaticanus (fourth century); C. Caesarean text form in Codex Washingtonianus (fifth century).; D. Western text in Codex Bezae (fifth century). And mixed text form in Codex Ephraemi (fifth century). See E. J. Epp, G. D. Fee, *Studies in the Theory and Method of New Testament Textual Criticism*. Studies and Documents, Founded by Kirsopp and Silva Lake. Vol. 45 (Grand Rapids: W.B. Eerdmans,1993).

[380] For fifteen types of variant readings, compare J. H. Greenlee, *Introduction to New Testament Textual Criticism* (Grand Rapids: W. B. Eerdmans, 1964), 63–68.

Greenlee stated, "The variants which require consideration in textual criticism, however, arose for the most part in the earliest period of textual history."[381] The canonization of the New Testament in the fourth century created pressure not to change the holy texts, but the intention never entirely disappeared. After centuries, it happened that copyists who were confronted with old and unusual forms or words chose more eloquent or well-known expressions at that time. And to complete the picture, already early (end of second century) people tried to restore variant readings by comparing texts from different origins, resulting in mixed texts.

From the nineteenth century, scholars decided to give prominence to the oldest variants; that is, from the oldest manuscripts (from circa AD 250–500). It is sad that in the later documents, especially of the Byzantine text form, many *harmonistic* variants occur (the translation of the King James Version goes back to this text form). Of course, changing old texts was not permitted, either from a literary or from a religious standpoint. After the canonization of the New Testament, the tendency slowly grew to add parallel clauses from other Bible books, especially in the Gospels. Until late in the Middle Ages, this occurred in the Byzantine tradition (in Greece and Turkey). It was felt that this was not adding to the Word of God, as the changes had been sourced from other parts of the written Word. It is a pity that text critics have lost interest in the Byzantine text form because of its many changes. However, it may still function as a source of possibly original readings. This tradition of manuscripts is from circa 400 and 1000–1500 and covers about 95 percent of handwritten texts of the New Testament. There are variant readings of little or no importance for the meaning of a passage, but there are also those of a more serious character. Let's look at two examples.

10.7.2 Intentional Text Alterations

First, an example of a Byzantine harmonistic text addition: In Mark 14:68 (KJV) we read after Peter's first denial, "And he went out into the porch; *and the cock crew.*" Two denials later we read, "But he began to curse and to swear, saying, I know not this man of whom ye speak.

---

[381] J. H. Greenlee, idem, 60.

And the second time *the cock crew.* And Peter called to mind the word that Jesus said unto him, 'Before the cock crows twice, thou shalt deny me thrice'" (Mark 14:71–72). The question is, why didn't Peter realize the first time the cock crowed that he was doing wrong? And that is also what we learn from the other Gospels—that Peter broke down in tears as soon as he heard the cock.

Current translations leave out "and the cock crew" of verse 68 because about five of the oldest manuscripts don't have this clause in verse 68. It is found, however, in nearly all Byzantine manuscripts; a harmonistic addition from verse 72 (the same words and so "admissible"; and the cock crowed). Copyists probably felt it a necessity to mention the first time the cock crowed to make the story complete and the second instance of crowing (72) reasonable. However, they may not have realized that when a cock begins to crow in the early morning, this usually happens two times in succession (or three times).

A second example of a less convincing variant reading in the Alexandrian text is in John 1:18. However, the Byzantine text seems to deliver the original reading: "No man hath seen God at any time, *the only begotten Son,* which is in the bosom of the Father, he hath declared him" (KJV). Modern translations have the Alexandrian reading: "*the only begotten God,* who is in the bosom of the Father, He has explained Him." (NASB). Paraphrasing the New International Version: "God the One and Only, who is at the Father's side." A text substitution has taken place. Which of the two words is original? God or Son? Because of the stronger value of the word God, an accidental copy error is to be excluded.[382] Modern scholars have given prevalence to the word God as original, according to old manuscripts (8) of Alexandrian origin (circa 250–400). The word Son is supported by many documents from later time, from about the year 400 and onward (Caesarean and Byzantine text forms).

At first, looking at the result, it must be said that the King James Version reading flows easily as the connection between the Father and the Son is related. The Alexandrian variant is less easy, not to say strange: "the only begotten God ... in the bosom of the Father." This is also the opinion of the committee installed by the United Bible Societies to comment on conjectural emendations in the text of the

---

[382] In fact, there is a difference here of only one letter: Θ or Υ.

New Testament.[383] They call the variant reading of the only begotten Son "undoubtedly easier." Nevertheless, the committee blames copyists for having chosen it and judges that "the only begotten God" is original, according to the oldest Alexandrian texts.[384]

However, some old Alexandrian texts also follow the reading of "the only begotten Son," together with Caesarean and Byzantine texts. It is not enough to consider only the oldest variant readings; we also must consider the wide, scattered range of the alternative readings. In this case, insufficient attention has been given to *congruence with the book*, the Gospel of John. The term "the only begotten Son of God" is firmly established in this Gospel (John 1:14; 3:16, 18) and "the only begotten God" is missing not only in John but in the entire New Testament.[385] And so it does not seem appropriate to play down the important biblical expression "the only begotten Son of God."

It looks like a text change to support a stronger doctrinal emphasis. The Alexandrian culture of faith was imbued with Docetism, the teaching that Jesus was more God than man. He would have had no real human body but a spiritual one, and so he did not suffer on the cross, according to this doctrine. Consequently, it would not be very impressive in the Egypt region to speak of the only begotten Son, and so an early copyist made it the only begotten God. It should be noted that the great church councils from 325 until 451 are all related with the definition of the two natures of Jesus, which would end in the formula: *vere Deus, vere homo* (truly God, truly man).

Congruence with book and author should be a must in conjectural emendations to prevent system forced solutions—the system that the older text is the best (original) by definition. What would be the reaction of a member of the committee who brought his car to the garage to repair a damaged spot in the red paintwork, and when

---

[383] B. M. Metzger (ed.), *A Textual Commentary on The Greek New Testament* (London, New York: United Bible Societies, corrected ed. 1975).

[384] It is an old rule that *lectio difficilior praestat* (the difficult reading has prevalence), and this was beneficial in the past to define text families of manuscripts. The starting point was that accidental mistakes go from strong to easy expressions, but the rule lectio dif. praes. does not give full weight to the fact that intentional changes have the disposition to go from easy to strong.

[385] For the first letter of John, see 3:23; 4:9, 14; 5:10–13, 20.

he returned, he saw a totally different shade of red on the repaired spot? He would not be amused, would he? It is the same with text emendations: *They should be in harmony with the book.* It is a mistake to suppose that congruence with the book is not necessary, based on the supposition that the oldest variant reading is always the best. It is remarkable that in the last case, the Byzantine text has the best reading, and it would be a great loss to forget the value of this old and worthy text tradition. This text grew on the old missionary region, where once the apostle Paul had founded the church and where the foundation was laid for the canonization process of the New Testament books. It is to be expected that a number of valuable variant readings have been preserved in texts from this region.

The variant readings are a result of the sheer quantity of copies of the New Testament that we possess from the first century to roughly the twelfth century—more than five thousand documents (small pieces, pages, chapters, books, and even complete New Testaments). Already some 150 years ago, Dr. Ph. Schaff stated: "It is the natural result of the great wealth of our documentary resources; it is a testimony to the immense importance of the New Testament; it does not affect, but it rather insures, the integrity of the text; and it is a useful stimulus to study."[386] The wealth of copies is, in fact, a testimony to the overwhelming tradition of the New Testament writings in history. Fortunately, the variant readings do not impact on Christian doctrines of faith or ethics, as they are estimated to be only a small part of the entire text.[387] The study of the variants is very useful, not only for the study of the meaning of the text but because they also

---

[386] Ph. Schaff, *Companion tot he Greek Testament and the English Version* (New York: Harper & Brothers, 1883), 177.

[387] N. L. Geisler and W. E. Nix calculated on the observations of F. J. A. Hort and B. F. Westcott as follows: "Only about one-eighth of all the variants had any weight, as most of them are merely mechanical matters such as spelling or style. Of the whole, then, only about one-sixtieth rise above 'trivialities,' or can in any sense be called 'substantial variations.' Mathematically this would compute to a text that is 98.33 percent pure." N. L. Geisler and W. E. Nix, *A General Introduction to the Bible* (Moody Press: Chicago, 1968), 365. (As quoted in J. McDowell 1972, 45.) Although the current estimate may have changed by new insights, the results will be comparable.

make it possible to speak of a history of the text that is visible, among other things, through the copied variant readings.

But what about Matthew 5:18, one may ask, where Jesus said that "not the smallest letter or stroke shall pass from the Law"? If Jesus said from the Old Testament that not one single letter would disappear from it, didn't he mean the same rule for the New Testament? Moreover, everyone who is somewhat informed also knows that in the tradition of the Old Testament, tiny variant readings play a significant role. So it is a common question for the Old and the New Testament to consider. Therefore, let's have a closer look at Matthew 5:17–19:

> [17] Think not that I have come to abolish the law and the prophets; I have come not to abolish them but to fulfil them.
> [18] For truly, I say to you, till heaven and earth pass away, not an iota, not a dot, will pass from the law until all is accomplished.
> [19] Whoever then relaxes one of the least of these commandments and teaches men so, shall be called least in the kingdom of heaven; but he who does them and teaches them shall be called great in the kingdom of heaven.

The kernel of the matter is that Jesus, in verse 17, says that he came to fulfill the Law, and saying so, he declared to be the Messiah as only he could do. This has a far-reaching consequence for the further sayings of the Lord here. In verse 18, he does not refer to the end of the world concerning the fulfillment of the Law.[388] History cannot fulfill the Law; only the Messiah can. The Law could not be fulfilled in any other way, not even in the course of time until the end of the world. His reference to the end of the world has to do also with the *preaching after his fulfillment of the law*. Those who will preach the Gospel but leave out the smallest of the commandments will be

---

[388] Jesus said what everybody believed, that the temple text of old would remain intact, the Law and the prophets. The same is to be observed in Luke 16:16–17; here, Jesus does not make a general statement for history but for his own time. After the destruction of the temple in AD 70, the temple text disappeared (compare section 9.10.1 and 10.7.2, notes).

called least, but those who will teach, including them all, will be called great in the kingdom.

Conclusion: After the phrase "till heaven and earth pass away," an enumeration follows of three things until the end of history:

1. Jesus's perfect work until his resurrection and ascension, while the Law (and the temple) remains intact (v. 17)
2. The proclamation of the kingdom thereafter, with the serious problem of those who don't do that as it should be (v. 19a)
3. Those who will do that properly (v. 19b)

What does that mean for the phenomenon of the variant readings?

10.8 Delivered into the Hands of Men

It is a great advantage of the documentation theory that we know how, for decades, the apostles watched over the Gospels they had published and over their distribution. Passages such as the apostolic manifesto (1 John 1:1–4) and others are very clear about it, and by that we know that the *common* text (i.e., apart from the variant readings) of the Gospels is reliable. Another fruit of the documentation theory is the fixed canon of the New Testament books, instead of the flexible canon of modern theology. And so we also know that the common text of the letters is reliable. The documentation theory presents a reliable basis in the texts for congruent decisions in text critical questions. No doubt all sorts of text-critical questions will remain within the discipline of text restoration, but the congruent approach, presented above, may furnish fair and satisfactory answers in significant cases.

The number of variant readings in the New Testament doesn't need to surprise or to disturb any Christian, as they are the natural consequence of the wealth of documentary sources of the Christian faith. Nevertheless, any Christian can feel concerned when confronted with the idea that the Word of God doesn't seem to be as perfect as is always taught. This is indeed a serious question, as well as how to deal with it. When the words of Jesus were secured by speedy writers, stenographers and preserved in the Gospels, aren't we back to the drawing board if errors slipped into the text later on? In that case, aren't we confounded before we begin? How is it possible that the

Word of God seems imperfect? Indeed, it is not possible to use the word *perfect* in this respect, with the meaning *smooth and clean*. Perfect is to be understood here in a different way. There are holes in the text, so to speak, where it is uncertain what the original reading is in the case of two (or even more) good possibilities of variant readings. There is something positive, however, about the existence of these perceived holes.

The New Testament did not drift through history smoothly and undamaged; it was *delivered into the hands of men.* Jesus also did not drift through life smoothly and undamaged. At the end, he also was delivered into the hands of men, and his body received holes through the tortures of flagellation and crucifixion. Yet he remained the same speaking Word of God. In its transmission, the New Testament is a type of Jesus Christ *in his deliverance.* In spite of the holes in the text, the New Testament speaks God's message unambiguously. When we speak about the truth of God's Word, it is only possible in relation to Jesus, who himself is the truth. And so it is no loss that the text of the New Testament contains a relatively small number of tiny holes, in spite of the accurate work of Jesus's speedy writers and stenographers.

Can we say in honesty that we possess the words of Jesus? The answer is yes! Jesus on the cross, with holes in his body through flagellation, crown and nails—he remained the same. His wounds proclaimed what he had done during his life on earth. In the same way, the holes in the transmitted text of the New Testament refer in a special way to the deliverance of the Lord. The state in which Jesus *was* is now the state of God's Word. In the despised state of Jesus, salvation was revealed to humankind; in the same despised state, the Word reveals that salvation to the world. The cross is not wisdom for the world, and neither is the Word of God. The miracle is that the Word is still the bright, shining light of God's salvation, as Jesus promised, "Heaven and earth will pass away, but my words will not pass away."

Appendix

Highlights of the Passion and Resurrection Story

In this appendix, four examples of analytical reading are treated to show the important applications of it. The most frequent questions are as follows:

1. What happened during Jesus's passion?
2. What was said exactly?
3. How do the different reports in the Gospels contribute to a more complete picture of what happened?
4. How can we explain seeming contradictions?

1. Confrontation at Night

Question 1. What happened when Jesus came before the Jewish council? Is there a living pattern?

Connected with Jesus's condemnation to death are several remarkable aspects. First, there were two condemnations strictly spoken: one at night, after his arrest (Matthew and Mark), and one on the morning after, for the second time (Luke). Second, there are four confessions of Jesus about his identity. That is quite a lot. The best way to discuss these aspects is to follow the course of the events.

After his arrest, Jesus was brought before the high priests in the dead of night. They had the assistance of the complete priestly council.[389] In this council, a preliminary examination took place, as it was only a priestly council. We may suppose that Joseph of

---

[389] In Greek, the word *sunedrion* has a broad meaning—any assembly (esp. of magistrates, judges, ambassadors), whether convened to deliberate or to pass judgment (Thayer, *A Greek-English Lexicon of the New Testament*). It is possible to suppose that there was only one *sunedrion* in Israel called Sanhedrin. In that case, the council that examined Jesus at night took a final decision in the morning thereafter. Maybe according to a custom that a judgment of death was to be given by day and not by night, it is also possible to take two councils. At night, a complete priestly council (Matthew 26:59; Mark 14:55) examined Jesus, and the morning thereafter the final judgment was given by the Sanhedrin, which was the highest council of

Arimathea and Nicodemus were clerks who reported the process and the results of it. We may deduce that from the following considerations:

At dawn on the morning after Jesus's arrest, the complete Sanhedrin was gathered to judge Jesus. This council consisted of a priestly party, augmented with representatives of the people (Matthew 27:1; Mark15:1; Luke 22:66). We have to notice that Joseph was "a respected member of the council" (Mark 15:43) and Nicodemus was "a ruler of the Jews" (John 3:1), which certainly meant that he also was a member of the great Sanhedrin.[390] Later on, these men were responsible for Jesus's funeral (John 19:38–42), and by that it is certain that they did not agree with the judgment of the Sanhedrin to which they belonged. About Joseph, it is explicitly remarked, "He was a member of the council [the great Sanhedrin is meant, Luke 22:66], a good and righteous man, who had not consented to their purpose and deed, and he was looking for the kingdom of God."[391] That means that Joseph and Nicodemus were writers, clerks who recorded what was said in the great Sanhedrin.[392] To maintain their independence in their work, they were not entitled to vote in the case of a death penalty. Joseph and Nicodemus certainly attended the latter meeting. It was possible for them to disagree with the final decision taken by the Sanhedrin that morning (Luke 22:66–71). We read about the moment of that decision: "And they all said, 'Are you the Son of God, then?' And he said to them, 'You say that I am.' And they said, 'What further testimony do we need? We have heard it ourselves from his own lips.'" Analytical reading shows that with "they all" and "they," Luke intends to say that they all agreed with the condemnation

---

priests, scribes, and elders (representatives) of the people (Matthew 27:1; Mark 15:1; Luke 22:66).

[390] About Nicodemus's position as member of the Sanhedrin, see also John 7:26, 48; Luke 23:13, 35; 24:20. And H. L. Strack, P. Billerbeck, *Das Evangelium nach Markus, Lukas und Johannes und die Apostelgeschichte Erläutert aus Talmud und Midrasch* (München: C. H. Beck'sche Verlagsbuchhandlung, 1924, repr. 1974), 412–413.

[391] Luke 23:50–51.

[392] There were at least two clerks, as one was to record votes of acquittal and the other, votes of condemnation. *Mishnah*, Sanhedrin 4, 3.

of Jesus. It was only possible for Joseph and Nicodemus to attend this council without giving their approval if they belonged to the clerks of the court.

The question of why there were two condemnations can be answered now. The first condemnation was only preliminary, and the second was the definitive judgment of the complete Sanhedrin. Subsequently, we have to look at the question of why there were four confessions of Jesus about his identity.

The course of the first confrontation at night is not quite clear. Witnesses testified against Jesus, but Matthew says, "They sought false testimony against Jesus, that they might put him to death." The witnesses were brought one by one into the hall to testify, and then they were taken out. The "false aspect" of the process was probably the lack of a correct interrogation of the witnesses; that was the task of the judges.[393] An intense interrogation was necessary, as according to the law, two or three testimonies had to be convincing for there to be a judgment of death penalty. If this occurred insufficiently or remained undone, the testimonies easily could be taken as true. After the witnesses, the moment came for Jesus to defend himself, as defense lawyers were not usual in court. And the high priest Caiaphas rose to invite Jesus to speak. "Have you no answer to speak? What is it that these men testify against you?"

Caiaphas upheld a semblance of truth. Superficially, it seemed as if honest people were discussing a serious matter, but in the meantime, Caiaphas used a centuries-old trick: put the accused under the pressure of the common will of the group, and everything he says will be used against him. Even the slightest nervousness will be taken as a sign of guilt. However, Jesus did not play the game, he remained silent, painfully so for everyone present. In that moment of silence, everyone felt that the lack of examination of the witnesses was the norm. And therefore, after Jesus's confession, the general relief consequently followed. "Why do we still need witnesses?"

---

[393] *Mishnah*, Sanhedrin 4 and 5.

Table 1

Before the Council		
Matthew 26:62–68	**Mark 14:60–65**	**Luke 22:66–71**
I. 62 And the high priest stood up and said, "Have you no answer to make? What is it that these men testify against you?" 63 But Jesus was silent. IV. And the high priest said to him, "I adjure you by the living God, tell us if you are the Christ, the Son of God." 64 Jesus said to him, "You have said so. But I tell you, hereafter you will see the Son of man seated at the right hand of Power, and coming on the clouds of heaven." 65 Then the high priest tore his robes, and said, "He has uttered blasphemy. Why do we still need witnesses? You have now heard his blasphemy. 66 What is your judgment?" They answered, "He deserves death." 67 Then they spat in his face, and struck him; and some slapped him, 68 saying, "Prophesy to us, you Christ! Who is it that struck you?"	II. 60 And the high priest stood up in the midst, and asked Jesus, "Have you no answer to make? What is it that these men testify against you?" 61 But he was silent and made no answer. III. Again the high priest asked him, "Are you the Christ, the Son of the Blessed?" 62 {And} Jesus said, "I am; and you will see the Son of man seated at the right hand of Power, and coming with the clouds of heaven." 63 {And} the high priest tore his garments, and said, "Why do we still need witnesses? 64 You have heard his blasphemy. What is your decision?" And they all condemned him as deserving death. 65 And some began to spit on him, and to cover his face, and to strike him, [and] saying to him, "Prophesy!" And the guards received him with blows.	V. 66 [And] When day came, the assembly of the elders of the people gathered together, both chief priests and scribes; and they led him away to their council, and they said, 67 "If you are the Christ, tell us." But he said to them, "If I tell you, you will not believe; 68 {and} if I ask you, you will not answer. 69 But from now on the Son of man shall be seated at the right hand of the power of God." 70 {And} they all said, "Are you the Son of God, then?" {And} he said to them, "You say that I am." 71 {And} they said, "What further testimony do we need? We have heard it ourselves from his own lips."

(See Table 1.) The records of Matthew and Mark are parallel (at night). The underlined signal words (And, And) show that the passages I and II give almost the same information. There are some differences, however, in the Greek expressions of the direct speeches, so it was said twice. In Matthew, the high priest only stands, but in Mark, he also moved into the center of the court. And so Mark gives the second utterance of the high priest.

The signal words of the passages III and IV show that the description of Mark is first (Again: asyndetically connected, and so uninterrupted). Matthew with *And* gives interruption and follows later. This is also to be seen from *Then* (Matthew 26:67, uninterrupted) in contrast with Mark 14:65—*And* (interrupted).

As Jesus kept silent (I and II), Caiaphas did not succeed in finding a point of contact with Jesus. Going into the center, he asked again why he did not react to the charges. But Jesus continued his silence. It seems that Caiaphas saw that his intimidation trick was starting to turn against him. What now? There was no progression in the case. Certainly, everyone in the council felt the lack of a proper interrogation of the witnesses. The silence became painful. But then Caiaphas grabbed at a straw, as the witnesses were worthless. He decided to put forth a straight question about Jesus's identity: "Are you the Christ, the Son of the Blessed?" (III).

And now Jesus's reply was unambiguous: "I am." And immediately he linked to a prophecy concerning his return to the Father and a later come-back to earth: "And you will see the Son of man seated at the right hand of Power, and coming with the clouds of heaven." According to these records, the high priest rented his clothes (III). First, he tore his *chitonous*, his undergarments, usually worn next to the skin (not his garments, as the Revised Standard Version says).[394] With both hands, he took it and tore it apart, as if to get fresh air. This

---

[394] The translation in the RSV of "his garments" (plural) may be inspired by the parallel of Matthew 26:65, "his robes" (plural). In that case, the translators supposed that Matthew and Mark gave different descriptions of the same moment of Jesus's interrogation. However, we have to deal with two confessions of Jesus and with two moments of rending clothes of the high priest. At first he tore apart his undergarments, which were worn next to the skin and partly hidden under the beard. Over this he wore his outer garment. The second time he rent "his garments.," *ta himatia* (i.e., his

was a dramatic moment because a high priest was not allowed to tear his garment, at least not when he was functioning in the temple.[395] That was not the case now, but undoubtedly, his action shocked the people as much as Jesus's pronouncement.

Caiaphas could be glad, as Jesus's reply was unambiguous. "Why do we still need witnesses? You have heard his blasphemy. What is your decision?" The process took a new direction without witnesses. A condemnation could follow quickly from this moment onward. For that to happen, a second confession from Jesus was necessary to exclude mistakes. This was the general custom in jurisprudence, also by that of the Romans (living pattern).[396] Part IV begins with an and-sentence, which shows an interruption between Matthew 26:63a and 63b. Again, Caiaphas puts forth the question of Jesus's identity but stronger now, with the addition, "I adjure you by the living God ..." and by a different choice of words, "Are you the Christ, the Son of God (instead of the Blessed)?" Now he used the blasphemous (in his opinion) expression "the Son of God."[397] The repeated question was answered by Jesus with a repeated positive answer, and that was

---

undergarments), which already had a rip from the top down together with his outer garment.

[395] Leviticus 21:10.

[396] Plinius Minor, in a letter to Emperor Trajan (98–117 AD), wrote about the Christians in Asia Minor: "In the meantime, I now handle it this way with those who are turned over to me as Christians. I ask them directly, in person, if they are Christian, I ask a second and third time to be sure, and indicate to them the danger of their situation. If they persist, I order them led dispatched (= executed)." (*Epistulae ad Trajanum*, Transl. William Harris, Prof. Em. Middlebury College; http://www.earlychristianwritings. com/text/pliny2.html). And Polycarp (AD 156), who was examined by the proconsul before he died as a martyr, was asked three times to give up his faith (*The Martyrdom of Polycarp*, 9–11, in: Kirsopp Lake, *The Apostolic Fathers II*. LCL 025N (London: W. Heinemann, and New York: G. P. Putnam's Sons, 1917): 323–27. Pilate asked two times whether Jesus was the king of the Jews, as this was a serious accusation with regard to the Roman government in the Jewish land.

[397] In Isaiah 9:6k the Christ is called *Eel Gibboor* (Hebrew): Mighty God. There can be no doubt about this meaning, as in Isaiah 10:21, the same expression with this meaning is formulated: "A remnant will return, the remnant of Jacob, to the *mighty God*." The Sanhedrin didn't reckon with

enough evidence for his condemnation by the council. The clerks did their job, and the record of the process was enough legal evidence later on, in combination with the testimonies of the members of the council. After Jesus's second confession, the high priest took his garments, his undergarments and the outer garment, and completely ruined them both in one go.

Jesus had checkmated himself. It didn't take much time now to finish the matter, and he was taken out. The next morning, an extra meeting was inserted for the complete Sanhedrin: priestly representatives, scribes and elders, and rulers of the people. That is described in Luke's record. Of course, Luke made no mention of the fact that Caiaphas gave a summary of what had happened the night before. All the members understood that the records of the night before would be enough evidence for Jesus's rejection. Denials could not help him anymore. The members of the highest court in Israel had the right and the duty to hear Jesus, and he was brought in. In Luke's record, we again meet the twofold question of Jesus's identity (living pattern). First, the question of being the Messiah: "If you are the Christ, tell us" (v. 67). Second, the question of being the Son of God: "Are you the Son of God, then?" (v. 70). Jesus confirmed the two questions, and again the matter was done.

The Sanhedrin decided to transfer him to Pilate. It was a Jewish festival day, and a trial was not only uncommon then but even forbidden. The Sanhedrin, however, could hold that they did not have a trial, as they didn't have the right to condemn someone to death. They had only made up their minds. On the other hand, the Romans, as Gentiles, were not prevented from having a trial. Legally, they had only organized Jesus's extradition to the Romans, and the latter would put him to death. The Romans would then be responsible, and the members of the Sanhedrin could keep their hands clean.

Finally, we may look at the records we have discussed. Later on, the records of that night and morning, which were made by the clerks, reached the disciples of Jesus. The first report, the teaching record of Matthew, was made out of the second confession of Jesus, because

---

the fact that the prophets of old spoke in this sense about the Messiah to come as Son of God.

it was conclusive. The second report, the public record of Luke, contained the description of the full Sanhedrin of that morning. That was really important for the public, as Jesus's case became a public matter in that council. The remnant record of Mark was built up around that stirring moment of Jesus's first confession.

There are two different types of problems in relation to the confrontation between Jesus and the priestly council: general problems and those that are related to the so–called oral tradition. A more general question is, for example, Was the priestly council allowed to judge Jesus after drinking wine some hours earlier during the meal of Passover? These types of problems are rather easy to solve. About the drinking of wine, we know generally that in Judaism, there are two evenings for the celebration of Passover. We learn the same thing from the Gospels. The Gospel of John, especially, remarks that the members of the Sanhedrin didn't want to enter the praetorium of Pilate, as they wanted to eat the Passover that evening.[398] Jesus and his disciples had already celebrated the feast the evening before. The custom of two Seder evenings was certainly a benefit for the priests, as they had one day more to slaughter the lambs for the people in Jerusalem. And that is, of course, the answer: the priests ate the Passover the second day to be sure that they could work in the temple without having drunk alcoholic liquids. And so they were also ready to examine Jesus, not having used wine the evening before.

The questions connected with the theory of the oral tradition are rather problematic with regard to this moment in Jesus's story. They are many. First, the Sanhedrin, according to Matthew and Mark, gathered at night and, according to Luke, in the morning. That's a real difficulty—or rather, a contradiction. Second, there's the question of whether there ever was a condemnation by the Sanhedrin, as the Gospel of John doesn't say anything about it. Third, the testimonies of witnesses in Mark differ completely from those in Matthew. The

---

[398] John 18:28. Maybe the custom of two evenings for Passover could develop from Exodus 12:6. The fourteenth day of the month is mentioned here, and in the evening, the lamb should be eaten. Is that the evening after daylight of the fourteenth? That evening belongs, by Jewish custom, to the fifteenth. Or is the evening of the fourteenth strictly meant? In that case, the evening before the daytime of the fourteenth is meant; that is, the evening following the daytime of the thirteenth.

explanation is that Matthew—by copying the Gospel of Mark—edited his material so freely with embellishments that Mark's Gospel is hardly able to be recognized anymore in Matthew's Gospel. Fourth, the two questions of Caiaphas and the two confessions of Jesus are very different in wording, when we compare Matthew and Mark. One supposes again that these changes did not actually happen but were results of the oral tradition. Or maybe Matthew transferred Mark's report according to his own insights, writing his Gospel. Anyway, within the exegesis of the oral tradition, it is improper to assume that Caiaphas asked Jesus twice concerning his identity. That this was the general custom in jurisprudence is not referred to in commentaries, as the two confessions are seen as such "a fine illustration" of how things were changed by the oral tradition. Fifth, the high priest ruined his undergarments (Mark), whereas according to Matthew, he tore his garments. Which of the Gospels is right, and which is wrong? What really happened? Defenders of the oral tradition have said that he probably didn't tear his clothes at all, for it is difficult to suppose that such an action of the high priest would be forgotten and get changed within the oral tradition. They suppose that it was an invention of the Gospel writers to dramatize their stories. All these scholarly problems that are connected with the theory of the so-called oral tradition are, in fact, denials of the reliability of the Word of God. And within the explanation of the documentation theory, all of these problems disappear like snow under a hot sun, as we have seen.

In the previous paragraph, we collected the problems one has to deal with in the exegesis of the oral tradition. It is clear that the oral tradition has logical explanations, based in all cases on two mottos: "Changed in the course of time" or "Changed by a gospel writer when he composed his gospel." The advocates of the oral tradition should ask themselves whether they are making their listeners wise or keeping them ignorant. However, what are considered as contradictions and embellishments in the oral tradition are, in fact, specific observations of the eyewitnesses. There is no need to speak of deformation of the texts within it. On the contrary, they contain a mass of sound information worth knowing and that brings us nearer to the Lord. As we have seen, with this theory an impressive reconstruction of the course of events and the course of the spoken word is possible. In other words, it is impressive to see the *consistency of Gospel texts* when read analytically.

2. The Trial before Pilate (First Session)

Question 2. Exactly what was said between Jesus and Pilate?

The Jewish council sent Jesus to Pilate, the governor. From there, Pilate sent him to Herod, who in turn sent Jesus back to Pilate. And so there were two sessions in which Pilate examined Jesus. However, after the first meeting, he was already convinced of Jesus's innocence.

Table 2

John 18:28–32
[28] Then they led Jesus from the house of Caiaphas to the praetorium. It was early. They themselves did not enter the praetorium, so that they might not be defiled, but might eat the passover. [29] So Pilate went out to them and said, "What accusation do you bring against this man?" [30] They answered him, "If this man were not an evildoer, we would not have handed him over." [31] Pilate said to them, "Take him yourselves and judge him by your own law." The Jews said to him, "It is not lawful for us to put any man to death." [32] This was to fulfill the word which Jesus had spoken to show by what death he was to die.

(See Table 2.) The first public confrontation between Pilate and the leaders of Jerusalem is recorded by John. Pilate immediately took the initiative and asked what accusation they had against Jesus. They failed to reply with any accusation that would have resulted in their objective of having Jesus put to death. Then the trial really started with the first accusations (Luke).

Table 3

Before Pilate		
Matthew 27:11–14	**Mark 15:2–5**	**Luke 23:2–5**
II b. ¹¹ <u>Now</u> Jesus stood before the governor; and the governor asked him [the question saying], "Are you the King of the Jews?" Jesus said, "You have said so." V a. ¹² [<u>And</u>] But when he was accused by the chief priests and the elders, he made no answer. ¹³ Then Pilate said to him, "Do you not hear how many things they testify against you?" ¹⁴ [<u>And</u>] But he gave him no answer, not even a single charge; so that the governor wondered greatly.	II a. ² <u>And</u> Pilate asked him [the question], "Are you the King of the Jews?" And he answered him [answering said], "You have said so." V b. ³ <u>And</u> the chief priests accused him of many things. ⁴ {And} Pilate again asked him [the question saying], "Have you no answer to make? See how many charges they bring against you." ⁵ But Jesus made no further answer, so that Pilate wondered.	I. ² {And} <u>they</u> began to accuse him, saying, "We found this man perverting our nation, and forbidding us to give tribute to Caesar, and saying that he himself is Christ a king." II a. ³ {And} <u>Pilate</u> asked him [saying], "Are you the King of the Jews?" And he answered him [answering said], "You have said so." III. ⁴ {And} Pilate said to the chief priests and the multitudes, "I find no crime in this man." IV. ⁵ <u>But they</u> were urgent, saying, "He stirs up the people, teaching throughout all Judea, from Galilee even to this place."

(See Table 3.) In the passages cited, a numbering has again been introduced to fix the order of the occurrences. Luke's report gives an uninterrupted description, as it is composed on *speaker returns* instead of and-sentences, in contrast with Matthew and Mark, who have several and-sentences.

The fact that Luke has a continuous succession makes it easy to analyze these passages. It is possible to establish five steps: (1) first accusations, (2) examination by Pilate[399], (3) Pilate's conclusion: innocent, (4) new accusations and his Galilean origin, (5) Jesus's silence and Pilate's encouragements to speak up.

II a. After the first accusation, the interrogation started. Luke has "asked him saying" (v. 3). The twofold introduction "asked him saying" does not introduce the direct speech that follows but rather the entire examination (asked is examined). A direct speech of the examination is introduced by the simple introduction, *saying*. This question and answer is also given in Mark.

II b. Matthew gives the second question about Jesus's kingship. Jesus's answer has been presented completely, as a simple introduction precedes it: "You have said so!"

III. Pilate immediately considered the fact that anybody was permitted to say anything about him that he wanted to, as long as he was not a criminal or a rebel against the nation. All the other accusations he had heard didn't seem to point in that direction, and so he concluded, "I find no guilt in this man."

IV, V a, V b. Then the second phase of accusations followed. In Matthew and Mark Pilate asked twice why Jesus didn't react to the new accusations, but he remained silent. As Pilate had heard that his origin was Galilee, he decided that it was Herod's task to judge Jesus. Herod governed Galilee, and so he was the right person for the job; the accusation that Jesus had stirred up the people should be taken seriously (IV).

The writers, probably members of the Sanhedrin (Joseph of Arimathea and Nicodemus), following the trial were poised between hope and fear. They did not comprehend what was happening. They must have done their work only mechanically. The teaching report of Matthew contains only the beginning and the end of

---

[399] There are two different verbs for "to ask": (1) *erota-oo*, ask, examine; covers the complete examination of Jesus by Pilate. (2) *eperota-oo*, put a question; refers to one single question and not to the whole examination in Matthew 27:11, Mark 15:2, 4.

the first examination. It has the simplest composition: three and-sentences. As often, Matthew is concise and to the point. The public record (Luke) gives more information. Speaker returns (without specific conjunctions) ensure that the occurrences were described continuously. Mark's remnant record is as short as that of Matthew and has been composed in the same way. The question is when these reports were arranged from the notes. After each occurrence, as it is most likely that it was part of the working method.

Table 4

A Personal Interview
John 18:33–40
[33] Pilate entered the praetorium again and called Jesus, and said to him, "Are you the King of the Jews?" [34] Jesus answered, "Do you say this of your own accord, or did others say it to you about me?" [35] Pilate answered, "Am I a Jew? Your own nation and the chief priests have handed you over to me; what have you done?" [36] Jesus answered, "My kingship is not of this world; if my kingship were of this world, my servants would fight, that I might not be handed over to the Jews; but my kingship is not from the world." [37] Pilate said to him, "So you are a king?" Jesus answered, "You say that I am a king. For this I was born, and for this I have come into the world, to bear witness to the truth. Everyone who is of the truth hears my voice." [38] Pilate said to him, "What is truth?" And when he said the following, he had gone out to the Jews [Judeans] again, and told them "I find no crime in him. [39] But you have a custom that I should release one man for you at the Passover; will you have me release for you the King of the Jews?" [40] They cried out again, "Not this man, but Barabbas!" Now Barabbas was a robber.

(See Table 4.) After the first public trial, Pilate had a short personal conversation with Jesus. He asked him again about his kingship, but it was difficult for Pilate to understand Jesus being the king of truth. And with that, the conversation ended with Pilate's question, "What is truth?"

John continues his story in verse 38b with the second part of Jesus's public trial before Pilate, after Jesus's visit to Herod. In this part of Jesus's trial, Barabbas was chosen to be set free, to the disadvantage of Jesus. John uses an and-sentence in verse 38b to make clear that something happened in between—Jesus's visit to Herod.

"And when he said the following, he had gone out to the Judeans again 'I find no crime in him.'" The second part of Jesus's trial was characterized by Roman violence. At first the flagellation followed by the dress up party: Jesus dressed as a king, with a crown of thorns and a purple robe—the first mockery. Then the presentation of Jesus to the people "Behold the man!" (John 19:5). At last Pilate delivered Jesus to be crucified and the second mockery occurred when the soldiers had gathered the whole battalion. Now Jesus wore the *purple* robe (Mark 15:17) and over it a *scarlet* mantle (Matthew 27:28).

3. Jesus's Death

Question 3. How do the reports in the Gospels contribute to a complete picture of Jesus's last moments?

In the Gospels, we possess four reports about Jesus's death. These reports form a good illustration of the working method of Jesus's writers. The parallel reports that were made during Jesus's work were a teaching record, a public record, and a remnant record. These reports were preserved in the Gospels of Matthew, Luke, and Mark. Messianic reports came in the Gospel of John.[400] As we examine and discuss the records concerning Jesus's death, it is notable that each was built on one of Jesus's last sayings. Each pronouncement tells us

---

[400] Sometimes John makes references to the scriptures, which demonstrates that his reports got their final form after the event of the resurrection. This occurrence gave John a complete view of Jesus's Messianic calling. And so his references to the scriptures made his reports about the Passion and resurrection into Messianic reports. The prologue of the Gospel of John already shows the Messianic character of his Gospel.

something about the intention and color of the report to which it belongs.

Why hast thou forsaken me? (1)

Table 5

Passing Away
Matthew 27:46–50
[46] {And} about the ninth hour Jesus cried with a loud voice [saying], "Eli, Eli, lama sabachthani?" that is, "My God, my God, why hast thou forsaken me?" [47] {And} some of the bystanders hearing it said, "This man is calling Elijah." [48] And one of them at once ran and took a sponge, filled it with vinegar, and put it on a reed, and gave it to him to drink. [49] But the others said, "Wait, let us see whether Elijah will come to save him." [50] {And} Jesus cried again with a loud voice and yielded up his spirit.

(See Table 5.) Chosen as the central saying in the teaching report of Matthew is "Eli, Eli, lama sabachthani?"[401] That is, "My God, my God, why hast thou forsaken me?" With the twofold introduction in verse 46 (cried … saying), Matthew indicates that something more was said. Maybe the words omitted in Matthew are "Eloi, Eloi, lama sabachthani?" as Mark gives them, and they were *"at* the sixth hour." It is not possible to decide whether the exclamation in Mark was first or if it was Matthew's, as he gives as time *"about* the ninth hour." That means Matthew's shout was probably before the ninth hour.

Matthew frequently puts God's activity in the center in his teaching report. That's also the case here. People wondered whether God would intervene at the last moment by a saving action of Elijah. Maybe Jesus's disciples also had an expectation like that—a high hope that could be the reason for the writers to continue their work. But a rescuing act from God's side didn't occur. However, God acquitted himself well when Jesus died. The curtain of the temple was torn in

---

[401] The variant reading *Lema* is more probable. Maybe Aramaic, but in Hebrew it is also possible.

two, the earth shook and rocks were split, and tombs were opened (v. 51). That was God's work, of which Matthew gives the most complete information. Most striking, therefore, is that he chose to relate Jesus's pronouncement that God had forsaken him in this teaching report. The disciples must have also had a feeling of desolation, in spite of the signs of God. After the resurrection, Matthew had to admit these signs: Yes, the Father was there also at Golgotha.

Why hast thou forsaken me? (2)

Table 6

The Curtain of the Temple
Mark 15:34–38
[34] And at the ninth hour Jesus cried with a loud voice, "Eloi, Eloi, lama sabachthani?" which means, "My God, my God, why hast thou forsaken me?" [35] And some of the bystanders hearing it said, "Behold, he is calling Elijah." [36] {And} one ran and, filling a sponge full of vinegar, put it on a reed and gave it to him to drink, saying, "Wait, let us see whether Elijah will come to take him down." [37] {And} Jesus uttered a loud cry, and breathed his last. [38] And the curtain of the temple was torn in two, from top to bottom.

(See Table 6.) In Mark's report, the exact time is unique—"*at* the ninth hour Jesus cried."

There must have been a clear time indicator in Jerusalem, maybe for the hours for offering and prayer. The ninth was an hour of prayer (Acts 3:1). Mark presents a remnant record, and it has nearly the same atmosphere of desolation as that of Matthew, with the same issues: Jesus's desolation, the feeling of the people that God might intervene by an act of Elijah, and the tearing of the curtain of the temple. The same writers worked on these reports.

Generally, one assumes that *the curtain* means that which was inside the temple, between the holy and the holiest place. However, this is not certain. It is more probable that it means the curtain outside the entrance of the temple house. When the large doors of the temple house were open by day, a magnificent curtain filled the opening (Strack-Billerbeck, I, 1045. "With regard to the question whether in Matthew 27:51 [or Mark 15:38] the first or the last curtain is meant, only theological considerations can turn the scale."). Billerbeck himself chose the last (inside) curtain, as is usually done because of the idea that the way to the holiest was opened when Jesus died.

In the documentation interpretation, the first (outside) curtain is more probable, as the tearing of it is described in the synoptic Gospels as a part of the occurrence on Golgotha; that means some impression about it was accessible for the people near the cross, when it happened. The eyewitnesses of Jesus wrote what they saw and heard at the moment of writing. Later, perhaps, they could more precisely put into words what had happened, as the distance between the cross and the temple was considerable. Certainly the open place before the temple was filled with people for the ninth hour to pray together in the temple on this day of preparation, and on that very moment, the curtain split from top to bottom. Calling and shouting must have filled the air. The two high temple doors were then closed, and maybe the people were sent away from the temple. Something of the shouts must have reached the people who were on Golgotha.

Jesus gives the spirit.

Table 7

Luke 23:44–46
[44] [And] It was now about the sixth hour, and there was darkness over the whole land until the ninth hour,
[45] while the sun's light failed; {and} the curtain of the temple was torn in two.
[46] [And] {Then} Jesus, crying with a loud voice, said, "Father, into thy hands I commit my spirit!" {And} having said this he breathed his last.

(See Table 7.) The public report of Luke starts with the tearing of the curtain. That indicates the public character of this event, which was seen by many. Luke's report also gives the impression that the first (outside) curtain was torn.

In his reports, a word of the Lord is also mentioned. "Father, into thy hands I commit my spirit!" That was Jesus's last word as he gave up his spirit. In Luke's report, the work of God is not central, but just as often, Jesus's work as a human being is so. Luke is extremely short; nothing about his desolation, nothing about the desolation of the surrounding people. He simply says, with this last utterance of Jesus, that he died in harmony with the Father. That is completely different from Mathew and Mark. Certainly Luke expressed a pious Jewish ideal—to die at peace with God; that was important for the public to hear.

It is finished!

Table 8

After the Vinegar
John 19:28–30
[28] After this Jesus, knowing that all was now finished, said (to fulfill the scripture), "I thirst."
[29] A bowl full of vinegar stood there; so they put a sponge full of the vinegar on hyssop and held it to his mouth.
[30] When Jesus had received the vinegar, he said, "It is finished"; and he bowed his head and gave up his spirit.

(See Table 8.) John's report shows the Messianic calling of Jesus. That becomes clear from his saying, "It is finished!" It might have been better as *accomplished* or *fulfilled*. He had completed his Messianic vocation.

After the Sabbath, he arose from the dead. The eyes of the disciples were opened, and they saw Jesus in glory. Then they started to see that Jesus had fulfilled his Messianic calling as the suffering servant of God. The Gospel of John is soaked in this divine paradox. The Messianic vocation is also visible in the words "I thirst!" and in the drinking of the vinegar. In Psalms 69:21, David (and therefore also the Son of David) says, "And for my thirst they gave me vinegar to drink."

It is difficult to decide when the reports about Jesus's death were made from the first notes. The synoptic records are professionally made up, concentrating only on the essentials of the story. It is very possible, therefore, that they worked out their notes that evening, as usual, shortly after the occurrences of that noon. John's report gives the impression of victory and fulfillment of the scriptures (28), which implies a last compilation after the resurrection.[402] In any event, the professional working method of the writers guaranteed the lasting quality of these reports.

Now we have to answer the question raised at the start: Do the reports in the Gospels contribute to a complete picture? Not always, but often it will be possible to paint a complete picture with complementary Gospel records. This is indeed the case with the story of Jesus's death.

Four reports concerning Jesus's death show the same event from different perspectives. Matthew and Mark describe the feeling of desolation while God seemed to be absent in life. Jesus undoubtedly had the insight that God was present, but all the more painful, then, was his perception of being separated from his heavenly Father by the charge of sin. Luke, however, shows how Jesus died, reconciled with God. John shows how the Lord accomplished his Messianic calling through suffering. These are indeed three different but relevant perceptions connected with the death of Jesus. These perceptions are important for us also. Frequently, we often do not recognize God's presence, even when he is near (Matthew, Mark). We may experience God's caring presence, even in our last moments (Luke). Finally, the faithful also have a Messianic calling in life: victory, though not without a measure of suffering (John).

4. Jesus's Resurrection

Question 4. How do we explain the many seeming contradictions in the resurrection story?

In many instances, the resurrection story makes a rather chaotic impression. There are numerous details that at first glance seem to contradict each other. The method of explanation is generally that these so-called contradictions are products of the oral tradition. Most of them, however, turn out better than expected. One who puts the messages together accurately receives a superb picture of the occurrences of that morning.

The women on their way to the tomb

---

[402] After Jesus's resurrection, the disciples came to understand that what had happened was according to the scriptures (John 20:9; Luke 24:25–27).

Table 9

Early in the Morning			
Matthew 28:1	**Mark 16:1–2**	**Luke 23:56–24:1**	**John 20:1**
II. [1] Now after the sabbath, toward the dawn of the first day of the week, Mary Magdalene and the other Mary went to see the sepulchre. [2] And behold, there was a great earthquake; ...	[1] And when the sabbath was past, Mary Magdalene, and Mary the mother of James, and Salo'me, bought spices, so that they might go and anoint him. III a. [2] And very early on the first day of the week they went to the tomb when the sun had risen.	[56] then they returned, and prepared spices and ointments. [And] On the sabbath they rested according to the commandment. III b. [1] But on the first day of the week, at early dawn, they went to the tomb, taking the spices which they had prepared.	I. [1] Now on the first day of the week Mary Magdalene {came} [went] to the tomb early, while it was still dark ...

(See Table 9.) How many women went to the tomb? Were there three women (Mark 16:1–2), two (Matthew 28:1), or only one (John 20:1)? Were there two angels (John 20:12; Luke 24:4), or one (Matthew 28:5; Mark. 16:5)? Did the women go to the tomb before dawn (Matthew 28:1; John 20:1), at sunrise (Luke 24:1), or after sunrise (Mark 16:2)? These questions include eight problems. How do we come to the right answers?

The first of the women on the road that morning was Mary Magdalene. It was still dark, before dawn (I). She first picked up "the other Mary"; it was still before dawn (II). The other Mary is also called Mary, mother of James and Joses.[403] Then on the road to the tomb, they picked up Salome (III a, III b). But before they came to Salome, there was a violent earthquake (Matthew). They did not

---

[403] Mark 15:40, 47; 16:1.

know that an angel at that very moment had rolled the stone away. When they were all three underway, the sun had risen (Mark).

A question that is also frequently stated is this: How is it possible that the women went to the tomb bearing ointments when they knew that the tomb was closed with a heavy stone? And isn't it a contradiction that they knew that Jesus had been anointed already at his burial by Joseph of Arimathea and Nicodemus?[404] For a person of distinction many ointments at his burial were an honor. It was also possible to put them around the body or to scatter or sprinkle them over the body later on.[405]

Nevertheless, they knew that there was a heavy stone in front of the tomb. Indeed, that was a subject of discussion while they were going to the tomb garden. Who would be able to roll the stone away?[406] They probably supposed that they had time enough to solve this problem, but first, they wanted to inspect the sepulcher. After that, one of them could go to Joseph of Arimathea for approval and help to enter. Apparently none of them was informed about the Roman guards watching the tomb; it seems that the installation of the guards had taken place extremely inconspicuously.[407]

From where did the women get the spices and ointments? This frequently has pointed to a so-called contradiction between Luke and Mark with regard to this matter. Did the women prepare spices on the day Jesus died, before night set in, as Luke remarks? Or did they buy spices on the first day of the week, as Mark says? The answer must be quite simple. The spices were prepared partly on the afternoon after the burial (Luke), but it was not sufficient, as time was short, and so they bought more after the Sabbath. That was the evening after the second Sabbath[408] and preceding the resurrection.

---

[404] Nicodemus used a mixture of myrrh and aloe, about a hundred pounds' weight (John19:39).

[405] At the burial of king Herodes there were five hundred servants with perfumery behind the bier to leave it in the sepulchre. Flavius Josephus, *Antiquities*, 17, 199.

[406] Mark 16:3.

[407] Matthew 27:62-66.

[408] Exodus 12:16, Leviticus 23:6 show that there was a Sabbath following on Passover. This Sabbath and the weekly Sabbath formed that year a couple of two Sabbaths (comp. Matthew 28:1). The translation of Ferrar Fenton has

Six of the eight problems mentioned earlier in this section have been solved now; only the question of the number of angels is still unanswered. We will return to this later. The report concerning the angel who descends then follows. The beginning of the resurrection ...

The tomb is opened.

Table 10

He Rolled Away the Stone
Matthew 28:2–4
[2] for an angel of the Lord descended from heaven and came and rolled back the stone, and sat upon it. [3] His appearance was like lightning, and his raiment white as snow. [4] {And} for fear of him the guards trembled and became like dead men.

(See Table 10.) The first angel in the story descended from heaven. He had no time for the guards, as he rolled the stone away without asking permission. The soldiers felt assaulted and thought they were going to die.

How interesting is that behavior of the angel. Rolling that stone away was absolutely forbidden. Then he took a seat on that stone; it looks as if he made himself comfortable. He didn't behave like a watcher who stands beside the door or who paces back and forth regularly. The soldiers of the guard looked at the tomb to do their job, while the angel looked in the opposite direction to do his job. And how effective was the behavior of the angel, relative to that of the soldiers. They "trembled and became like dead men." Then the soldiers gathered their last strength to escape.

Meanwhile, the women, ignorant of what had happened, were on their way to the tomb. There was a short period in which no human being was present at the sepulcher; within that short interval, the resurrection occurred. Jesus arose and left the tomb. Everything seemed quiet when the women arrived. The only strange thing they saw was the stone rolled away; even the angel in front of the tomb

here correctly: 'After the Sabbaths...'. Jesus was three days in the grave: the day of Preparation and the two Sabbaths that followed.

had disappeared. It has been supposed that Jesus went out into the garden to say his morning prayers, while the angels followed him as his servants. (More about the second angel in the following paragraphs.)

First reaction of the women

Table 11

Women in Doubt		
Mark 16:3–4	**Luke 24:2**	**John 20:1–2**
I. ³ And they were saying to one another, "Who will roll away the stone for us from the door of the tomb?" II a. ⁴ And looking up, they saw that the stone was rolled back—it was very large.	II b. ² {And} they found the stone rolled away from the tomb,	II c. ¹ and saw that the stone had been taken away from the tomb. III. ² So she ran, and went to Simon Peter and the other disciple, the one whom Jesus loved, and said to them, "They have taken the Lord out of the tomb, and we do not know where they have laid him."

(See Table 11.) The women did not enter the sepulcher. Mary Magdalene ran to the disciples (III), while the others stayed behind. Mary told the disciples her premature conclusion that Jesus's body had been stolen from the tomb. Remarkably, she said, "And we do not know where they have laid him." This makes clear that in the Gospel of John, in which only Mary Magdalene is mentioned, other women also are included in the story. Hereafter follows the moving story of Peter and John, who inspected the tomb.

Peter and John inspect the tomb.

Table 12

Peter and John at the Grave
John 20:3–10
³ Peter then came out with the other disciple, and they went toward the tomb. ⁴ They both ran, but the other disciple outran Peter and reached the tomb first; ⁵ and stooping to look in, he saw the linen cloths lying there, but he did not go in. ⁶ Then Simon Peter came, following him, and went into the tomb; he saw the linen cloths lying, ⁷ and the napkin, which had been on his head, not lying with the linen cloths but rolled up in a place by itself. ⁸ Then the other disciple, who reached the tomb first, also went in, and he saw and believed; ⁹ for as yet they did not know the scripture, that he must rise from the dead. ¹⁰ Then the disciples went back to their homes.

(See Table 12.) Peter and John saw the linen cloths in which the body of Jesus had been wrapped.[409] They lay there in the same state as during the burial, but now without the body of Jesus. The napkin was in the same state, still wrapped, but in another place.[410] This was a staggering experience for Peter and John.

Jesus could not have been taken out of the cloths, for then the complete form would have been disturbed, and the cloths would not lie in the proper position where Jesus had lain. But what then? Unrolled and again wrapped wasn't an option either, what with all the hard crusts of dried blood and old ointments. It surpassed their comprehension, but only one conclusion was possible. Jesus had stood straight up through the cloths. In the same way as walls and doors couldn't stop him, when he appeared to his disciples, as John immediately tells after this passage of the tomb inspection (John 20:19). John started to believe that a miracle had happened, and they returned. One thing was clear; it was impossible that the body had been stolen. If that had

---

[409] Luke 23:53.

[410] John uses the perfect *entetuligmenon* for the napkin. This is the Greek perfect that means *wrapped*, not rolled up (RSV). The notion of the Greek word is that it is rolled around something else. It is the same verb (*entulissoo*) as used in Luke 23:53 for the entire body of Jesus—wrapped in a linen shroud.

been the case, the cloths would have been gone also. To get a complete picture, we may suppose that a second angel had entered the tomb with heavenly clothes. He had shoved away the napkin and left the tomb to wait outside for Jesus's coming out.

The women and the angels

Table 13

The Women and the Angels			
Matthew 28:5–7	**Mark 16:5–7**	**Luke 24:3–8**	**John 20:11–14**
III. ⁵ But the angel [answering] said to the women, "Do not be afraid; for I know that you seek Jesus who was crucified. ⁶ He is not here; for he has risen, as he said. Come, see the place where he lay. ⁷ Then go quickly and tell his disciples that he has risen from the dead, and behold, he is going before you to Galilee; there you will see him. Lo, I have told you."	V. ⁵ And entering the tomb, they saw a young man sitting on the right side, dressed in a white robe; and they were amazed. ⁶ {And} he said to them, "Do not be amazed; you seek Jesus of Nazareth, who was crucified. He has risen, he is not here; see the place where they laid him. ⁷ But go, tell his disciples and Peter that he is going before you to Galilee; there you will see him, as he told you."	I. ³ but when they went in they did not find the body. II. ⁴ [And] While they were perplexed about this, behold, two men stood by them in dazzling apparel; IV. ⁵ {and} as they were frightened and bowed their faces to the ground, the men said to them, "Why do you seek the living among the dead? ⁶ Remember how he told you, while he was still in Galilee, ⁷ that the Son of man must be delivered into the hands of sinful men, and be crucified, and on the third day rise." ⁸ And they remembered his words,	VI. ¹¹ But Mary stood weeping outside the tomb, {and} as she [then] wept she stooped to look into the tomb; ¹² and she saw two angels in white, sitting where the body of Jesus had lain, one at the head and one at the feet. VII. ¹³ [And] They said to her, "Woman, why are you weeping?" She said to them, "Because they have taken away my Lord, and I do not know where they have laid him." ¹⁴ Saying this, she turned round …

(See Table 13.) The speeches of the angels to the women are basically problematic in the resurrection story.

There are three, with considerable mutual differences. Is there better evidence that the oral tradition has struck also at the core message of the Christian belief? The oral tradition has ensured that the event at the sepulcher, whatever it might have been, developed into a happening with angels and an empty sepulcher, in which some women played a central role. The Gospel of Mark and of John let the angel(s) speak to the women in the tomb, while Matthew and Luke paint the picture that the angels spoke with them outside the tomb. Moreover, the deviations of the speeches reflect changes that could only grow due to the oral tradition, as the defenders of it claim. And so it seems that the Gospels deliver a real chaotic picture of what happened at the tomb. Many hold that the Gospels together offer a completely unbelievable report about Jesus's resurrection from a historical point of view. So let's have a closer look at all the ins and outs.

Shortly after Peter and John left the sepulcher, Mary Magdalene arrived again at the garden of the tomb. There, she met the other women, who had been waiting at the entrance of the garden. Now they also entered the sepulcher, and they also did not find the body of Jesus (I). They went out and, being uncertain what to do, found themselves in the presence of two angels (II).[411] One of the angels started to speak and offered to enter with them to "see the place where he lay" (III).[412] This angel had said more, as becomes clear from the twofold introduction: "answering said." Of course, he first tried to put them at ease and announced that he had an important message for them and for Jesus's disciples. That was the sign for one of the women to take out her writing tablet to note the message (III). A *sjaliach* was a messenger, who delivered a message literally as it was spoken. Salome was the shorthand writer, as we will see.[413]

---

[411] Important is the and-sentence of Luke 24:4, which shows that there was an interval of time between verses 3 and 4, during which the women could go outside of the tomb.

[412] The repeated encouragement of the angels to see the place where Jesus had lain underlines that there was the evidence they needed.

[413] See section 4.3–4.

When the angels saw how the women looked at the ground (Luke 24:5) and that their words didn't seem to have any impact, one of them repeated the message but now with the remark that it was Jesus himself who had foretold his crucifixion and resurrection (IV). And the remembrance of Jesus's words had more effect. Then the women followed the angels, entering the tomb to see the place where Jesus had lain (V). Inside, the angels took a seat near that place to indicate the spot. John says, "One at the head and one at the feet."

When one of the angels saw that the women were again filled with fear, he started to speak to them, trying to comfort them, and for the third time the women heard the message about Jesus's resurrection— but now while they were looking at the empty cloths. Mechanically, Salome also noted these words of the angel (V).

By analytical reading, it is easy (after seeing the previous three paragraphs) to meet the criticism. It is clear that each speech of the angels brought new elements: first, the resurrection: second, Jesus's own predictions about it; and third, in the tomb, looking at the cloths, the encouragement to not be amazed and to see the place where he had lain. This was the living pattern of diatribe style of teaching to which the angels adapted themselves. New elements made it possible to repeat what was already said, and that's what happened here. So there is little or no reason for criticism. Then the outcome of the story follows.

Mary Magdalene could not remain there in the sepulcher, so she went outside. What is the use of an empty shroud? The angels could say what they wished, but she didn't see Jesus. The words of the angels remained secret language to her. She didn't want to remain inside that dark tomb, and so she went out. Outside, she turned, bent down, and looked, weeping, into the sepulcher, maybe to see whether the other women had followed her (VI). But then her eyes were caught by the bright angels, and one of them asked why she was so sad: "Woman, why are you weeping?" And in spite of all the good words of the angels, she said that she was missing the body; she turned, determined to seek it (VII).

Jesus meets the women

Table 14

The Women Meet Jesus			
Matthew 28:8–10	**Mark 16:8–11**	**Luke 24:9–11**	**John 20:14–18**
I b. 8 [And] So they departed quickly from the tomb with fear and great joy, and ran to tell his disciples. II. 9 And behold, Jesus met them and said, "Hail!" ... IV a. {And} they came up and took hold of his feet IV c. and worshiped him. 10 Then Jesus said to them, "Do not be afraid; go and tell my brethren to go to Galilee, and there they will see me."	I a. 8 And they went out and fled from the tomb; for trembling and astonishment had come upon them; ... Vb. ... and they said nothing to any one, for they were afraid. 9 Now when he rose early on the first day of the week, he appeared first to Mary Magdalene, from whom he had cast out seven demons. VI. 10 She went and told those who had been with him, as they mourned and wept. 11 But when they heard that he was alive and had been seen by her, they would not believe it.	VI. 9 and returning from the tomb they told all this to the eleven and to all the rest. 10 Now it was Mary Magdalene and Joanna and Mary the mother of James and the other women with them who told this to the apostles; 11 [kai] but these words seemed to them an idle tale, and they did not believe them. VII. But Peter rose and ran to the tomb; stooping and looking in, he saw the linen cloth by themselves; and he went home wondering at what had happened.	III. 14 and saw Jesus standing, but she did not know that it was Jesus. 15 Jesus said to her, "Woman, why are you weeping? Whom do you seek?" Supposing him to be the gardener, she said to him, "Sir, if you have carried him away, tell me where you have laid him, and I will take him away." 16 Jesus said to her, "Mary." She turned and said to him in Hebrew, "Rabboni!" (which means Teacher). IV b. 17 Jesus said to her, "Do not hold me, for I have not yet ascended to the Father; but go to my brethren and say to them, I am ascending to my Father and your Father, to my God and your God."

				V a. [18] Mary Magdalene went and … VI. said to the disciples, "I have seen the Lord"; and she told them that he had said these things to her.

(See Table 14.) The reports concerning the women leaving the tomb seem to give rather complex information. It is therefore important to bring some order by determining the sequence of the activities.

The first messages (I a, I b) show that the other women also left the tomb with Mary Magdalene. They were trembling (especially Mary Magdalene) and astonished (the others), as Mark states. Matthew has the words "with fear" (probably Mary Magdalene) and "great joy" (the others). The clause "and ran to tell his disciples" is to be taken as connected with "great joy" and with Salome and Mary, the mother of James; certainly not with Mary Magdalene, who was still in fear and despair.

In II, III the women met Jesus, who greeted them in a friendly manner. Mary Magdalene was the first of them, and Jesus asked her, while she was still weeping, "Woman, why are you weeping? Whom do you seek?". These friendly words made her forget her previous suspicion about a theft, and she asked him to show her the body, if he maybe had laid it elsewhere. She was ready to take it with her—she supposed to speak with the gardener. Jesus didn't leave her in uncertainty any longer and said, "Mary." And then the veil was removed; Mary recognized Jesus. She knelt, holding his feet, as did also the other Mary (IV a). Jesus wanted them not to hold him (IV b) but to go to his disciples to bring them the message of his resurrection (IV c).

The information makes clear why Matthew speaks concerning two women from the beginning of his story. From the first moment that the women met the angels, Salome was the writer, and as such, she followed the activities. Matthew describes these activities as having been done by Mary Magdalene and Mary, the mother of James. From the moment that the angel started to speak and announced that he had a message for the disciples, she understood that she was the person to make notes, as she regularly did. Jesus's writers were accustomed to strange occurrences when they took the minutes. And so we have a detailed description of all the ins and outs of the resurrection story.

It is not difficult to imagine what happened when the soldiers came into Jerusalem with their information about the angel and the opening of the tomb. Of course, the priests didn't know what to think about it. They had to inform the high priest about it. They gathered and decided that they needed firsthand information, and so new guards were sent to the sepulcher. Nobody was allowed to enter anymore. It took some time, and within that short period, everything as described in the Gospels took place. Peter and John inspected the tomb; the women had a meeting with angels and at last with Jesus. They went to the disciples to bring their message, and Peter, for a second time, went to the tomb (VII).

And from then it was over. New guards closed the garden; nobody was permitted to enter anymore. When the garden later on was opened for the public, the tomb was cleared and nothing of the linen cloths was left. The features of the resurrection were erased. Thanks to the adequate actions of three women, Christianity possesses the everlasting reports of Jesus's resurrection. In our analysis, each of the reports gets a logical and accurate place in the entire picture.

It has been often taken as an absurdity that Jesus was not recognized by Mary Magdalene. She had followed and served him for some years. Without pronouncing a definite statement about it, it goes too far to call it an absurdity or contradiction. She left the dark tomb and looked into the daylight, and so she saw only a dark silhouette in front of her. Because of her tears, it was certainly impossible to see sharply and recognize Jesus.

Is there a contradiction in the reporting of the women to the disciples? According to Mark 16:8, the women seem to tell nothing to the disciples concerning the resurrection after their experiences at the grave. How short-sighted! In Mark 16:10, we are told that

Mary Magdalene went to the disciples to tell them. This is fully in accordance with Matthew, who shares that the women left the sepulcher to tell the disciples (28:8), just like Luke (24:10) and John (20:18). The meaning of Mark 16:8 must be that they didn't speak to any person on the road. They didn't greet anybody. In Mark 16:10 we read clearly that they indeed went to the disciples to tell them what they had seen and heard. The three women didn't go directly to the disciples. They went first to the other women, as, according to Luke 24:10, the three were accompanied by other women on their visit to the disciples. But they didn't believe them; the disciples remained in unbelief, while the women had been transformed by joy.

When Jesus appeared that evening to his sad disciples, he first comforted them.[414] One week later, when Thomas was with them, he blamed them for their unbelief, that they didn't accept the message of the women about his resurrection. He blamed them also for their hardness of heart.[415]

There were a lot of good reasons for them to start believing prudently. First, there was an open and empty tomb. Maybe they were not aware of the guards who had been installed and who had fled away later on. Second, there was a shroud, which, in the form of an empty cocoon, witnessed to an unexplainable, staggering miracle. Third, there were the reports transmitted by the women about the words of the angels and of Jesus himself. Fourth, the reports referenced Jesus's prediction about the crucifixion and the resurrection. That was undeniable, and even the women remembered that when the angels spoke about it. Fifth, they were dealing with adult, intelligent women who transmitted written reports. Their behavior could not be taken as exaggerated or oversensitive. Finally, there was the personal testimony of Mary Magdalene. She had come to them at first in complete panic, but later a strange metamorphosis took place. She was radiant with happiness. All this should have given them a new insight and room in their hearts for a divine intervention.

How was it possible that these men, who could not believe

---

[414] John 20:19–23.
[415] Mark 16:14.

293

in Jesus's resurrection, were sent out by the Lord to preach the message of his resurrection to the world? Two great gifts made it possible: (1) the *power of the Holy Spirit*, and (2) the *accurate reports* that were prepared and collected by Jesus's speedy writers and stenographers. Therefore, Jesus prophesied (John 14:26), "But the Counsellor, the Holy Spirit, whom the Father will send in my name, he will teach you all things, and bring to your remembrance all that I have said to you." Moreover, this was not only for them, but is also for us.

Bibliography

Modern Authors

Aland, K. *Synopsis Quattor Evangeliorum.* 8th ed. Stuttgart: Württembergische Bibelanstalt, 1973.

Aland, K. and B. Aland. *The Text of the New Testament.* Translated by E. F. Rhodes. 2nd ed. Grand Rapids: W. B. Eerdmans, 1995.

Alexander, L. C. A. *Luke—Acts in its Contemporary Setting.* Oxford D. Phil. diss, 1977.

Archer, G. L. *Encyclopedia of Bible Difficulties.* Grand Rapids: Zondervan, 1982.

Baarlink, H. (red.) *Inleiding tot het Nieuwe Testament.* Kampen: Kok, 1989.

Bakhuizen van den Brink, J. N. *Handboek der Kerkgeschiedenis I.* The Hague: Daamen NV, 1965.

Birkeland, H. "The Language of Jesus." *Avhandlinger utgitt av Det Norske Videnskaps: Akademi i Oslo,* II, (July 1954): 6–40.

Black, M. *An Aramaic Approach to the Gospels and Acts.* Oxford: Clarendon Press, 1946.

Boge, H. *Griechische Tachygraphie und Tironische noten: Ein Handbuch der antiken und mittelalterlichen Schnellschrift.* Berlin: Akademie Verlag, 1973.

Bruce, F. F. *The Books and the Parchments.* 6th rev. ed. London, Glasgow:Pickering & Inglis, 1978.

Bruce, F. F. *The Acts of the Apostles: The Greek Text with Introduction and Commentary.* Grand Rapids: W. B. Eerdmans, 1952.

Bruce, F. F. *De Betrouwbaarheid van de Geschriften van het Nieuwe Testament.* Internationale Bijbelbond: Telos, 1977. Translation of *The New Testament Documents. Are They Reliable?* Downers Grove Il: Inter-Varsity Press, 1972.

Bruggen, J. van. *Die geschichtliche Einordnung der Pastoralbriefe.* Wuppertal: Brockhaus Verlag, 1981.

Carson, D. A. and R. T. France, J. A. Motyer, G. J. Wenham. *New Bible Commentary. 21st Century Edition.* Leicester UK and Downers Grove US: Inter-Varsity Press, 1994.

Charles, R. H. *The Apocrypha and Pseudepigrapha of the Old Testament*, vol. 1—2. Oxford: Clarendon Press, 1913.

Clarke, A. *Clarke's Commentary, Part III, Matthew–Revelation*. Nashville: Abingdon Press, 1824.

Cook, E. M. *Solving the Mysteries of the Dead Sea Scrolls*. Carlisle UK: The Paternoster Press, 1994.

Dalman, G. *Jesus–Jeschua*. Leipzig: Hinrichs'sche Buchhandlung, 1922.

Danby, H. *The Mishnah*. London: Oxford University Press, 1933.

Emerton, J. A. "Maranatha and Ephphatha." *The Journal of Theological Studies*. Oxford, University Press. 18 (1967): 427–431.

Epp, E. J. and G. D. Fee. *Studies in the Theory and Method of New Testament Textual Criticism*. Grand Rapids: W. B. Eerdmans, 1993.

Gallagher, E. L. and J. D. Meade. *The Biblical Canon Lists from Early Christianity*. Oxford: University Press, 2017.

Goodspeed, E. J. *Matthew, Apostle and Evangelist*. Philadelphia and Toronto: Winston, 1959.

Greenlee, J. H. *Introduction to New Testament Textual Criticism*. Grand Rapids: W. B. Eerdmans, 1964.

Gummere, R. M. *Epistels of Seneca II*. LCL. London: W. Heinemann, and Cambridge MA: Harvard, Univ. Press, 1920.

Guthrie, D. *New Testament Introduction*. London: Inter-Varsity Press, 1985.

Harris, W. V. *Ancient Literacy*. Cambridge and London: Harvard University Press, 1989.

Hawkins, J. C. *Horae Synopticae*. 2nd ed. Oxford: Clarendon Press, 1968.

Helmbold, W. C. *Plutarch's Moralia VI*. LCL. London: W. Heinemann, and Cambridge MA: Harvard University Press, 1939.

Henry, M. *Commentary on the Whole Bible*. Grand Rapids: Zondervan, 1961.

Johnen, Ch. *Geschichte der Stenographie I*. Berlin: Ferdinand Schrey, 1911.

Ker, W. C. A. *Martial Epigrams II*. LCL. London: W. Heinemann, and New York: G. P. Putnam's Sons, 1920.

Kuyper, A. *Encyclopedia of Sacred Theology its Principles*. Translator J. H. De Vries, New York: Charles Scribner's Sons, 1898. Later: *Principles of Sacred Theology*. Grand Rapids: Eerdmans, 1954.

Lauffer, S. *De Klassieke Geschiedenis in Jaartallen.* Utrecht/Antwerpen: Het Spectrum, 1969. Transl. J. H. Schmitz, *Abriss der Antiken Geschichte.* München: R. Oldenbourg, 1964.

Lewis, C. S. "Modern Theology and Biblical Criticism." In *The Essential C. S. Lewis,* edited by Lyle W. Dorsett. New York: Macmillan, 1988

Linnemann, E. *Is There a Synoptic Problem?* Grand Rapids: Baker Book House, 1992.

Lowe, M., and D. Flusser. "A Modified Proto-Matthean Synoptic Theory." *New Testament Studies.* Cambridge, University Press. 29 (1983) 25–47.

Marshall, I. H. *The Gospel of Luke. A Commentary on the Greek Text.* The International Greek Testament Commentary. Exeter: Paternoster Press, 1978.

McDowell, J. *Evidence that Demands a Verdict.* San Bernardino: Campus Crusade for Christ International, 1972.

Mentz, A. *Ein Schülerheft mit Altgriechischer Kurzschrift.* Bayreuth: Gauverlag Bayerische Ostmark, 1940.

Mentz, A. *Geschichte der Kurzschrift.* Wolfenbüttel: Heckner, 1949.

Mentz, A. *Geschichte und Systeme der griechischen Tachygraphy.* Berlin: Verlag von Gerdes & Hödel, 1907.

Merx, A. *Die Vier Kanonische Evangeliën.* Berlin: Reimer, 1911.

Metzger B. M., red. *A Textual Commentary on the Greek New Testament.* Corrected edition. London and New York: United Bible Societies, 1975.

Millard, A. *Reading and Writing in the Time of Jesus.* New York: University Press, 2000.

Kirsopp Lake, *The Apostolic Fathers II.* LCL, London: W. Heinemann, and New York: G. P. Putnam's Sons, 1917

Milne, H. J. M. *Greek Shorthand Manuals, Syllabary and Commentary.* London: Egypt Exploration Society, 1934.

Moo, D. J. *The Letter of James. An Introduction and Commentary.* Tyndale New Testament Commentaries 16. Grand Rapids: W. B. Eerdmans, 1986.

Morag, S. "Ephphatha (Mark VII.34): Certainly Hebrew, not Aramaic?" *Journal of Semitic Studies.* Oxford, University Press. 17 (1972): 198–202.

Morris, L. *Luke. An Introduction and Commentary.* Tyndale New Testament Commentaries 3. Grand Rapids: W. B. Eerdmans, 1988.

Mussies, G. "Greek as the Vehicle of Early Christianity." *New Testament Studies.* Cambridge, University Press. 29 (1983) 356–369.

The New Testament in Hebrew and Dutch. London: The Trinitarian Bible Society. 1990.

Nestle-Aland, Novum Testamentum, 28th Rev. Ed., Stuttgart: Deutsche Bibelgesellschaft, 2012.

Perrin, B. *Plutarch's Lives VIII.* LCL. London: W. Heinemann and New York: G. P. Putnam's Sons, 1919.

B. Perrin, *Plutarch's Lives X.* LCL. London: W. Heinemann, and New York: G. P. Putnam's Sons, 1921

Paulys Real-Encyclopädie XI der Classischen Altertumswissenschaft. Bnd. XI.2. Stuttgart: Metzler, 1922.

Porter, S. E. "Thucydides 1.22.1 and Speeches in Acts: Is There a Thucydidean View?" *Novum Testamentum.* Leiden: Brill. 32 (1990): 121–142.

Rabbinowitz, I. "Did Jesus speak Hebrew?" *Zeitschrift für die Neutestamentliche Wissenschaft.* Berlin: De Gruyter. 8 (1962): 229–238.

Richards, E. R. *The Secretary in the Letters of Paul.* Wissenschaftliche Untersuchungen zum Neuen Testament 42–2te Reihe. Tübingen: J. C. B. Mohr / Paul Siebeck, 1991.

Robinson, J. A. T. *Redating the New Testament.* London: SCM Press LTD, 1976.

Shackleton Bailey, D. R., *Cicero's Letters to Atticus.* Vol. V, Books XI–XIII. Cambridge: University Press, 1966.

Smith, C.F. *History of the Peloponnesian War.* LCL. London: Harvard University Press, 1919.

Stonehouse, N. B., *The Apocalypse in the Ancient Church, A Study in the History of the New Testament Canon.* Goes: Oosterbaan & Le Cointre, 1929.

Stonehouse, N. B. *Origins of the Synoptic Gospels.* London: Tyndale Press, 1964.

Stott, J. R.W. *The Letters of John. An Introduction and Commentary.* Tyndale New Testament Commentaries 19. Grand Rapids: W. B. Eerdmans, 1988.

Strack, H. L. and P. Billerbeck. *Das Evangelium nach Markus, Lukas und Johannes und die Apostelgeschichte*. Kommentar zum Neuen Testament aus Talmud und Midrasch, Band II. München: Beck'sche Verlagsbuchhandlung, 1974.

Streeter, B. H. *The Four Gospels, a Study of Origins*. 4th ed. London: MacMillan and Co., 1930.

Wenham, J. *Christ and the Bible*. Guildford: Eagle Inter Publishing Service, 1993.

Wenham, J. *Redating Matthew, Mark & Luke*. London: Hodder & Stoughton, 1991.

Whiston, W. *The Works of Josephus*. 12th ed. Peabody MA: Hendrickson Publishers, 1996.

Wikenhauser, A. *Einleitung in das Neue Testament*. 5th ed. Freiburg im Breisgau: Herder, 1963.

Yonge, C. D. *The Works of Philo*. 2nd ed. Peabody, MA: Hendrickson Publishers, 1993.

Zahn, T. *Geschichte des Neutestamentlichen Kanons II*. Leipzig: Deichert'sche Verlag, 1890.

Zahn, T. *Grundriss der Geschichte des Neutestamentlichen Kanons*. Leipzig: Deichert'sche Verlag, 1901.

Zahn, T. *Einleitung in das Neue Testament I*. 3th ed. Leipzig: Deichert'sche Verlag, 1924.

Zahn, T. *Das Evangelium des Matthäus*. 4th ed. Leipzig, Erlangen: Deichert'sche Verlag, 1922.

Dictionaries and Grammars

Bauer, W. *Wörterbuch zum Neuen Testament*. Berlin/New York: Walter de Gruyter, 1971.

Blass, F. and A. Debrunner. *Grammatik des Neutestamentlichen Griechisch*. Göttingen: Vandenhoeck & Ruprecht, 1965.

Dalman, G. *Grammatik des Jüdisch-Palästinischen Aramäisch*. Leipzig: Hinrichs Verlag, 1905.

DeWitt Burton, E. *Syntax of the Moods and Tenses in New Testament Greek*. 3d ed. Edinburg: T. & T. Clark, 1955.

Fanning, B. M. *Verbal Aspect in New Testament Greek*. Oxford: Clarendon Press, 1990.

Jastrow, M. *A Dictionary of the Targumim, the Talmud Babli, and Yerushalmi, and the Midrashic Literature I–II.* New York: Shalom, 1967.

Kittel, G., G. Friedrich, and G. W. Bromiley (transl.) *Theological Dictionary of the New Testament.* I–X. Grand Rapids: Eerdmans, 1993. Translated from *Theologisches Wörterbuch zum Neuen Testament.* Stuttgart: W. Kohlhammer Verlag.

Liddell, H. G., R. Scott and H. S. Jones. *A Greek–English Lexicon.* New Edition, Clarendon Press, Oxford, 1966.

Moulton, J. H. *A Grammar of New Testament Greek, I Prolegomena.* Edinburgh: T&T Clark, 1908.

Moulton, J. H. and G. Milligan. *The Vocabulary of the Greek Testament Illustrated from the Papyri and Other Non-Literary Sources.* Grand Rapids: W. B. Eerdmans, 1985.

Pring, J. T. *The Oxford Dictionary of Modern Greek.* 6th ed. Oxford: Clarendon Press, 1987.

Segal, M. H. *A Grammar of Mishnaic Hebrew.* Oxford: Clarendon Press, 1927.

Stevenson, W. B. *Grammar of Palestinian Jewish Aramaic.* London: Oxford University Press, (repr.) 1956.

Thayer J. H. *A Greek–English Lexicon of the New Testament.* Grand Rapids: Baker Book House, 1977, (repr.) 1991.

Turner, N. *A Grammar of New Testament Greek, III Syntax.* Edinburg: T&T Clark, (repr.) 1993.

Index

A

Alexander 38, 53, 69, 79, 240, 295
Alexandrian text 254, 255
Amphilocius of Iconium 242
analytical reading xi, 159, 160, 161, 162, 170, 171, 180, 184, 192, 218, 219, 221, 263, 265, 289
and-style 97, 141
Antonius 42
apostolic canon 231, 234
apostolic manifesto 13, 14, 16, 17, 19, 87, 101, 103, 115, 128, 130, 229, 243, 258
Aquila 43, 44, 49, 57, 58
Aramaic xv, 3, 19, 20, 21, 22, 23, 24, 25, 26, 27, 28, 29, 30, 31, 32, 33, 34, 35, 91, 124, 125, 127, 129, 202, 277, 295, 298
Aristeas 24, 25, 38, 39, 56
asyndetic connection 138, 139
Athanasius 47, 239, 240, 241, 242, 243
Atticus 50, 51, 52, 53, 298
Augustine 47, 237, 240, 241, 242
Augustus 44, 49, 57, 58, 62

B

Bartimaeus 163, 165, 167
Basil the Great 47
Boge, H. 42, 58, 295
Byzantine text 252, 253, 254, 255, 256

C

Caesarean text 252
Calvin 9, 202, 248
canon xiv, 117, 119, 129, 225, 226, 227, 228, 230, 231, 232, 233, 234, 235, 238, 239, 240, 241, 242, 243, 245, 246, 247, 249, 252, 258, 296, 299
canon formula 228, 239, 241, 242, 243, 252
Carson, D. A. 18, 80, 296
Catilina 40, 41
Cato the Younger 40, 41
Chaerammon of Panechotes 49
Chaldaïsti 25, 32
Chrysostomus 242
church fathers 10, 23, 46, 47
Cicero 40, 41, 42, 43, 46, 48, 49, 50, 51, 52, 53, 54, 55, 56, 57, 58, 59, 60, 62, 70,

V

variant reading 18, 252, 253, 254, 255, 256, 257, 258, 259, 277
Vipsanius Filagrius 43, 44, 49, 57, 58

W

wax tablet xiii, 13, 45, 71, 74, 97, 138, 142

Z

Zahn, T. 26, 29, 124, 240, 299